A Political Nation

A Political Nation

Nation

New Directions in
Mid-Nineteenth-Century
American Political History

Edited by GARY W. GALLAGHER
and RACHEL A. SHELDEN

University of Virginia Press   *Charlottesville and London*

University of Virginia Press
© 2012 by the Rector and Visitors of the University of Virginia
Printed in the United States of America on acid-free paper

First published 2012

9 8 7 6 5 4 3 2 1

LIBRARY OF CONGRESS CATALOGING-IN-PUBLICATION DATA

A political nation : new directions in mid-nineteenth-century American political history
/ edited by Gary W. Gallagher and Rachel A. Shelden.
   p.   cm.
Includes bibliographical references and index.
   ISBN 978-0-8139-3282-8 (cloth : alk. paper) — ISBN 978-0-8139-3283-5 (e-book)
   1. Federal government—United States—History—19th century. 2. Secession—
United States—History. 3. States' rights (American politics)—History—19th century.
4. United States—Politics and government—1849–1877. 5. United States—Politics and
government—1845–1849. 6. United States—Politics and government—1841–1845.
7. Political culture—United States—History—19th century. 8. Political parties—United
States—History—19th century. I. Gallagher, Gary W. II. Shelden, Rachel A., 1981–
   JK311.P65 2012
   973.6—dc23
                                                                    2011045308

These essays are offered with profound gratitude and appreciation to MICHAEL F. HOLT, *a mentor and colleague whose scholarship places him in the forefront of historians shaping the field of nineteenth-century American political history.*

Contents

III Parties and Federalism in the Era of the Civil War and Reconstruction

Acknowledgments

The editors incurred many debts in the course of preparing this volume for publication. We offer our warmest gratitude to the contributors, who found time amid the pressures of other obligations to prepare their essays and respond cheerfully to our numerous inquiries. At the University of Virginia Press, Dick Holway took an early interest in the project and helped guide it toward completion at every stage. Raennah Mitchell and Mark Mones similarly helped with many details, and George Roupe exhibited skill and patience in the editing process. Lastly, Michael Morrison and Michael Perman read the manuscript for the Press, carrying out that task in exemplary fashion. They offered criticism in the best sense of the word—sometimes pointed, always helpful, and illustrative of their sense of disinterested professionalism.

A Political Nation

Introduction

GARY W. GALLAGHER and RACHEL A. SHELDEN

This is a book about traditional American political history in the mid-nineteenth century. It is a book about elections, voters, and issues. It is about political parties and factions. It is about consensus and conflict in American political life. It is about the structures of the United States Congress, state and local governments, and other political organizations. But most importantly, this is a book about political *leaders*—the people who made policy, ran for office, influenced elections, and helped to shape American life from the early years of the Second Party System to the turbulent period of Reconstruction.

The study of American political leadership is not new. Until the mid-twentieth century, scholars typically told the story of American history through the prism of presidential and congressional politics. Over the past five decades, scholars have moved away from studying leadership, embracing fields such as social and cultural history and borrowing methodology from other disciplines in the humanities. In the 1960s and 1970s, historians used new social science techniques to enhance our understanding of political participation. They analyzed roll-call voting and electoral behavior to explain shifting party allegiances, creating what came to be called the "New Political History." Their dominance proved to be somewhat short-lived, as historians became increasingly dissatisfied with a narrow focus on elections, voters, and especially presidential politics.[1]

Since the 1980s and 1990s, political historians have completed a shift away from leadership, focusing instead on three new areas of study. The first emphasizes the somewhat nebulous concept of political culture. Borrowing heavily from cultural history and anthropology, these scholars seek to understand the broad context within which politicians operated. They focus on the unspoken ideas, attitudes, cultural norms, and social constraints that influenced political behavior, such as codes of honor and etiquette in early nineteenth-century America.[2]

Other social and cultural historians, particularly those in African American and gender studies, also have entered the realm of political history. These scholars embrace an expansive definition of "politics" that includes the everyday behavior of average Americans and marginalized groups. The simple act of a slave breaking a rake in defiance of his master or a woman bringing her family to an evangelical revival could be considered political. This kind of work demonstrates that although many people could not exercise traditional American rights such as voting or running for office, they still engaged in inherently political behavior.[3]

Perhaps the biggest influence on recent political history has come from outside the discipline. A new generation of historians is working closely with political scientists to examine political structures and institutions. These scholars are fascinated by the tension between an expanding American government and persistent antistatist attitudes from the founding period to the present. Rather than honing in on political leaders, these historians highlight constraints posed by preexisting political institutions such as the postal system, lobbying restrictions, or the welfare state. In this literature, the institutions themselves became crucial actors in American political development.[4]

Because of these new developments in the field, political history has thrived in the twenty-first century. We know more about cultural and institutional behavior than ever before,[5] and, somewhat surprisingly, interest in traditional political issues and personalities also has been rejuvenated. In the last few years, political culture and American political development have provided a framework for historians—young and old—who are eager to return to questions of political leadership. As a result, scholars of "traditional" political history have begun to spark new and interesting debates.

Academics should welcome this development for two reasons. First, as the popularity of books by nonprofessional historians such as Doris Kearns Goodwin and David McCullough demonstrate, the American reading public remains eager for new studies of traditional American politics.[6] While most academic historians do not write best sellers, their work does influence popular literature. Closing the gap between popular and academic history could further revitalize public interest in our discipline.[7] Second, a renewed interest in traditional political history gives scholars the opportunity to revisit and reevaluate older scholarship with political culture and institutional constraints in mind. Historians can breathe new life into federal, state, and local politics; partisan activities; elections; caucuses; and especially the politicians themselves.

Some of the most exciting new work on American politics and political actors focuses on the mid-nineteenth century. For several generations, the political history of the period 1840–77 has carried a theme of failure; after all, politicians in the antebellum years failed to prevent war, and those of the Civil War and Reconstruction failed to take advantage of opportunities to remake the nation.[8] Recent books and articles by Yonatan Eyal, Joanne Freeman, Russell McClintock, Elizabeth Varon, and others have moved beyond these older debates to ask new questions about mid-nineteenth-century American politics and politicians.[9]

The essays in this volume seek to contribute to this revival of traditional American political history. The book is divided into three chronological sections. The first three essays examine antebellum topics with an eye toward how political actors behaved within their cultural surroundings. Rachel Shelden investigates living arrangements in Washington, DC, to reexamine how the Texas annexation controversy of 1843–45 influenced party and sectional cohesion. She shows that congressmen made strong friendships in the boardinghouses and hotels of Washington, particularly among their partisan colleagues. Such friendships led to increased cross-sectional cooperation, particularly on party issues like annexation.

Mark Neely similarly reevaluates party politics through the prism of political culture. Using the murder of Bill Pool, a New York City political organizer, as a test case, Neely demonstrates that violence played a critical role in party organization. Historians, he argues, have much work ahead if we are to understand how violence influenced party politics. Jean Baker hopes to spark more interest in the civic culture of American women in the mid-nineteenth century. She provides a new model for evaluating women's political behavior by dividing female actors into three groupings: benevolent activists, political integrationists, and partisan enablers.

Language, rhetoric, and ideology were also critical to mid-nineteenth-century political culture. Daniel Crofts, William Freehling, and William Cooper use these tools to reevaluate the secession crisis in the second section of this collection. Crofts explores the little-studied Opposition Party of the late 1850s, drawing on the rhetoric of slave protection deployed by Southern politicians in the mid-nineteenth century to explain why the party achieved moderate success. Crofts shows how Southern Unionists embraced proslavery rhetoric to win elections. Freehling emphasizes the importance of rhetoric among secessionists. Historians are right to emphasize slavery's crucial role in the coming of the Civil War, he concedes, but the rhetoric of state rights should not be ignored. Freehling uses the legal and ideological culture of the South to shed new light on the meaning of state rights. While Freehling revisits an old debate over Civil War causation through the lens of political culture, Cooper urges historians to ask new questions about the behavior of political leaders during the secession crisis. He suggests historians have dwelled too often on whether President-Elect Abraham Lincoln's behavior during the secession winter was inept or shrewd. Instead, Cooper suggests that historians need to better understand the cultural milieu in which Lincoln operated.

The third group of essays investigates cultural and institutional influences on politicians in the Civil War and Reconstruction years. Each author stresses the role of federalism in understanding American political behavior. As Sean Nalty points out, looking at the state level is crucial to understanding the growth and appeal of the Union Party during the Civil War years. While scholars have questioned the legitimacy of the national party, Nalty demonstrates that Pennsylvania's Union Party members had a broad base with a shared commitment to fighting corruption. State-level politics in the Reconstruction South also looked markedly different from national trends. By examining Alabama's legislature, J. Mills Thornton shows that postbellum politicians often proposed policies that had more to do with class conflict than racial standing. These legislative proposals had a significant (and sometimes positive) impact on legislation for freedpeople during Reconstruction.

While Southerners struggled to reestablish themselves economically after the war, Northerners found themselves in the midst of bitter partisan battles and factional divisions. Erik Alexander examines the difficulties Northern Democrats faced in trying to unite their party and win elections during Republican-dominated Reconstruction. He argues that Democrats operated under the assumption that political parties were fluid—a widely held belief that dated back to the antebellum era—and saw the 1868 election as a critical turning point for their party's chances. Democrats were not the only ones to worry about party cohesion. Brooks D. Simpson investigates Republicans during Reconstruction, arguing that in addition to national unity and freedpeople's rights, the party of Lincoln was inordinately interested in maintaining party dominance at the federal and state levels. Ultimately, Simpson uses the culture of the Reconstruction period to show that Republicans did what was possible in the context of political, institutional, and ideological constraints in which the party tried to achieve its goals.

The historians in this volume share an enormous scholarly debt to Michael F. Holt. Since the late 1960s, Holt has set a standard for impeccably researched and skillfully argued studies in American political history. His work has covered politics from every angle, including relationships on the individual, city, state, party, and national levels. From his first book, *Forging a Majority: The Formation of the Republican Party in Pittsburgh, 1848–1860*, to his latest, a biography of Franklin Pierce, Holt has reshaped our understanding of political engagement in the mid-nineteenth century. Among other contributions, his work has highlighted the fragility and fluidity of politics in the mid-nineteenth century, dramatically influenced studies of the coming of the Civil War by insisting that politics (or a lack thereof) were the critical ingredient in disunion, and demonstrated the importance of examining politics from every governmental level and grappling with the intricacies of the federal system.[10]

Because of his tremendous impact on the field, Holt's work served as a starting point for each of us in evaluating the ways in which mid-nineteenth-century Americans framed and participated in political affairs. He repeatedly showed us that they understood their own lives through the prism of politics. Most important, he challenged us to think about the political process in complex ways. These essays serve as a tribute to him and will, we hope, help spur further study of American politicians and political history.

Notes

1. Many of these historians drew from an earlier argument made by Thomas Cochran that scholars were too focused on political elites. Thomas C. Cochran, "The 'Presidential Synthesis' in American History," *American Historical Review* 53 (1948), 748–53. Some of the seminal works in the New Political History include Lee Benson, *The Concept of Jacksonian Democracy: New York as a Test Case* (Princeton, NJ: Princeton University Press, 1961); Paul Kleppner, *The Third Electoral System, 1853–1892: Parties, Voters, and Political Cultures* (Chapel Hill: University of North Carolina Press, 1979); Joel Silbey, *The Shrine of Party: Congressional Voting Behavior, 1841–1852* (Pittsburgh: University of Pittsburgh Press, 1967).

2. Glen Gendzel, "Political Culture: Genealogy of a Concept," *Journal of Interdisciplinary History* 28:2 (Autumn 1997), 225–50; Catherine Allgor, *Parlor Politics: In Which the Ladies of Washington Help Build a City and a Government* (Charlottesville: University of Virginia Press, 2000); Joanne Freeman, *Affairs of Honor: National Politics in the New Republic* (New Haven, CT: Yale University Press, 2001).

3. See Steven Hahn, *A Nation under Our Feet: Black Political Struggles in the Rural South from Slavery to the Great Migration* (Cambridge, MA: Belknap Press of Harvard University Press, 2003); Stephanie McCurry, *Masters of Small Worlds: Yeoman Households, Gender Relations, and the Political Culture of the Antebellum South Carolina Low Country* (New York: Oxford University Press, 1995). Also see Jeffrey L. Pasley, Andrew W. Robertson, and David Waldstreicher, *Beyond the Founders: New Approaches to the Political History of the Early American Republic* (Chapel Hill: University of North Carolina Press, 2004).

4. See Meg Jacobs, William J. Novak, and Julian E. Zelizer, eds., *The Democratic Experiment: New Directions in American Political History* (Princeton, NJ: Princeton University Press, 2003); Richard J. John, *Spreading the News: The American Postal System from Franklin to Morse* (Cambridge, MA: Harvard University Press, 1995); Brian Balogh, "Reorganizing the Organizational Synthesis: Federal-Professional Relations in Modern America," *Studies in American Political Development* 5 (1991): 119–72; Jacob S. Hacker, *The Divided Welfare State: The Battle over Public and Private Social Benefits in the United States* (New York: Cambridge University Press, 2002).

5. For example, having focused much of their effort on the twentieth century, scholars in the field of American political development have only recently begun to examine nineteenth-century institutions. See Brian Balogh, *A Government Out of Sight: The Mystery of National Authority in Nineteenth-Century America* (New York: Cambridge University Press, 2008).

6. Doris Kearns Goodwin, *Team of Rivals: The Political Genius of Abraham Lincoln* (New York: Simon & Schuster, 2005); David McCullough, *John Adams* (New York: Simon & Schuster, 2001).

7. See Gordon Wood, "Defending the Academicians," *Washington Post*, November 17, 2009; Wood, *The Purpose of the Past: Reflections on the Uses of History* (New York: Penguin, 2008).

8. Historians often refer to antebellum politicians as a "blundering generation," whether or not these men can be blamed for causing the Civil War. James G. Randall coined the term in 1940. Randall, "The Blundering Generation," *Mississippi Valley Historical Review* 27:1 (June 1940): 3–28. A useful summary of the blundering generation thesis can be found in Michael Perman, ed., *The Coming of the American Civil War*, 3rd ed. (Lexington, MA: D. C. Heath, 1993). Eric Foner provides a comprehensive summary of Reconstruction historiography in *Reconstruction: America's Unfinished Revolution, 1863–1877* (New York: Harper & Row, 1988). Foner's groundbreaking work shows Reconstruction through the eyes of freedpeople. Like many of his colleagues, Foner argues that Republicans failed to take advantage of the opportunities that Reconstruction offered.

9. Yonatan Eyal, *The Young America Movement and the Transformation of the Democratic Party, 1828–1861* (New York: Cambridge University Press, 2007); Joanne Freeman, "The Culture of Congress in the Age of Jackson," *History Now* 22 (December 2009); Russell McClintock, *Lincoln and the Decision for War* (Chapel Hill: University of North Carolina Press, 2008); Elizabeth Varon, *Disunion! The Coming of the American Civil War, 1789–1859* (Chapel Hill: University of North Carolina Press, 2008). Also see Jon Grinspan, "'Young Men for War': The Wide Awakes and Lincoln's 1860 Presidential Campaign," *Journal of American History* 96:2 (September 2009): 357–78; Byron E. Shafer and Anthony J. Badger, eds., *Contesting Democracy: Substance and Structure in American Political History, 1775–2000* (Lawrence: University Press of Kansas, 2001).

10. The major themes of Holt's scholarship can be explored in *The Political Crisis of the 1850s* (New York: W. W. Norton, 1983), *Political Parties and American Political Development: From the Age of Jackson to the Age of Lincoln* (Baton Rouge: Louisiana State University Press, 1992), *The Rise and Fall of the American Whig Party: Jacksonian Politics and the Onset of the Civil War* (New York: Oxford University Press, 1999), and the most recent revised edition of *The Civil War and Reconstruction* (New York: W. W. Norton,

2001; cowritten with David Herbert Donald and Jean Harvey Baker). See also "An Elusive Synthesis: Northern Politics during the Civil War," in James M. McPherson and William J. Cooper Jr., eds., *Writing the Civil War: The Quest to Understand* (Columbia: University of South Carolina Press, 1998), 112–34.

I

Political Culture in
Antebellum America

Not So Strange Bedfellows

Northern and Southern Whigs and the
Texas Annexation Controversy, 1844–1845

RACHEL A. SHELDEN

American politicians were not primarily motivated by sectional concerns in the early 1840s. Local and state bias, regionalism, party loyalty, class, and a wide variety of other concerns were as influential, if not more important, to the political actors in Washington. In no case is this variety of interests more salient than in the debate over Texas annexation in 1844 and early 1845. Focusing primarily on the Whig Party, this essay demonstrates that sectionalism was only one of many concerns during the "annexation crisis" of the 1840s. Furthermore, although the issue of annexation produced some sectional friction, the Whig Party retained a surprising degree of intersectional comity and cooperation on Texas.

I examine the Whigs in this essay for two reasons. First, the Whig Party is traditionally perceived as the less cohesive of the two political organizations. Some historians have gone so far as to question whether the Whig Party ever existed, citing sectional disagreements among party members as evidence of its incoherence.[1] A second reason is that some scholars have identified the Texas controversy as the primary cause of the Whig Party's demise and, therefore, the beginning of a breakdown of the Second Party System. As a result, many point to the Texas controversy as a crucial turning point on the path to Civil War.[2]

One reason historians argue that Texas was such a sectionally divisive issue is that they have often been swayed by the testimony of Americans in the 1850s, whose retrospective view of annexation included division and dissent. A closer look at Washington politicians' behavior during the annexation controversy itself reveals a different story. This essay traces the month-to-month negotiations and conversations of Northern and Southern Whig leaders regarding Texas annexation from 1844 to 1845. The thoughts, words, and actions of Whigs who lived during this period clearly illustrate that when the issue of Texas annexation was on the table, it was not so disruptive. Nor would it fundamentally alter sectional relationships within the party system immediately following the passage of the joint resolution in March 1845. Rather, the party remained overwhelmingly united throughout the controversy.[3]

The extent of party unity in 1844 and 1845 can be demonstrated in three ways. First, members of the Whig Party from both sections felt both a personal and a professional bond while living in Washington in the mid-1840s. These Northerners and Southerners did more than interact with one another in the halls of Congress. A wide variety of evidence, from boardinghouse records and personal letters to public statements and travel accounts, illustrates that Whigs from all states made friendly relationships with one another.

Second, Whigs did not necessarily feel a *sectional* rift among them, in large part because the North and the South were not such distinct entities. The "West" and the border states did not necessarily belong to one section or another. Whigs frequently excluded South Carolina when they talked of the South because of its disunionist past. Similarly, some party members excluded known abolitionist areas when they talked of the North. Overall, for Whigs, the United States was not cleanly divided down the middle. It was a country made up of different regions, different states, and different localities, all of which included members of the Whig party. Finally, there was not a "Northern" view of Texas on the one hand and a "Southern" view on the other. Party members from both sections had a variety of motivations for opposing annexation, including party reasons, state reasons, local reasons, personal reasons, moral reasons, economic reasons, or some combination thereof.

Ultimately, Whigs *were* united in a crucial way: they were committed to fighting tyranny and to preserving the Union. Therefore, the context in which President John Tyler pushed for annexation is crucial to understanding Whig behavior. Tyler was a rogue leader who had abandoned the party and had already upset other Whigs by blocking their economic agenda. This economic agenda was critical to maintaining a healthy and happy Union. Tyler's tyrannical behavior and his casual disregard for the Union fueled Whig opposition to his Texas proposal.[4]

Thus, while sectionalism played a role in the Texas controversy—as it did in all territorial and slavery disputes in the mid-nineteenth century—the annexation debate was primarily partisan, not sectional. Whigs who did support Texas statehood were motivated primarily by political concerns, not sectional ones. Nor was the Whig Party rent by sectional dispute. Rather, Whigs rejected Texas annexation and found themselves unified as they faced the next territorial challenge: war with Mexico.

On the eve of the Twenty-Eighth Congress's arrival in Washington in December 1843, Whig spirits were high. Although the divisive influence of John Tyler had produced disastrous defeats in the fall elections of 1841 and off-year congressional elections in 1842, the Whigs had a minor comeback in 1843. Signs of recovery from economic downturn had reaffirmed Whigs' economic principles and renewed a sense of unity among the party's members. Ultimately, Tyler's Democratic-leaning politics had created some intraparty divisions, but partisanship remained strong in the early 1840s.[5]

Two hundred and seventy five politicians descended upon the House and Senate in December 1843. The House was primarily Democratic, consisting of 147 Democrats, 72 Whigs, and 4 others. The Senate was significantly more contentious, containing 23 Democrats and 29 Whigs.[6] Upon arriving in Washington, the members found housing in local boardinghouses and hotels, while a few obtained private housing in Georgetown or near the White House. Boardinghouses were the most common residence of members. According to one historian, these houses consisted of "mutually exclusive, closely knit, voluntary associations . . . where members took their meals together, lived together in the same lodginghouse, and spent most of their leisure time together."[7] The following tables illustrate that Whigs and Democrats did not divide themselves into sectional houses. In both parties, a high percentage of Northerners and Southerners chose to live with one another.[8]

As table 1 demonstrates, members lived more often in cross-regional boardinghouses than in regional ones (26–13). Furthermore, nearly as many cross-sectional boardinghouses existed as sectional ones (17–22). Table 2 shows that almost three times as many boarders lived in cross-regional boardinghouses (147–54), while nearly as many members lived in cross-sectional houses as sectional ones (91–110). Of the 101 Whigs in the Twenty-Eighth Congress, more than half lived in cross-regional houses, while nearly two-fifths lived in cross-sectional lodgings.

Some cross-sectional Whig examples included Miss Polk's lodgings on Pennsylvania Avenue, near the corner of Third Street, which housed Delaware senator Richard Bayard, New York representatives J. Philips Phoenix and William Moseley, and Representative Kenneth Rayner, a North Carolinian. Half a block from Miss Polk's, Senators William Sprague of Rhode Island and John Henderson of Mississippi shared lodgings at Mr. Gilbert's. Virginia senator William Rives and New Jersey representative William Wright lived together at Mrs. Ulrick's, opposite the State Department.

These boardinghouse arrangements also offer evidence to the strong partisanship in Washington at this time. Very few boarders lived with opposite-

TABLE 1 **Regional and sectional dispersion of boardinghouses in the first session of the Twenty-Eighth Congress**

Boardinghouse type	No. of houses	Whig houses*	Democratic houses*
Regional	13	5	8
Cross-regional**	26	9	13
Cross-sectional**	17	6	9
Cross-party**	5	—	—

Source: *Congressional Directory for the First Session of the Twenty-Eighth Congress of the United States of America* (Washington, DC: Wm. Q. Force, printer, 1843–44). Although the directories give detailed living information, the numbers are necessarily estimates. Some members arrived late to the session and were not included in the directory. Others moved midsession to a different house or hotel.

* "Whig houses" denotes boardinghouses with only Whig members; "Democratic houses" denotes houses with only Democrat members.

**Numbers for cross-sectional boardinghouses and for cross-party boardinghouses that were also cross-regional are included in the cross-regional numbers.

party members, and when they did, it was usually one Democrat and several Whigs or vice versa. In H. V. Hill's boardinghouse, for example, Thomas Gilmer, a close friend of Tyler, boarded with several southwestern Democrats. Members from the same state also boarded together. In Mr. Whitney's boardinghouse, for example, two Democrats and one Whig boarded together, all from Ohio. The arrival of a member of the opposing party could also prompt a boarder to search for alternate housing. In one such example, Spencer Jarnagin, a Whig senator from Tennessee, left Mrs. Adams's boardinghouse in midsession. According to Jarnagin, "The true reason I left at the time I did was because Mrs. Adams took a Loco to board without consulting any of us."[9]

Thus, the Twenty-Eighth Congress opened with more party agitation than sectional division. Upon their arrival in Washington, members looked forward to dedicating their work to revisiting the Tariff of 1842, internal improvements, and other routine matters. Yet as congressmen settled themselves in Washington, they quickly became distracted by the possibility of Texas annexation.

The United States had entertained the possibility of annexing Texas since at least 1825, when John Quincy Adams, then president, and Henry Clay, then secretary of state, attempted to acquire all or a large part of Texas through negotiations with Mexico. When this sale fell through, President Andrew Jackson and Martin Van Buren, his secretary of state, attempted to purchase

TABLE 2 Regional and sectional dispersion of Whig and Democrat boarders in the first session of the Twenty-Eighth Congress

House type	No. of boarders	Whig boarders	Democrat boarders	Senate boarders	House boarders
Regional	54	14	40	8	46
Cross-regional*	147**	57	90	30	117
Cross-sectional*	91**	37	54	20	71
Cross-party*	29	17	12	3	26

Source: *Congressional Directory for the First Session of the Twenty-Eighth Congress of the United States of America* (Washington, DC: Wm. Q. Force, printer, 1843–44).

*Numbers for cross-sectional boardinghouses and for cross-party boardinghouses that were also cross-regional are included in the cross-regional numbers.

**Includes the three delegates (all Democrats) representing territories, one each from Florida, Wisconsin, and Iowa.

Texas again in 1829. The face of the issue changed in 1835 when Texas settlers, many of whom were of U.S. origin, revolted against Mexico and declared themselves independent. Concerned about their foreign policy relationship to Mexico, American politicians did not immediately respond to Texans' wishes to become part of the United States. Several attempts to forge a treaty between the United States and Texas failed in the late 1830s, but Tyler made the acquisition a priority as early as 1841.[10]

The only thing standing in Tyler's way was Secretary of State Daniel Webster, the last remaining member of William Henry Harrison's cabinet. Webster, like most Whigs, opposed all territorial expansion, on the grounds that it was both unproductive and unsettling to the Union. Webster refused to negotiate a treaty for Texas while serving in his cabinet post, but the Massachusetts statesman eventually tired of aiding a rogue president and resigned in May 1843. In his place, Tyler appointed Virginian Abel Upshur, a proslavery extremist, who was as committed to Texas annexation as the president.[11]

Upshur immediately set the annexation wheels in motion. Over the summer, newspapers all over the country had published reports and editorials claiming that the administration was negotiating a secret treaty with Texas. The newspaper reports were enough to create tremendous controversy nationwide. As the session began, large numbers of petitions appeared daily protesting or encouraging the possibility of annexation. Letters and speeches of several prominent members of the Whig and Democratic Parties fueled such agitation.[12] Finally, when Upshur died in an accident aboard the *Princeton,* Tyler would appoint the most divisive replacement possible: South

Carolinian John C. Calhoun. Calhoun, who did not believe in political parties and swore allegiance only to the South, presented annexation as a proslavery, sectional measure and was willing to use every tool possible to acquire the territory. It took Calhoun only a few weeks to complete the treaty.[13]

Amid this agitation, congressmen in Washington looked to their party leaders for guidance on how to handle the Texas controversy. As the long-standing leader of the Whig Party, Kentuckian Henry Clay took the helm in framing party policy. Out of Congress and campaigning seriously for the Whig presidential nomination, Clay traveled throughout the South in the spring of 1844, talking with Whigs about the Texas issue. Aware that annexation had caused a stir in Washington and the North, he wanted to determine just how badly Southerners wanted Texas. By late March, after a few weeks of travel, Clay had determined that Southerners were not united in favor of the measure. As he told his friend John Crittenden, "Of one thing you may be certain, there is no such anxiety for the annexation here at the South as you might have been disposed to imagine."[14]

As a result of his trip, Clay determined that he could safely come out against annexation. Thus, on April 27, the *Washington National Intelligencer* published a letter from Clay to its editors, strongly arguing against immediate annexation. Among other reasons for his opposition, Clay argued that the measure was unconstitutional and that it would prove detrimental to the Union. He explained, "No motive for the acquisition of foreign territory would be more unfortunate ... than that of obtaining [Texas]. ... Such a principle, put into practical operation, would menace the existence, if it did not certainly sow the seeds of a dissolution of the Union." Henceforth, this letter was referred to among Whigs as Clay's "Raleigh Letter."[15]

One historian has argued that Clay badly misread sentiment in the South. Visiting primarily wealthy areas, Clay encountered Whigs who were planters and merchants, Southerners who tended to oppose migration west. Contrary to what Clay believed, many Southerners *did* favor annexation, a fact that does much to explain the waning support for Clay among local Whigs in the South in the 1844 presidential election. Yet Clay was right on one front. Most of the Southern Whig policy makers in Washington opposed the measure, albeit for a variety of different reasons. In fact, opinions on the Texas matter greatly varied among Whig congressmen and state leaders in both the North and South.[16]

Some Southern Whigs believed that annexation was unconstitutional. D. F. Caldwell wrote to Daniel Barringer, a North Carolina representative, "If we have the power to annex Texas, we have the power to annex Cuba, Great

Britain & even all of Europe. . . . No such power [is] to be found in this constitution." Similarly, David Campbell, the former governor of Virginia, wrote to his nephew, William, a former Tennessee representative, deploring the efforts of Democrats to obtain Texas. To Campbell, "Nothing could furnish stronger evidence of the desperate conditions of the Democratic party than their attempts to seize the Texas question and appropriate it to themselves as a party measure. . . . They have forgotten all sense of selfrespect [sic] for their country and for its constitution."[17]

Other Southerners opposed the measure for economic reasons. In a letter to North Carolina congressmen Daniel Barringer and T. L. Clingman, D. F. Caldwell explained, "I am decidedly of the opinion that the Annexation of Texas would prove a curse to [our] Southern states especially the cotton & sugar regions. Beyond doubt both those articles already very low would be reduced still further in price & as the price of cotton regulates everything, so the annexation would affect every thing."[18]

Perhaps the most important reason for Southern opposition to the measure was fear of disunion. The editors of the Whig organ in Washington, the *National Intelligencer*, hoped to prevent any sectional disagreement by illustrating the extent to which Whigs, North and South, agreed on the issue. Beginning in April and extending through the summer, the *Intelligencer* published excerpts from Southern Whig papers demonstrating the degree of comity between the sections. Among these was a report from the Tennessee legislature, which rejected annexation in favor of cross-sectional cooperation. The report from the legislature read, "Well satisfied that for political reasons, wholly disconnected with the question of slavery, our brethren of the North and East will be averse to annexation, *the committee would deprecate the necessity of agitating the subject.*"[19]

Many Whigs from the South corresponded openly with their Northern friends about the possible pitfalls of annexation. In late March, North Carolinian Willie P. Mangum sent a letter to William Hayden, a Boston Whig. Mangum opposed annexation for its potential to cause a disruption in the Union. Hayden's response thanking Mangum demonstrates the degree of cross-sectional comity felt by the two men. Hayden praised Mangum's effort to explain "the feelings and intentions of our Southern & Western friends in the Senate." The letter had greatly allayed the fears of his Northern cohorts. "Not that *I* have ever doubted the honor or fidelity of our Southern & Western friends in that body," Hayden explained. "I had carefully watched their course—and, from the past, was led to rely upon their future faithfulness. But I had no means at hand to satisfy those around me, upon that point."[20]

Mangum and others helped quell the anxiety of Northerners who feared the South would unite in favor of annexation, a popular (though false) rumor in the North. Like their Southern brethren, these Northerners were concerned with the effects of annexation on both the success of the Whig Party and the perpetuity of the Union. As William Dayton, a Whig senator from New Jersey, wrote to former Massachusetts senator Leverett Saltonstall, the sectional bent of the Texas controversy could "drive away . . . even the prudent men of the north [and] do more to foment abolition than all the fanatics of the north could accomplish." Dayton and others feared that Southern insistence on Texas would enliven an extremist spirit in the North that could be avoided through continued cooperation between the Northern and Southern wings of the party. Yet most Northern Whig leaders believed that Southern Whigs would stay true to the party. William Seward, a New York Whig, explained that each section was "imbued with that devotedness to the principles and policy of the region to which he belongs, which marks the faithful representation, and imbed with that comprehensive patriotism, which teaches us that personal and local interests must always be subordinate to the security, welfare, and harmony of our common Country, and to the inestimable blessings of Liberty and Union."[21]

Thus, when the president sent his completed treaty to the Senate on April 22, Whigs were already largely united against annexation. Furthermore, both the members who favored and those who opposed the treaty did so for a wide variety of reasons, not simply sectional allegiance. When the terms of the treaty were read, however, Whig solidarity became even greater. Southerners in particular opposed the treaty. For example, Senator Alexander Barrow of Louisiana changed his stance on Texas after some reflection. In a letter to the *New York Tribune*, Barrow explained that after "mature and calm" consideration, he had "arrived at the conclusion that there exists no State necessity for the measure, and that the ratification of the Treaty now before the Senate would not only involve the nation in an unjust war, but would, in an especial manner, prostrate the best interests of Louisiana." Barrow argued that, because he was a thoroughbred Southerner, he could speak for the South. He explained, "Possessing every motive, from birth, education, and long-cherished opinion and well matured convictions . . . [regarding] the institution of Slavery, I am decidedly of opinion that the Annexation of Texas to the United States will not give any additional security to the South; and that, on the contrary, our position will be weakened by such a measure." Similarly, the *Charlotte Journal* explained that there was "a disposition on the part of the Loco Foco party to join the malcontents of South Carolina in overthrowing our present government and establishing a Southern Confederacy with Mr. Calhoun at its head."[22]

In addition to fear of disunion, Whigs shunned the treaty as an attempt by the president to win votes in the upcoming election at the expense of the Union. Georgia representative Alexander Stephens abhorred the actions of the president, arguing: "The whole annexation project is a miserable political humbug got up as a ruse to divide and distract the Whig party at the South. . . . Tyler would willingly destroy a country which he has deceived and betrayed when he is satisfied that he can no longer be its chief ruler. It is all a trick—one of his desperate moves or strokes to produce dissention in the country for his own personal aggrandizement."[23]

When debate over the resolution finally began in Congress on May 10, Whigs from different parts of the South spoke out against annexation. These men presented a variety of reasons for opposing the measure, including the fact that Americans would be breaking their good faith with Mexico, inducing the probability of war with that country, and the treaty's provision to absorb Texas's debts. Yet, as they had in the preceding months, Whigs overwhelmingly opposed annexation because of its implications for the Union. Moreover, they blamed Tyler for his willingness to overlook the bill's sectional implications.[24]

For most Whigs, Tyler was using Texas for political gain. Spencer Jarnagin exclaimed that "the truth is, this whole business is a fraud, a plan, with which John Tyler intends, if he can, to bamboozle the American people in the approaching presidential election." Georgia senator John M. Berrien agreed that Tyler had "hoodwinked" Southerners especially into desiring Texas and argued that "when the American people have time deliberately to examine the question of Texian annexation, free from the excitement of a presidential canvass . . . it will be found to be neither a northern nor a southern question, but one in which the whole Union, whether for weal or wo [sic] alike and equally interested."

Furthermore, Southern Whigs scoffed at Tyler's ultimatum that Texas should be annexed "now or never." If this were really a choice, Virginia senator William Archer asked, then is there "room for hesitation? No! The loud exclamation! Let it go out from this hall—resound through this land—reverberate from Texas—Never! Oh, Never!" Archer's resounding "no" was emblematic of the Whig refrain in Congress. As Ohio representative Joshua Giddings reported to his daughter, "The Whig party *as a party* will take, indeed have taken determined ground against [annexation]."[25]

With such resounding Whig opposition, Tyler's treaty was doomed to failure. On June 8, the annexation treaty was laid on the table in the Senate and rejected by a vote of 16 to 35. Twenty-eight of 29 Whigs in the Senate voted against the measure; John Henderson of Mississippi was the one exception. Seven Van Buren Democrats joined with the Whigs in defeating the treaty. Whigs expressed great enthusiasm for the substantial defeat of the Texas measure. A Maryland representative, John Pendleton Kennedy, exclaimed, "The Texas flurry is over and I have hopes that before many weeks we shall hear no more about it. We hope that John Tyler [will] meditate over his failure in the [presidency] as well as in every thing else [he] has attempted during this [session] of folly and wickedness."[26]

As soon as Congress adjourned, Whigs began to seriously campaign for their presidential nominee, Henry Clay. Northern and Southern Whigs believed their prospects for winning the election were high. Yet, as a result of the 1844 Democratic presidential convention, Texas was sure to play a role in the campaign. During the convention, Democratic favorite Martin Van Buren was pushed aside by Southern Democrats, particularly Tyler and Calhoun sympathizers, in favor of a more obscure nominee, James K. Polk. While many Whigs considered Polk a less-than-serious choice, the selection of a proannexation man proved that Texas would be a prominent issue during the election. For in some sections of the South, such as Tennessee, Virginia, and Georgia, Whig constituents *wanted* Texas annexation. Although congressional Whigs had particularly resisted Tyler's terms, they knew the presidential canvass could prove challenging.[27]

Nevertheless, Whigs did not abandon their anti-annexation rhetoric. Even in parts of the South where local Democrats and Whigs alike approved of annexation, by no means did they make Texas a sectional issue. Whigs continued to vocally oppose the measure, citing numerous reasons ranging from economics to personal preference. Still, they remained united in excoriating annexation for its influence on Whig principles and the Union.

Clay continued to be the most vocal about his opposition to immediate annexation. In his famous "Alabama Letters," published on July 1 and 27, Clay echoed the standard Whig line about Tyler's irresponsible handling of annexation and the threat of disunion. Addressing the editors of the *Tuscaloosa Independent Monitor,* Clay explained, "I consider the Union a great political partnership; and that new members ought not to be admitted into the concern at the imminent hazard of its dissolution. Personally, I could have no objection to the annexation of Texas, but I certainly would be unwilling to see the existing Union dissolved or seriously [jeopardized] for the sake of acquiring Texas."[28]

Clay toed the Whig line, but he had clearly altered his approach from his "Raleigh Letter" of the previous April. Concerned about Polk's influence, Clay felt a need to appeal to future interest in Texas in the South. Many would later argue that these letters helped bring about Clay's defeat in the 1844 election. As one newspaperman explained, the Alabama Letters "fell like a wet blanket upon the Whigs, and enabled the Democratic managers to deprive him of the vote of New York." Michael Holt even calls Clay's letters "among the biggest mistakes of his long political career."[29] Regardless of what some Northern Whigs believed, however, Clay had not deviated substantially from his original arguments about Texas. The most important point to Clay was that annexation could endanger the Union. Although he was amenable to acquiring Texas, Clay believed that reasonable men throughout the Union would not sacrifice their principles for the measure.

Like Clay, some Whigs in Tennessee feared the effects of the Texas issue on the election, but they stuck to their principles. William Campbell wrote his Virginian uncle, "I think we will carry this state, but the contest will be hard. This rascally Texas question will mislead some. It is a question I have no patience with, as I am now [well] satisfied that the Burr conspiracy nor nullification were not more corrupt in their inception, and more dangerous to the union or the peace & prosperity of this republic than this Texas conspiracy." In Virginia, other prominent Whigs hoped to eventually annex Texas but agreed with Clay that it must be completed under proper terms. William Cabell Rives wrote as much to Clay, explaining that he had "been led to the conclusion that a large majority of your friends in Virginia are in favor of the acquisition of Texas, but they are, like myself, anxious to commit so great a question to an able & patriotic guardianship." Although Rives knew local Virginia Whigs greatly favored Texas, he was still committed to receiving the territory properly, and under the guidance of Henry Clay. As a result, many Southern Whigs campaigned against *immediate* annexation in their states.[30]

Amid the difficulties of the presidential canvass, Whigs also found time to visit their friends in other states. The Texas controversy both in Congress and during the campaign had done nothing to diminish the cross-sectional friendships that congressmen had made in Washington. Thus, in August and September, Rives, Crittenden, and Berrien all traveled to the North to visit with their Northern counterparts. Rives visited several areas of Massachusetts, dining with Joseph Grinnell and even going on a fishing expedition with Grinnell and John Quincy Adams. In mid-September, Robert Winthrop invited Leverett Saltonstall to a dinner attended by Grinnell, Jacob Miller (a Whig senator from New Jersey), Adams, and Berrien, who was visiting the area. Some Northerners also visited friends in other regions. John Pendleton Kennedy wrote to his wife in mid-June that "old Mr. Adams has promised he will makes us a visit before he goes north, this summer—perhaps some day next week."[31]

Cross-sectional visits did much to show the Northern and Southern public that Whigs were united. Newspapers served a similar purpose. As the presidential canvass continued, newspapers tried to promote cross-sectional unity among their readers by citing editorials from all over the country that opposed annexation. Such demonstrations were particularly important in the North, where Clay's Alabama Letters had unsettled some local Whigs. Throughout the summer, *New York Tribune* editor Horace Greeley published several reports insisting that Southern Whigs opposed acquiring Texas. On September 12, Greeley editorialized, "We receive at least One Hundred Whig journals printed in the Southern States. Of those, *not one advocates the Annexation of Texas in this Country on the terms of Tyler's Treaty, not Immediate Annexation at all.*" Furthermore, he explained, "A larger portion of the Whig Press of the South is either indifferent or resolutely efficiently hostile to Annexation *under any circumstances.*"[32] The *Washington National Intelligencer,* which had a wide audience in the North, published similar editorials and ran weekly, sometimes daily, records of Southern Whig papers arguing against annexation.

Regardless of this cross-sectional comity, however, in November 1844 the Whigs lost the presidential election in a close contest. Northern and Southern Whigs alike lamented the loss and speculated about the cause of their defeat. Some Southerners blamed the Democratic victory on the Texas issue. Just after the election, Arthur Campbell expressed this opinion to his brother James. He wrote, "For any one now to say that the Texas question has no influence on the Presidential election only makes a fool or an ass of himself."[33]

While several local Whigs echoed Arthur's insistence that Texas controlled the election, his opinions were uncommon among national Whig leaders. Even Arthur's brother, David, disagreed. He later wrote Arthur, "The election was decided, as you know very well, by the people of New York & Pennsylvania, Michigan & Maine, on considerations and feelings unconnected with any great national principles or interest." Modern analysis of the 1844 presidential election has demonstrated the validity of David Campbell's reasoning. Although the annexation issue certainly contributed to the success of the Liberty Party, particularly in New York, Texas could not be blamed for the election.[34]

Although the actual impact of annexation on the election was minimal, the *perceived* influence of the Texas issue may have heightened sectional tension in localities throughout the South in the winter of 1844–45. Discord also grew in December when South Carolina and Massachusetts became embroiled in a controversy over the Negro Seamen's Act. When, in late November, the Massachusetts legislature sent Samuel Hoar to Charleston to investigate the impact of the act on black Northerners, the South Carolina legislature expelled the former congressman.[35]

The expulsion caused a flurry of anger among Northern newspapers and legislatures. Yet in both sections, and particularly among Washington politicians, many realized that South Carolina did not speak for the whole South. After hearing of the expulsion, Maryland Whig John Pendleton Kennedy told his wife, "I advise [the Massachusetts men] to pass an act in their Legislature abolishing South Carolina, and declaring [it] to be absolutely null and void. I dont know any thing else that will meet the case." Furthermore, neither Hoar's expulsion nor postelection frustration split the party in half along sectional lines. As members filed back to Washington for the second session, Northern and Southern Whigs again occupied boardinghouses together (see tables 3 and 4).[36]

The second session boardinghouse arrangements demonstrate that neither the Texas issue nor other sectional disagreements had severed friendships between Northerners and Southerners. Roughly the same number of Whigs lived in cross-regional boardinghouses, and many more chose to

TABLE 3 Regional and sectional dispersion of boardinghouses in the second session of the Twenty-Eighth Congress

Boardinghouse type	No. of houses	Whig houses*	Democratic houses*
Regional	5	2	3
Cross-regional**	35	14	21
Cross-sectional**	14	10	4
Cross-party**	5	—	—

Source: Congressional Directory for the Second Session of the Twenty-Eighth Congress of the United States of America (Washington: Wm. Q. Force, Printer, 1845).

*"Whig houses" denotes boardinghouses with only Whig members; "Democratic houses" denotes houses with only Democrat members.

**The cross-sectional numbers are included in the cross-regional numbers. Cross-party boardinghouses that are cross-regional are included in the cross-regional category as well.

TABLE 4 Regional and sectional dispersion of Whig and Democrat boarders in the second session of the Twenty-Eighth Congress

House type	No. of boarders	Whig boarders	Democrat boarders	Senate boarders	House boarders
Regional	12	5	7	2	10
Cross-regional*	168**	78	90	29	139
Cross-sectional*	102	53	49	18	84
Cross-party*	32	9	23	9	23

Source: Congressional Directory for the Second Session of the Twenty-Eighth Congress of the United States of America (Washington: Wm. Q. Force, Printer, 1845).
    *Numbers for cross-sectional boardinghouses and for cross-party boardinghouses that were also cross-regional are included in the cross-regional numbers.
    **Includes the three delegates (all Democrats) representing territories, one each from Florida, Wisconsin, and Iowa.

live in cross-sectional apartments. William Archer and John Berrien moved into Mr. Gurley's lodgings with William Hubbell, a New York representative, and Jacob Preston, a Maryland congressman. Daniel Barringer renewed his rooms at Dr. Mayo's on B Street, sharing quarters with Representatives Edward Morris of Pennsylvania, Caleb Smith of Indiana, Robert Schenck of Ohio, and Jonathan White of Kentucky. By the second session, only five Whigs who lived in boardinghouses chose to isolate themselves by region or state.

As Whigs got themselves settled in Washington in December, party members considered how to approach the new administration. They quickly determined that the party should stick to its principles as a minority but let the Democrats pass legislation without significant impediment. The strategy was basically to allow the Democratic Party to dig its own grave. Clay outlined this approach in a letter to Crittenden in late November. "We should adhere to our principles," Clay wrote, but Democrats "ought to be allowed to carry their own measures, without any other opposition than that of fully exposing their evil tendency to the people."[37]

A shrewd politician, Clay realized that, with the Democrats in power, Polk's party would be blamed for any future policies, including the annexation of Texas. While Clay still opposed the measure, he understood that some Southerners, particularly in Tennessee and Georgia, had difficulty justifying their anti-annexation votes to their constituents. Thus these Southern Whigs could vote for their constituents' wishes, and Polk would be held responsible for the war with Mexico that annexation would likely bring. Democrats would bear the electoral responsibility for that policy in the next election.

As Whigs suspected, the Democrats pressed for annexation as soon as the session began. In his annual message to Congress on December 3, Tyler recommended that Congress annex Texas by joint resolution of both houses. Members responded favorably, submitting seven resolutions to the Senate and ten to the House of Representatives. Of these, only two came from Whigs, one in each body. Milton Brown, a Tennessee Whig, was the culprit in the House. Brown believed that, because of the House's large Democratic majority, Texas was an unbeatable issue, and he was reluctant to let Democrats get all the credit for a matter widely supported by his constituents. Brown's plan brought Texas into the Union as a state rather than a territory, made the United States responsible for the disputed boundary with Mexico, and forced Texas to pay its public debt while retaining its lands. Brown's proposal also stipulated that as many as four additional states could be carved from Texas and that future Congresses must admit them as slave states if their residents so desired.[38]

On January 23, House Democrats held a caucus to discuss their prospects. Most did not believe that a solid majority—105 Democrats and 8 Whigs—could be counted on to vote for the treaty. Yet Milton Brown's proposal was sure to appeal to more Southern Whigs and therefore give the measure a greater chance of passing. Thus when Brown's resolution came before the House on January 25, Democrats seized it, and the resolution passed 120–98. Twenty-eight Northern Democrats voted with the minority.[39]

Although some Whigs did break ranks, only eight voted for the measure: four from Tennessee, including Brown, John Ashe, Joseph Peyton, and William Senter; Alexander Stephens and Duncan L. Clinch of Georgia; James Dellet of Alabama; and Willoughby Newton of Virginia. These representatives came from states where local clamoring for Texas was highest. Furthermore, Virginia, Tennessee, and Alabama had congressional and state elections scheduled for 1845, while Georgia had gubernatorial elections scheduled for that year.[40]

Arguments made by three of these men illustrate the extent to which annexation served a primarily *partisan* purpose rather than a sectional one. For example, Newton, the only Virginia Whig representative up for reelection, explained his vote in a letter to his constituents dated February 4, 1845. He told them that Northerners should not be blamed for their votes against Texas. Yes, many wanted to use their political power to prevent slavery's extension, but, he argued, "it is natural that they should entertain these views; and their motives being pure, we have no right to condemn them." Furthermore, Northerners' antislavery motives were not to be confused with abolitionism: "So mad, impracticable, and destructive a scheme can of course find no countenance, except among those who are phrensied by fanaticism."[41]

Although Newton's letter carefully omitted any mention of the impending Virginia elections and the pressure he may have felt to approve the treaty, his letter does much to explain the course taken by these eight Southern Whigs. Far from resenting Northerners, Newton understood that sometimes the interests of slaveholding states countered the interests of the nonslaveholding states. Significantly, Newton justified his position to his *constituents,* not other congressmen; although his argument contained sectional elements, he did not emphasize sectional antagonisms, and he even acknowledged the existence of wise men in the North. Newton did not disavow fidelity to the party nor to his Northern brethren but calmly stated that he voted for the measure because it was in Virginia's interest.

Joseph Peyton similarly attempted to justify his vote to William Campbell. The Tennessee representative argued that annexation was "inevitable sooner or later," and he believed it was vastly important to his state "regardless of when the measure could be achieved." Yet Peyton did not shun the Whig Party in favor of Southern solidarity. He wrote, "I do not see how it is to injure us as a party abroad, or in other states. Questions will arise when men must go according to the peculiar interest or feelings of their people, regardless of party, & it may be done, without affecting the general party organization." In fact, by preventing Democrats from using Texas as a party issue, Whigs were likely to *improve* their chances in the upcoming election.[42]

Boardinghouse arrangements for the second session further demonstrate that the eight Whigs voting for annexation were not all North-hating Southerners. Newton, Ashe, and Dellet lived at Mrs. Potter's, a large, cross-sectional boardinghouse that also housed three Southern members who voted against Brown's resolutions. Stephens lived at Mrs. Carter's with one Rhode Island and one Massachusetts representative, both of whom opposed the measure. Clinch lived in a private residence near the White House. Of the eight rogue Whig representatives, only three lived in regional boardinghouses: Brown and Senter boarded with Henry Grider, a Kentucky Whig who voted against the annexation bill, and Peyton, who lived with the Tennessee Whig senator, Ephraim Foster, who would be responsible for the Senate version of Brown's resolutions.[43]

More important, the vast majority of the Whigs voted against annexation.

Seventeen Southern party members opposed the measure, including the entire delegations of North Carolina, Kentucky, Maryland, and Delaware. Seventy-two Whigs in total voted against annexation, 90 percent of the Whigs in the House. Whigs who voted against the measure also understood it as a partisan matter. After the vote, Joshua Giddings reported that the Southerners who voted for annexation "disgraced" the Whigs, but "they will be discarded from the party. No northern whig will ever associate with them I hope. Every whig from Kentucky North Carolina Maryland and Delaware stood firm and when the vote was taken a whig from Maryland remarked My God and said he 'are there eight whigs who will assist in carrying out this [damnable] deed?'"[44]

Northern Whigs were not the only ones who felt that the Southern rogues disgraced the party. A Georgian wrote to John Berrien, "What then may I expect from the future when I see two of the most prominent Whigs of my own state, its sole representatives in the popular branch of the national legislature, joining in a most palpable and dangerous assault upon the constitutional prerogatives of the Senate?" Similarly, George Tucker wrote Rives from the University of Virginia that, although he held a significant stock interest in Texas, he was appalled by the House resolutions and would "be rejoiced to hear that this most glaring of all violations of the Constitution" would fail in the Senate.[45]

The ensuing debate over annexation in the Senate also gave several Southern Whigs the opportunity to vocally oppose the measure. For example, Rives gave a weighty speech against Texas in mid-February, detailing the constitutional objections to Texas annexation by joint resolution. He explained that he was in favor of annexation, not because it would benefit Virginia or the South, but because he regarded "the acquisition of Texas as a great national object, only calculated to strengthen the whole confederacy." Yet, regardless of the benefits Texas might give to the country, it was his "responsibility as a senator of that ancient Commonwealth," to oppose the measure "if Texas can now be acquired only by a sacrifice of the constitution." Rives's speech mirrored other speeches given by Southern Whig senators. Archer, in particular, seconded Rives's assertions regarding the unconstitutionality of the measure.[46]

Northerners also argued against annexation for constitutional reasons. Many of them appealed to all Southerners—Democrats, too—by arguing that annexation would violate "the integrity of the states," in the words of New Jersey's William Dayton. Dayton, like other Northern Whigs, drew a distinction between himself and the abolitionists of the North. His objection to the measure did not lie in a wish to end slavery. As he told the Senate, "I am no fanatic myself, nor do I sympathize with such as are so." Several Northern Whigs seconded Dayton's assertion that reasonable men of the North rejected annexation for constitutional reasons, not antislavery reasons. These men wanted to demonstrate that they were sensible to the interests of their Southern counterparts.[47]

Notwithstanding continued Whig resistance, by February 20, hints that the Senate would pass the joint resolution became stronger. Willie Mangum told a friend that the measure would definitely pass with the votes of three Whigs. Clearly distressed, Mangum wrote, "The annexation in this form will excite a deep feeling in the North, North east & East. It will stir to its foundation the abolition and antislavery feeling, & lead not remotely I fear, to a state of things to be deplored by every friend of the Country." Yet Mangum took solace in the fact that most Whigs remained true to their party principles. "The Whigs are at ease," he explained. "They are quiet, cherishing no excessive feeling, but as a mass devoted to the principles of their Cause."[48]

On February 27 the Senate convened to vote on the measure and passed an amended joint resolution, 27–25. Three Whigs—all Southerners—voted in favor, including John Henderson of Mississippi, Henry Johnson of Louisiana, and William Merrick of Maryland. The rest of the affirmative votes came from twenty-four Democrats, while Whigs cast every negative vote. Even Spencer Jarnagin, who had offered the Milton Brown counterpart to the Senate, voted against annexation.[49]

Although the Texas bill passed, the Whig Party had not experienced a great rupture. Three Whigs broke with the party to vote for the measure. Yet Henderson had cast his vote in favor the previous June as well. Thus two Whigs effectively departed from the party line. Furthermore, Whigs had pursued the strategy that Clay and others had outlined in November and December, stipulating that the party should adhere to its principles but allow the Democrats to pass their policies with little resistance. Given this political context, Whigs were not divided; rather, they showed overwhelming solidarity.

After the Senate voted in favor, the measure was sent back to the House for a final vote. This time, the joint resolution passed by an overwhelming majority of 132 to 76. Yet, in this case, six of the eight Whigs who had initially voted in favor changed their votes to the negative, and one other abstained from voting. Dellet was the only Whig member to vote yea. As Foster had done in the Senate, Milton Brown rejected his own resolution.[50]

Many Whigs in the South reacted to the vote with disgust, particularly for those who had voted for the measure. In a March 10 diary entry, John Pendleton Kennedy wrote, "Merrick of Maryland, whose fidelity to the Whigs has always been more than doubtful, has proven [false] at the last moment and [gone] with the Locos. Thus Texas comes in by an act of treachery." Ambrose Barber, a correspondent from Macon, Georgia, wrote to Berrien, thanking him for his efforts to avert the measure's passage. Unfortunately, he told his friend, "acquiescence will give validity to the act, and constitutional liberty, under the guardianship of Democracy, may be swallowed up into the grave of despotism." Upon hearing the news, Clay declared, "God Save the Commonwealth!"[51]

Yet the Whigs, as a party, were not defeated: Whigs had not ruptured permanently over Texas; they had simply lost the vote. Northern Whigs did not blame Southerners for the success of annexation; they blamed Democrats. And they would continue to fight Democrats for their party's survival, a crucial strategy in promoting party unity. No issue was more unifying than the war with Mexico. Whig predictions that annexation would produce a war were not immediately realized, but in May 1846 Polk's attempt to acquire California incited conflict with Mexico. Although congressmen differed in votes for manpower and supplies for the army, inside and outside of Congress, Whigs condemned the conflict.[52]

Whigs also remained cross-sectionally united in the capital city. After the summer recess, the new Congress returned to Washington in the fall of 1845. The 1844 elections had produced some gains for the Democrats in Congress, and when the 286 members gathered for the first session, Democrats held the balance in the Senate, 34 to 22. In the House, 142 Democrats took their seats along with 79 Whigs and 6 members of the American Party. Although there were several new faces, Whigs' boardinghouse choices reflected no significant change in cross-sectional association. One hundred and seventy seven members lived in thirty-nine boardinghouses, only seven of which were regional.

As tables 5 and 6 demonstrate, Northern and Southern Whigs did not isolate themselves from one another when they returned to Congress in December 1845. In fact, more Whig boarders chose to live in cross-sectional houses during the Twenty-Ninth Congress than had done so in the Twenty-Eighth Congress. Although the number of Whig houses decreased, Whig solidarity remained high as the numbers of members in each boardinghouse grew. For example, Alexander Stephens remained in a cross-sectional boardinghouse, moving to Mrs. Carter's on Capitol Hill with Representatives Jacob Collamer of Vermont, Amos Abbott of Massachusetts, Andrew Steward and

TABLE 5 Regional and sectional dispersion of boardinghouses in the first session of
the Twenty-Ninth Congress

Boardinghouse type	No. of houses	Whig houses*	Democratic houses*
Regional	7	2	5
Cross-regional**	26	9	17
Cross-sectional**	17	6	11
Cross-party**	6	—	—

Source: *Congressional Directory for the First Session of the Twenty Ninth Congress of the United
States of America* (Washington: William Q. Force Printer, 1846).
*"Whig houses" denotes boardinghouses with only Whig members; "Democratic houses"
denotes houses with only Democrat members.
**Numbers for cross-sectional boardinghouses and for cross-party boardinghouses that
were also cross-regional are included in the cross-regional numbers.

Joseph Buffington of Pennsylvania, and Henry Cranston of Rhode Island.
Daniel King lived in Mr. Hyatt's on Pennsylvania Avenue with ten other rep-
resentatives from Massachusetts, New York, Ohio, and Kentucky. Critten-
den, who lived in a cross-sectional boardinghouse for both sessions of the
Twenty-Eighth Congress, moved to Mr. Stettinius's lodgings on Louisiana
Avenue with Spencer Jarnagin. Their messmates included Senator James
Pearce of Maryland and Representative Thomas Butler King of Georgia, as
well as three Ohioans, Senator Thomas Corwin and Representatives Robert
Schenck and Joseph Vance. Overall, the immediate effects of the Texas crises
had not resulted in divided living arrangements.

Sectionalism played a role in the conflict over Texas annexation, as it played
a role in the everyday lives of members. Still, historians should not consider
annexation an important stop on the road to disunion. Each member of the
Twenty-Eighth Congress was motivated by a series of interests, not all of
which were sectional. Moreover, not all members viewed Texas as a sectional issue, and as a party Whigs remained overwhelmingly united against
annexation.

Three points emphasize this cohesiveness. First, only three Whigs in the
Senate and eight Whigs in the House ever broke ranks from the party on
Texas issues. In fact, Whigs maintained greater party unity than the Demo-
crats in three out of the four votes taken in both houses on the measure.
Second, Whigs did not antagonize or verbally attack members in the other

TABLE 6   Regional and sectional dispersion of Whig and Democrat boarders in the first session of the Twenty-Ninth Congress

House type	No. of boarders	Whig boarders	Democrat boarders	Senator boarders	House boarders
Regional	25	4	21	7	18
Cross-regional*	152	64	88	21	131
Cross-sectional*	108	41	67	19	89
Cross-party*	20	11	9	3	17

Source: Congressional Directory for the First Session of the Twenty-Ninth Congress of the United States of America (Washington: William Q. Force Printer, 1846).

*Numbers for cross-sectional boardinghouses and for cross-party boardinghouses that were also cross-regional are included in the cross-regional numbers.

section. Those breaking party lines justified their votes primarily through arguments of state or local interest, not anti-Northern sentiment. Finally, the Texas issue did not injure relationships between Northern and Southern Whigs. When the members filed back to Washington for the Twenty-Ninth Congress, no sectional divide arose in the Whig ranks.

It is more than likely that the misinterpretation of sectionalism and the Whig Party in the Texas controversy has been clouded by later debates. Members used the memory of Texas annexation in their disputes over the Mexican War, the Wilmot Proviso, the Compromise of 1850, the Kansas-Nebraska Act, and other issues. Northerners and Southerners alike used the Texas controversy to justify their actions or create further discord between the two halves of the Union. Recollections of Texas, however, were not the same as the Texas controversy itself. The debates, letters, diary entries, travel accounts, boardinghouse records, and pamphlets referenced in this essay all demonstrate that Texas annexation did not create a sectional divide.

Notes

1. James L. Huston, review of *The Rise and Fall of the American Whig Party: Jacksonian Politics and the Onset of the Civil War,* by Michael F. Holt, H-Pol, H-Net Reviews, December, 1999; Eric Foner, *Free Soil, Free Labor, Free Men: The Ideology of the Republican Party before the Civil War* (New York: Oxford University Press, 1995), 9.

2. See for example Frederick Merk, *Slavery and the Annexation of Texas* (New York: Alfred A. Knopf, 1972); Joel Silbey, *Storm over Texas: The Annexation Controversy and the Road to Civil War* (New York: Oxford University Press, 2004), xvii; Peter Zavodnyik, *The Age of Strict Construction: A History of the Growth of Federal Power, 1789–1861*

(Washington, DC: Catholic University of America Press, 2007), especially 225–29; and William Freehling, *Road to Disunion*, vol. 1, *Secessionists at Bay* (New York: Oxford University Press, 1990), 449. In volume 1 of *Road to Disunion* Freehling was adamant that Texas annexation was "the largest turning point on the road to disunion" (353). He has since retreated somewhat from this claim in volume 2, *Secessionists Triumphant* (New York: Oxford University Press, 2007).

3. I chose to examine Washington politicians because of the erroneous contention that Whigs had nothing uniting them except a national party aimed at winning elections. Except for quadrennial national nominating conventions, Washington was the only place in the Union where Northerners and Southerners from both parties interacted on a daily basis. While other members of these two sections may have had yearly or even monthly economic transactions that brought them into contact with one another, politicians in Washington had daily if not hourly interaction and communication.

4. Thomas Brown, *Politics and Statesmanship: Essays on the American Whig Party* (New York: Columbia University Press, 1985), 11; Daniel Walker Howe, *The Political Culture of the American Whigs* (Chicago: University of Chicago Press, 1979), 32, 74.

5. Michael F. Holt, *The Rise and Fall of the American Whig Party: Jacksonian Politics and the Onset of the Civil War* (New York: Oxford University Press, 1999), 160–61; Joel Silbey, *The Shrine of Party: Congressional Voting Behavior, 1841–1852* (Pittsburgh: University of Pittsburgh Press, 1967); Thomas Alexander, *Sectional Stress and Party Strength: A Study of Roll-Call Voting Patterns in the United States House of Representatives, 1836–1860* (Nashville: Vanderbilt University Press, 1967), 31.

6. When Nathaniel Tallmadge, a New York Whig, left the Senate to become the governor of Wisconsin Territory in June 1844, he was replaced by Daniel Dickinson, a Democrat. Thus, the second session of the Twenty-Eighth Congress included twenty-eight Whigs and twenty-four Democrats.

7. James Sterling Young, *The Washington Community, 1800–1828* (New York: Columbia University Press, 1966), 98–102, 104 (quotation on 98).

8. For the purposes of this study, I used two different types of categorizations to analyze Whig boardinghouse arrangements. First, I divided the United States in 1843 into five "regions": New England (Maine, New Hampshire, Vermont, Massachusetts, Connecticut, and Rhode Island), the Middle Atlantic (New York, New Jersey, Pennsylvania, and Delaware), the Northwest (Ohio, Indiana, Illinois, and Michigan), the Southeast (Maryland, Virginia, North Carolina, South Carolina, Georgia, and Florida), and the Southwest (Louisiana, Mississippi, Alabama, Arkansas, Tennessee, Kentucky, and Missouri). Second, I divided the country into the two "sections" commonly associated with it—the separating line being slave and nonslaveholding states. I borrowed most of the framework for these divisions from Alexander, *Sectional Stress and Party Strength*, 5.

9. Spencer Jarnagin to his wife, Washington City, April 19, 1844, Spencer Jarnagin Papers, Southern Historical Collection, University of North Carolina, Chapel Hill.

10. Merk, *Slavery and the Annexation of Texas*, ix; Justin H. Smith, *The Annexation of Texas* (New York: AMS, 1971), 66, 103.

11. Holt, *Rise and Fall*, 176; Merk, *Slavery and the Annexation of Texas*, x, 33–34.

12. For petitions see *Congressional Globe*, 28th Cong., 1st Sess., April 1 and 3, 1844. For letters and speeches see Daniel Webster to Edward Everett, Boston, April 1, 1844, and

Daniel Webster to Charles Allen, March 13, 1844, in Charles M. Wiltse, ed., *The Papers of Daniel Webster, Correspondence*, vol. 6, *1844–1849* (Hanover, NH: University Press of New England, 1984), 41; "Letter of Mr. Walker of Mississippi, Relative to the Annexation of Texas," quoted in Merk, *Slavery and the Annexation of Texas*, 9.

13. To head off Calhoun's efforts, some Northern Whigs tried to prevent Tyler from offering the treaty to Congress at all. See *Congressional Globe*, 28th Cong., 1st Sess., March 15 and 25, 1844. Before sending the Texas documents to the Senate, Calhoun wrote a letter to British minister Richard Pakenham, resurrecting correspondence between the British minister and Abel Upshur. Pakenham had written Upshur in late February, transmitting a dispatch from his government that mentioned Great Britain's wish to eventually eliminate slavery throughout the globe. Calhoun submitted the Pakenham correspondence to the Senate with the treaty, attempting to revive American concern that the British were interested in acquiring Texas to abolish slavery in the United States. See Merk, *Slavery and the Annexation of Texas*, 57; and Smith, *The Annexation of Texas*, 194–96.

14. Henry Clay to John J. Crittenden, Savannah, March 24, 1844, in Melba Porter Hay, ed., *The Papers of Henry Clay*, vol. 10 (Lexington: University Press of Kentucky, 1991), 13.

15. Henry Clay to the editors of the *Washington Daily National Intelligencer*, Raleigh, April 17, 1844, in *Papers of Henry Clay*, 10:41. Clay was not the only national party leader to publicly resist annexation. Clay's letter to the *National Intelligencer* appeared on the same day, April 27, as a statement from Martin Van Buren, the man thought to be the heavy favorite for the Democratic presidential nomination in 1844. Van Buren submitted a letter to the *Washington Globe*, expressing his opposition to annexation.

16. Holt, *Rise and Fall*, 178–79.

17. D. F. Caldwell to Daniel Barringer, April 10, 1844, Daniel Morneau Barringer Papers, Southern Historical Collection, University of North Carolina, Chapel Hill; David Campbell to William B. Campbell, Montcalm, April 10, 1844, Campbell Family Papers, Perkins Library Special Collections, Duke University.

18. D. F. Caldwell to Daniel Barringer and T. L. Clingman, May 11, 1844, Barringer Papers.

19. *Washington National Intelligencer*, April 2, 1844.

20. William Hayden to Willie P. Mangum, Atlas Office, Boston, April 6, 1844, Mangum Family Papers, Library of Congress.

21. William L. Dayton to Leverett Saltonstall, Senate Chamber, April 5, 1844, in Robert E. Moody, ed., *The Papers of Leverett Saltonstall, 1816–1845*, vol. 5, *January 1843–May 1845* (Boston: Massachusetts Historical Society, 1992), 213; William Seward to Severn Teackle Wallis and others, Auburn, April 5, 1844, William Henry Seward Papers, Rush Rhees Library, University of Rochester, microfilm.

22. *New York Tribune*, Monday, May 27, 1844; *Charlotte Journal*, May 3, June 7, July 18, 1844, quoted in Mark W. Kruman, *Parties and Politics in North Carolina, 1836–1865* (Baton Rouge: Louisiana State University Press, 1983), 110.

23. Alexander H. Stephens to James Turner, Washington, DC, May 17, 1844, in Ulrich B. Phillips, ed., "The Correspondence of Robert Toombs, Alexander H. Stephens, and Howell Cobb," *Annual Report of the American Historical Association for the Year 1911* 2 (1913): 57.

24. Tyler had sent the Texas treaty to the Senate on April 22, but it was immediately referred to the Committee on Foreign Relations, chaired by the anti-annexationist Whig

William Archer of Virginia. Archer's committee discussed the treaty and offered it back to the Senate "without amendment." Debate over Tyler's treaty was conducted in closed executive session, lasting until June 8. See Merk, *Slavery and the Annexation of Texas*, 69; and Smith, *The Annexation of Texas*, 258.

25. *Appendix to the Congressional Globe*, 28th Cong., 1st Sess., June 8, 1844; Giddings to his daughter, Washington City, April 28, 1844 (Giddings's emphasis), Joshua Giddings Papers, Ohio Historical Society, microfilm.

26. *Congressional Globe*, 28th Cong., 1st Sess., June 8, 1844. Also see Holt, *Rise and Fall*, 173. John Pendleton Kennedy to his wife, June 15, 1844, John Pendleton Kennedy Papers, Enoch Pratt Free Library, Baltimore, microfilm.

27. See Henry Clay to Willie P. Mangum, Ashland, June 7, 1844, Mangum Family Papers; Holt, *Rise and Fall*, 173.

28. Henry Clay to Stephen Miller, Lexington, July 1, 1844, *Papers of Henry Clay*, 10:78.

29. Ben Perley Poore, *Perley's Reminiscences*, vol. 1, reprint ed. (New York: AMS, 1971), 323 (quotation); Holt, *Rise and Fall*, 180.

30. William B. Campbell to David Campbell, Carthage, July 9, 1844, Campbell Family Papers; William C. Rives to Henry Clay, Castle Hill, July 15, 1844, William C. Rives Papers, Library of Congress.

31. Journal of William Cabell Rives, 1844, Rives Papers; Robert Winthrop to Leverett Saltonstall, Boston, September 16, 1844, *Papers of Leverett Saltonstall*, 245; John Pendleton Kennedy to his wife, June 15, 1844, Kennedy Papers.

32. *New York Tribune*, September 12, 1844.

33. Arthur Campbell to James Campbell, November 21, 1844, Campbell Family Papers. Holt explains that although Clay lost the electoral vote 170–105, Polk beat him by only 38,000 in the popular vote. The vote was so close that had he taken New York, Clay would have beaten Polk. Holt, *Rise and Fall*, 194.

34. David Campbell to Arthur Campbell, February 11, 1845, Campbell Family Papers; Lex Renda, "Retrospective Voting and the Presidential Election of 1844: The Texas Issue Revisited," *Presidential Studies Quarterly* 24:4 (Fall 1944): 839–41. Renda shows that Whigs actually experienced a resurgence in 1844 and Texas more likely helped rather than hurt the Whig cause.

35. Under this act, South Carolina could imprison free black seamen from the North upon their arrival in Charleston.

36. John Pendleton Kennedy to his wife, December 10, 1844, Kennedy Papers. Boardinghouses reshuffled from session to session as some closed for repairs or financial reasons. Some members did make boardinghouse plans over the summer or at the end of the first session, yet others took up rooms upon their arrival in Washington. If the election had produced a great migration out of cross-sectional boardinghouses, those numbers might be reflected in the records of the first session of the Twenty-Ninth Congress.

37. Henry Clay to John J. Crittenden, November 28, 1844, Clay Autograph File, Houghton Library, Harvard University.

38. See Merk, *Slavery and the Annexation of Texas*, 121; and Holt, *Rise and Fall*, 220.

39. Smith, *The Annexation of Texas*, 332. Illinois Democrat Stephen Douglas attached an amendment making explicit declaration that slavery should not exist north of the Missouri Compromise line.

40. *Congressional Globe*, 28th Cong., 2d Sess., January 25, 1845.

41. *Letter of Willoughby Newton, of Virginia, Addressed to his Constituents, Chiefly in Explanation and Defense of the Joint Resolutions, Passed by the House of Representatives for the Admission of Texas Into the Union* (Washington: J. and G. S. Gideon, 1845), Albert and Shirley Small Special Collections Library, University of Virginia.

42. J. H. Peyton to William Campbell, February 16, 1845, Campbell Family Papers.

43. *Congressional Directory for the Second Session of the Twenty-Eighth Congress of the United States of America* (Washington, DC: Wm. Q. Force, printer, 1843–44).

44. Joshua Giddings to unknown, January 25, 1845, Giddings Papers.

45. Charles J. Jenkins to John M. Berrien, Augusta, February 3, 1845, John M. Berrien Papers, Southern Historical Collection, University of North Carolina, Chapel Hill; George Tucker to William C. Rives, January 31, 1845, Rives Papers.

46. *Appendix to the Congressional Globe*, 28th Cong., 2d Sess., February 15, 1845.

47. Ibid., February 21, 1845. See, for example, the speech of Jacob Miller, ibid., February 21, 1845.

48. Willie P. Mangum to Tod R. Caldwell, February 20, 1845, in Henry Thomas Shanks, ed., *The Papers of Willie P. Mangum* (Raleigh, NC: State Department of Archives and History, 1955), 267.

49. Smith, *The Annexation of Texas*, 342–45; Holt, *Rise and Fall*, 221; *Congressional Globe*, 28th Cong., 2d Sess., February 27, 1845.

50. *Congressional Globe*, 28th Cong., 2d Sess., February 27, 1845. See also Smith, *The Annexation of Texas*, 349; and Holt, *Rise and Fall*, 221.

51. Diary of John Pendleton Kennedy, March 10, 1845, Kennedy Papers; Ambrose Barber to John Berrien, Macon, March 28, 1845, Berrien Papers; Henry Clay to John Berrien, March 19, 1845, Berrien Papers. Clay wrote a similar message to Kennedy on January 31 after the measure passed the House. Henry Clay to John Pendleton Kennedy, January 31, 1845, *Papers of Henry Clay*, 10:194. For similar Northern response, see William S. G. Brown to Hamilton Fish, Erie, March 18, 1845, Hamilton Fish Papers, Library of Congress; and Daniel P. King to Leverett Saltonstall, Washington, February 21, 1845, *Papers of Leverett Saltonstall*, 325.

52. Holt, *Rise and Fall*, 231–33.

Apotheosis of a Ruffian

The Murder of Bill Pool and American Political Culture

MARK E. NEELY JR.

In the early hours of a Sunday morning in February 1855, in a saloon on Broadway in New York City, an ex-policeman named Lewis Baker shot and mortally wounded a saloonkeeper named William Pool. Originally reported in the press as a Saturday night brawl among "pugilists," by the time of Pool's death—days later from a bullet in his remarkably sturdy heart—the event had somehow become the centerpiece of a vast public demonstration of political support for the cause of Know-Nothingism. The death of William Pool, perhaps because it occurred in the winter of an odd-numbered year and not in the summer of an even-numbered one, is best known in sports history and urban history, but its political features were important and should be better known to political historians. In political history, Pool's reputation was tied closely to nativism and the Know-Nothing Party, and the complete collapse of that organization by the end of the 1850s assured that Pool's fame would be only temporary. He had come close to fame: perhaps one hundred thousand New Yorkers watched his funeral procession, there was at least one lithographed portrait of him, and a statuary company was prepared to manufacture a plaster bust as well.

"You Can't Disfigure Me Any More Than I Am"

Whatever else it was, the death of Bill Pool was a landmark in the history of the Know-Nothing Party in New York City. His funeral, one of the largest in memory in the great city, marked, according to the *New York Herald,* the first mass public appearance of the Know-Nothing Party in the public spaces of New York City.[1] But in truth, the meaning of the death of Bill Pool remains elusive to any field of history—political, sports, urban, social.

Sports history properly lays claim to the interpretation of Pool's death be-cause one of the people involved in the brawls at the saloon that fateful night was John Morrissey. "Old Smoke" Morrissey was a famous bare-knuckle boxer whose "sports" career was on the rise in 1855, when the murder occurred. He had already fought a celebrated match with "Yankee" Sullivan in 1853. He had fought unsuccessfully with Pool in New York City in 1854, not exactly in a prizefight, apparently, but more as a matter of gang culture.[2] On the night of the murder in 1855, Pool had left his own saloon, which was called the Bank Exchange, to go to another, Stanwix Hall, where Morrissey was eating and drinking. Pool apparently did not know beforehand that Morrissey was there. There was very bad blood between them.

The prizefights between famous violent figures like Pool and Morrissey were unsupervised by any prizefighting authority or umbrella organization or corporation. The only referees were the pugilists' own gangs of supporters watching the two men fight. Accusations of cheating were common, and the partisans on the sidelines sometimes entered the frays themselves when things started going badly for their favorites. Therefore disputes over the prize money were rife. Those who held the money advanced by each side before the fight sometimes did not surrender the stakes because the fight was not fairly won in their eyes. Since eye gouging, chewing off lips and noses, and biting through cheeks were common tactics, it is difficult for an outsider to see what was fair and what not. But in the case of the Morrissey-Pool fight of July 1854, Morrissey claimed that Pool's partisans, who greatly outnumbered those in the crowd rooting for Morrissey, had pulled Morrissey down and themselves kicked him. Pugilists were violent men, and disputes over money could easily lead to more violence. By 1855 nothing had apparently really been settled between the two.

When Morrissey emerged from another room in the saloon that fateful winter night, the two men first argued at the nonpolitical level of "coward" and "liar." Morrissey abused and insulted Pool as a "black-muzzled son of a bitch" but also as an "American son of a bitch." Pool returned the abuse in kind: Morrissey was "an Irish bastard." Pool produced a revolver for a fight. Morrissey had none, apparently. A fight was averted, but Pool then got into a shouting match with a man named McGuire and challenged him to fight with butcher knives. McGuire backed down.[3] The police appeared, took Morrissey off, and at the later brawl in which Pool was shot, Morrissey was not present.[4] Morrissey's friends shot Pool.

There was nothing sporting about the death of Bill Pool; it was murder, pure and simple. And there was nothing sporting about the presence of pugilists, fighting men, and "shoulder hitters" (thugs who intimidated voters at the polls and knocked down party operatives at primary meetings) in politics.

The pugilists simply had the skill set the political organizers were seeking. At a certain level, the pugilists *were* the organizers. The sports historian Elliott Gorn, who has written about the overlap of sport and election violence, intimidation, and fraud, enhances the sporting quality of the men employed to do the bloody political work of the Second Party System by framing his discussion around the meaning of "bare-knuckle boxing." But these election thugs used more than their fists, as Bill Pool knew to his sorrow. The resort to firearms takes much of the quality of sporting honor out of the picture of this class of political operatives. Of course, these brutes had other occupations besides political violence. They were also prizefighters and saloonkeepers and gamblers. But a similar statement could be made about lawyers and newspaper editors. They had other occupations too, but they were the mainstays of the more visible and proper portion of political parties.

Gorn suggests that the pugilists were in some way offering a protest against Victorian middle-class values. They were in fact supporters of those values at least in some compartments of their lives. Bill Pool was married and fathered two children (only one of whom was still alive in 1855). Pool's self-conscious deathbed scene might be said to have come right out of the Victorian sentimental manual for passing to the great beyond. When he was near death, he revealed a fear of being buried underground and stipulated that he be laid to rest aboveground and asked that the son who had died in childhood be exhumed and placed on his breast. Surely such sentimentality—the spooky qualities aside—was comfortably Victorian. He asked his mother to read a chapter from the Bible to him, and when she asked whether he wanted to see a clergyman, he said he did. A very able Methodist minister delivered a sermon at the elaborate funeral. Pool was said always to have dressed respectably and to have behaved politely in ordinary society. He asked to be dressed in his coffin in a black suit, and he was.[5] One has to strain to find any systematic "affirmation" of working-class "culture" in the lives of these men.

If anything, the prizefight was a pale and distorted imitation of a pre-Victorian and aristocratic order. Indeed, the prizefight was in part a grisly lower-class imitation of the upper-class and aristocratic duel. When Morrissey had challenged Pool to fight back in the summer of 1854, for example, Pool could pick the weapons. In turn, Morrissey had the right to pick the dueling ground. Of course, men did not bet on duels, and betting was central to the prizefight—was a part of the very name of the enterprise—but the betters who followed the shadowy world of prizefighting were called "the fancy" and included men of wealth and property. The prize money was a step to respectability for the ruffians in the fight and could lead, as in Pool's case, to ownership of a saloon, or in Morrissey's, to considerable wealth and fame. One is reminded of an earlier and non-city-bred group of violent men, the Mountain Men of the early nineteenth century, who went west and braved terrible dangers and high mortality, not to escape civilization or middle-class values but to earn enough of the rewards from the fur trade to return and become members of the society they had once abandoned for the mountains.[6]

In America's confusion of social classes, in fact, dueling had been made bourgeois (and more deadly, by the common use of rifles as chosen weapons), and the old practice was in fact undergoing a renaissance all over the United State in the 1850s. All kinds of violence, except that against abolitionists, appears to have been on the rise in that decade.[7] After the Fugitive Slave Act of 1850, the antislavery forces were themselves contributing to the culture of violence by interfering with force against the apprehension of alleged fugitive slaves. From top to bottom, American society in the 1850s was wracked with violence. There were riots about capitalism in the Erie, Pennsylvania, railroad war, in which the violent crowds included women.[8] Volunteer firemen, noted for their hypermasculine feats of strength, frequently engaged in disgraceful, dysfunctional, and life-threatening fisticuffs as representatives of their distinct companies and engine houses in the cities. Instead of pouring oil on turbulent waters, religion—in the undisciplined form of street preaching—was playing a role in drawing crowds to the public parks and city hall steps and dockyard piers and stirring them up to rock-throwing and weapon-brandishing ethnic and religious violence, again in cities. Political violence was so routine that ward meetings were sometimes reported on in the press less for their political results than for the presence or absence of fighting and arrests by the police.[9] On top of all that, then the new wave of dueling swept through all the social classes of the country. These somewhat higher-class pugilists seem to have been inspired by the high-profile challenge to a duel over the Kansas-Nebraska Act issued by New York congressman Francis Cutting to John C. Breckenridge in late March 1854. The mania spread high and low in society. Eventually some African American men engaged in affairs of honor.[10]

For the men described as pugilists, rowdies, prizefighters, or shoulder hitters, fighting was central to their identities, and despite some obvious desires for respectability, they spent weekend nights at saloons and gambling dens, not at the hearth reading to the family circle. Indeed their lives of revolting and ruthless violence left some of them physically almost monsters. Patrick McLaughlin, the violent thug who led the group of Morrissey partisans back to Stanwix Hall and initiated the insults that led to the fatal brawl, was a grotesque specimen of street violence. Born in Ireland, he was a thief and fighter for all his mature life in the United States. He bit off a man's thumb or finger in a fight in the notorious Five Points neighborhood of New York City. Another brawler named Michael Murray bit off McLauhglin's nose in 1848. In turn, McLaughlin—he was called Paugene or Paudeen—bit off an adversary's lower lip. When Paugene challenged Pool to fight him in Stanwix Hall on February 25, 1855, there was already very bad blood between them, because Pool had tried to keep Paugene out of his saloon six weeks earlier because he was Irish. Paugene wanted to fight then and said, "You can't disfigure me any more than I am."[11]

Fighting was central to their identities, but so was politics. "Shoulder hitter" was political slang for an election bully. It was a political term. "Prizefighter" and "pugilist" were sporting terms. The press used them interchangeably in describing these men, whether on Election Day or on the docks biting each others' noses off purely for money and bragging rights.

The truly respectable classes did not see the respectable Victorian side of Pool, only the brawling and socially destructive side. From beginning to end the *New York Tribune,* Horace Greeley's reformist newspaper, treated the affair at Stanwix Hall as a tragicomic display of the consequences of drinking and carousing and cultivating violence. In the period after the assault but before Pool died of his wounds, the *Tribune* headed an article on the subject this way: "Freaks of the Fancy. Abortive Attempt to Murder Bill Poole. Morrissey's Midnight Merry-Making." The paper introduced the story that followed as a "piquant sketch of midnight amusements." The editors rather haughtily sniffed, "As the fun was all amongst themselves, and conducted appropriately in a liquor store, whereby the more orderly portion of the people were safe from danger, it is hardly worthwhile commenting on this entertainment."[12] The editors seemed interested at first in putting the episode to the good use of urban reform. "We trust," they wrote after Pool finally died of his horrendous wounds, "that this brutal homicide may have its use in putting a check upon that rampant ruffianism, fruit of political corruption, gambling, and the liquor-trade, with which the City has been too long afflicted and disgraced."[13] The other city newspapers followed suit in denouncing the crime, though they did not necessarily attempt to mount a crusade for good government and against drinking. After Pool's death the headlines were a bit more respectful of the dead: the *Tribune* described the event as "The Ruffian's Tragedy."[14]

"Exerting Considerable Influence in City Politics"

Whatever Pool's level of social respectability in society, he was, in New York City ward politics, a force to contend with. As late as 1862 Pool was still remembered by newspapermen as "the idol of the Ninth Ward" who "carried the votes of the people in his breeches pocket."[15] In their political capacity any resemblance to the rough-and-tumble mountain men breaks down, for there was nothing political about men like John "Liver-Eating" Johnson. But identity politics lay at the very heart of prizefighting in America in the 1850s. The hostile *Tribune* said of the victim, "He has been known as a political operator and a sort of contractor for carrying primary meetings, and managing conventions. It is said that he has for a few years past mostly controlled the Eighth and Ninth Wards, and has been an active member of the Whig Committee at the Broadway House, besides otherwise exerting considerable influence in City politics."[16] The election returns from the Eighth and Ninth Wards provide a warning that we cannot entirely trust what the newspapers said on the subject of shoulder hitters, the men who intimidated voters at elections and political party meetings. Pool did not really control those wards, but he apparently did an adequate job for his political allies.

New York City's wards were all Democratic in voting by the time of the Civil War, but Whigs and Know-Nothings like Pool were more competitive in the City than Republicans turned out to be. In 1852 Whigs had carried three of twenty wards even with their party crippled by an inept presidential candidate, Winfield Scott.[17]

Eulogists, like the author of the pamphlet biography published to benefit the Know-Nothings just after Pool's death, were willing to admit that Pool "was a smart electioneer at primary and general elections."[18] Whatever his methods, in the autumn elections of 1854, both of the wards associated with Pool turned in pluralities for the Know-Nothing mayoral candidate, James Barker. No doubt political feeling had been intensified and polarized by the notorious riot that occurred in the Ninth Ward on the Fourth of July in 1853. At that time, a parade of the Ancient Order of Hibernians, gotten up apparently to show their loyalty to the United States on the birthday of its independence, backfired when a commercial wagon driver tried to cross the line of the procession with his stage. The ensuing confusion apparently enraged the Irish Americans in the parade and probably the onlooking crowd too, the driver was beaten, and thirty-seven members of the parade were arrested after a wild melee of violence. The riot made news all over the country to the distress of the Irish Americans, who were generally blamed for brutally beating the hapless driver in a fit of uncontrollable rage. The event is interesting in itself for revealing the keen desire of the Irish Americans to identify with the American flag. In an indignation meeting afterward, Irish American speakers insisted that "they loved the country over which the stars and stripes flowed, and would, if it was necessary, lay down their lives in its behalf."[19]

If the American flag had not been appropriated completely to the cause of either side, the two sides had surely been politically polarized in the Ninth and Eighth Wards. The winner of the election citywide turned out to be the Soft-Shell Democrat Fernando Wood. The Whigs ran a merchant named Herrick, and the independent-minded Wilson H. Hunt, a Hard-Shell Democrat who also enjoyed reformist credentials, was a candidate too.[20] The results for the wards Pool played a role in are summarized in table 1.

The political situation was wildly complicated at the time, and it would be difficult to know the meaning of these figures even were we privy to the work of shadowy operatives like Pool. Fernando Wood, for example, was in 1854 not only the Democratic standard-bearer for mayor but also, until the scandal broke shortly before the election, secretly a member of the Know-Nothing Party.[21] Even the contemporary newspapers were baffled by the aldermanic race in the Ninth Ward, which the *Times* characterized as a "severe contest" among Whig, Hard, Soft, Know-Nothing, Temperance, and Independent candidates.[22] Returns for the gubernatorial race from the Eighth and Ninth Wards are noted in table 2. Pool may have been the boss of the Know-Nothing (and earlier, Whig) vote in one of the more closely contested areas of the city. "Boss" is not the right term, surely, but he had influence.[23]

Pool's influence over hundreds of Whig and later Know-Nothing voters may seem surprising, given his low-status occupations (he had been a butcher before becoming a saloonkeeper), but as the historian Tyler Anbinder points out in his history of the Five Points neighborhood (the Sixth Ward), common avenues to party leadership in such wards included saloonkeeping and membership in a volunteer fire department. Pool was a saloonkeeper and was affiliated with a volunteer fire company.[24] What might be a disqualification

TABLE 1   Eighth and Ninth Ward voting in 1854 New York City mayoral race

Ward	Herrick	Wood	Barker	Hunt
Eighth	339	937	1,188	1,064
Ninth	444	824	1,389	1,211

Source: Adapted from *New York Times*, November 9, 1854.

Ward	Clark (Whig)	Seymour (S)	Bronson (H)	Gilman (KN)
Eighth	733	1,251	245	946
Ninth	1,051	1,232	256	1,363

Source: Adapted from *New York Times,* November 9, 1854. The "S," "H," and "KN" designations are the ones used by the newspaper.

for a candidate for major office, keeping a saloon, was thus a qualification for a party operative at another level of the organization. In looking after the Know-Nothing interest in that part of the city, Pool was not on the side of the angels, but it looked as though he would soon be on the winning side. The *New York Times,* for example, noted that the most astonishing quality of the 1854 election was "the tremendous vote cast for the Know-Nothing Candidates."[25]

"The American Fighting Man"

Accounts of what happened on that cold night in February 1855 in Stanwix Hall vary, but the one I have stitched together here emphasizes the evidence of political motivation and connection. To begin with, Pool ran a saloon that did not willingly serve Irish Americans. Customers knew it as "an American house." Although some would proclaim "that Irishmen had as good a right to come there as other people," the bartenders "would tell them that they did not want any Irishmen to spend their money in the house." Pool himself said that he did not want any customers who did not eat meat on Fridays.[26] The saloon stood as an ethno-cultural statement, and much that went on inside it was charged with the animosities and tensions of identity politics. As it happened, Pool was mortally wounded in another saloon, but the ethnic tensions hung over his presence anywhere. He had been attacked the year before in Jersey City for wearing a Know-Nothing hat. Taunted that night in 1855 as a "pretty American son of a bitch," Pool replied with the confidence of a leader, "Yes I am—I am their standard-bearer."[27] He was the self-proclaimed standard-bearer of the Americans. The title was ambiguous, of course, as Pool was native born, but he was also likely an activist in the American or Know-Nothing Party.

On Saturday night, February 24, 1855, the affair began. Police intervened in the first brawl, described earlier in this essay, and carried Morrissey off. They persuaded Pool to go to a station to swear out a complaint, but Morrissey was released before arriving at any police station. Pool had nothing to do at the station house when he arrived there, and he returned to drink with his pals in the closed saloon (it was past hours and had to be closed on Sunday morning). Patrick McLaughlin then came into Stanwix Hall in company with Lewis Baker (the ex-policeman), Jim Turner (about thirty and once trained as a cooper), Cornelius Linn (a twenty-year-old jeweler from New York City) and Charles Van Pelt (a thirty-one-year-old butcher, also from New York City). They called out "the American fighting man."[28] Patrick McLaughlin spat three times in Pool's face. Nativist partisans later said that was done "to get him to fight so they could murder him without suspicion of premeditation."[29] That may well be true. The *Atlas,* which did not excuse the fracas, considered such insults as Pool had to bear that night full cause for violent retaliation.[30]

Pool, though he had a pistol when Morrissey visited the saloon, now went through a cock-of-the-walk challenge to fisticuffs. He would fight any of them for $500, he boasted, and plunked five $20 gold pieces into the hand of a friend named Dean. The visiting gang did not have $100 among them to match the earnest money for the fight. Turner, who may have been bent on Pool's murder for some time, had had enough. He threw his cloak on the bar and shouted, "Let's sail in, anyway." He had a five-shot Colt pistol and steadied it on his arm to shoot Pool but shot himself in the forearm. He fell with his arm shattered but kept firing and hit Pool in the knee. That was the beginning of the end of the American standard-bearer. Pool fell to the floor, and Baker, a large man, five feet ten inches tall, weighing 190 pounds, jumped on the wounded Pool, put a six-barrel revolver to his heart, and fired. It was amazing Pool lived as long as he did afterward, fourteen days, and his wound even invited medical explanations in the newspapers.

Pool's partisans had been too few and too late to act. His brother-in-law, Charles Lozier, tried to help but was shot twice by McLaughlin. The wild-shooting Turner apparently wounded his own ally Baker twice. Three of the gang fled to a gambling hall run by Johnny Lyng and were arrested there. Baker was likely with them, and perhaps because he had been a policeman, the investigating police conspicuously ignored an obvious hiding place.[31] With the help later of Alderman James Kerrigan, he fled, it was said, to the Canary Islands, and an expensive search at sea aided by the federal government failed to intercept him.[32]

For all the nativist drama and ethno-cultural hatred that framed the affair, there must have been more to it than that (but what else was involved we will not likely ever know). The fact is that Pool's murderer, the policeman Baker, was a Welshman, and therefore not likely a Catholic; moreover, he had once been the ally and protégé of the nativist Pool himself. One of the political powers wielded by men at Pool's level in the party organizations was the ability to find men paying jobs with the police department.

"Apotheosis of a Ruffian"

After the fight, with its mixed motives, nativist political forces took over the funeral arrangements. A "Pool Association" was formed immediately at his death, and its secretary was Christian W. Shaffer, a leading Know-Nothing speaker. Its chairman discouraged the wearing of any emblems that might have a "bad effect" on Pool's detractors and insisted that the law must take its course. Yet the funeral itself was arranged in defiance of such an idea. Indeed there was no other reason for a funeral spectacle—for the arrangement of an "apotheosis of a ruffian"—but to make a marching and rolling political statement, just as Pool's saloon was a political statement as edifice. The respectable *New York Tribune* expressed only shock and dismay at such a spectacle gotten up in behalf of a man like Pool. The public display reflected on the "respectability of a community." "A notorious fighting character," the editorial went on, "who kept a drinking and gambling house, whose associates were of the very dregs of society, men who live by corruption, violence, dicing, drabbing, and crimes that might make angels weep—this man—murdered by foul companions—received the ovation of a great public funeral."[33]

The funeral began at 2:00 on the afternoon of March 11, 1855. Pool was laid out in a broadcloth suit with a symbol of the Order of United Americans, an early nativist organization, on his body. An American flag was draped over the coffin, though Pool was not a veteran of the armed services.

The political parties and shoulder hitters could not control the press, religion, or the family. The opposition press—in this case, all of the press claiming respectability—said few kind words about Pool and the pugilists. Pool's widow, for her part, refused to allow a plaster death mask of her husband to be taken as the basis for a popular bust. If that happened, she said, Pool's face would look down on the crowds at every porterhouse in the city, and she wanted to avoid that.[34]

More worthy of lengthy comment was the role of institutional religion. The funeral began with a funeral sermon by J. B. Wakely of the Jane Street Methodist Church. He had a difficult role to play and might have lent his skills, which were considerable, to the forces that were turning Pool's brawling murder into a crusade for political anti-Catholicism. The established Protestant churches seem to have been faulted for giving the green light to the uneducated and ranting "street preachers," who, after the visit of the papal nuncio Gaetano Bedini to the United States, turned their rabble-rousing skills to militant preaching against the Catholic Church.[35] In fact, the record of the institutional churches in New York City was mixed, and many did not join the street preachers in focusing their message on anti-Catholicism.

The central message the Know-Nothings wished to drive home from Pool's death featured his alleged deathbed declaration, "I die a true American." Wakely repeated the slogan but declared, "We see the folly and danger of national prejudice. We cannot blame a man for loving his country. . . . A man cannot help being born in this place or that." He affirmed the right of Americans to defend themselves from violence aimed at them merely because they were Americans, but he insisted, in words directed to Pool's Order of United Americans, that the repentant Pool would say, "Let there be no violence in avenging my death." Overall, he depicted Pool as a victim of being motherless from the age of eighteen months, for thereby failing to benefit from the nurture of home values, and ultimately for not being home instead of in a saloon with toughs so late on the night he was murdered. "Home! Home!" was the simple message of the sermon. This Methodist minister did not indulge in anti-Catholic invective at the volatile moment or make Pool a martyr. The sermon did not seem to pacify the widow, who wept uncontrollably and declared that she could cope with death but not with murder. Wakely had essentially focused on the "striking defects" in Pool's character.[36]

The political anti-Catholic forces of the Pool Association took over from there, however. There were eight pallbearers for Pool's hearse, one of them an alderman. One was a celebrated prizefighter, Tom Hyer. Four white horses decorated with plumes pulled the hearse, which bore the motto "I die a true American" on either side. The procession included a hired musical group, the celebrated Dodsworth Band—fifty-two men strong. Representatives of two fire department engine companies (the Howard and the Live Oak) marched in the procession, as did a thousand men from the Organization of United Americans and five hundred Know-Nothings. Thus some two thousand men dressed in black broadcloth accompanied the ruffian's corpse to its final resting place. The Monroe Guard and the Alert Guard also marched. Delegations of nativists came from Albany, Philadelphia, and Baltimore. It took forty minutes for the procession to pass one point, and the *Tribune* estimated the procession itself at four thousand persons. Their estimate of the spectators ran to one hundred thousand, including people at windows and on rooftops and at balconies. The less hostile *Herald* estimated the crowd along the route at eighty thousand. The *Atlas* put the crowd at one hundred thousand and attributed the spectators' presence to the impression that Pool "fell a martyr to 'American principles.'"[37] The route was long, stretching from Pool's residence on Christopher Street to a ferry and then across the river to Greenwood Cemetery.[38]

The plea to avoid party emblems apparently went unnoticed, and the *Herald* trumpeted the "First Appearance of the Know Nothings in the Public Streets." The once-secret membership now identified themselves by wearing "narrow strips of red, white, and blue ribbon tied with black crape in their button holes." The Order of United Americans symbol on the corpse was, according to the *Herald,* part of Pool's own deathbed request.[39]

The *New York Atlas* printed an engraved portrait of Pool, based on a lithograph (which itself would likely have been based on a photograph). Pool appears in it with a waxed moustache. He wore a high collar and cravat and could pass for an old-fashioned aristocrat. He certainly did not look like the grotesque Paugene. Pool was apparently only thirty-one when he died, and occasions for formal photographs had probably not been many in his rough-and-tumble life. A somewhat ungrammatical nativist named William L. Knapp produced a pamphlet, based mostly on the testimony at the coroner's inquiry, entitled *The True Life of William Pool, Being a Correct History of His Grandparents and His Parents with a Full Account of the Terrible Affray at Stanwix Hall, in Which He Received a Fatal Wound.*[40] Pool's portrait, apparently based on yet another photograph, appeared as a smudgy woodcut on the paper wrapper of the pamphlet, and " I DIE A TRUE AMERICAN " was printed on the cover as well. This publication was the only item to appear that emphasized the genealogical credentials of Pool as a "true American." His maternal grandfather had been a soldier in the Revolution and in the War of 1812 and was said to have expressed disappointment that he was too old to serve in the Mexican-American War. Pool himself would have been too young to serve in the Mexican-American War.

"To Free the Body Politic from the . . . Putrid Excrescence"

Newspapers could make a political silk purse out of a sow's ear. The *New York Herald* well before Pool's death from the wounds received in the fracas had a myth all worked out, laying blame on a "factious conspiracy of jealous rivals in the same business":

> We may trace their origin to the principles of whiskey and ruffianism introduced years ago into the electioneering machinery of the two old

political parties, and kept up, more or less, to the present day. Gangs of these hired bullies have for years past been employed and subsisted by whigs and democrats, to manage, by brute force, our primary and our regular elections. . . . In our recent elections, the quiet and orderly discipline of the Know Nothings threw the pugilists entirely in the background. . . . This was the work of the mysterious Know Nothings in behalf of temperance, good morals, law and order.[41]

In other words, the *Herald* maintained in the face of mountains of public evidence to the contrary that the funeral of Bill Pool revealed a "Diseased Public Sentiment" in such an outpouring over the political ruffians of the old party system, when the Know-Nothings had shown the way to end the rule of liquor and violence. Yet Pool was himself a Know-Nothing, apparently, a saloonkeeper drinking with his cronies on the night of his murder, and no one could blink away entirely his brawling and irresponsible past as a consort of prizefighters like Tom Hyer. "When the Know Nothing revolution broke out," the *Herald* maintained, "and honest men began once more to rise up against this system of blackguardism and pugilism, the fighters were thrown out of employment."[42]

Ironically, the only political forces that proved able to exploit Pool's murder were in fact the ones in 1855 most responsible for perpetuating the problem of violence in American politics, the Know-Nothings and their allies, not those seeking a genuine solution to it. The cynical and flighty *New York Herald*, briefly infatuated with Know-Nothingism, chose to ignore the obvious truth of Pool's Know-Nothing affiliation and used the events as proof of the crying need for the good-government and clean-politics reforms that the American Party offered the country as a replacement for the corrupt old Whigs and Democrats who had relied on shoulder hitters and pugilists. Though Pool himself would have been only around eleven years old at the origins of the parties, the *Herald* linked Pool to the rise of mass political parties in the Second Party System: "Bill Poole was one of a class of men who rose into notoriety some twenty years ago when the fashion began of packing primary elections and selling the nominations. He and others by their superior physical strength and pugilistic ability completely excluded honest, respectable men from these assemblies, and for years were in the habit of selling every nomination to the highest bidder."[43]

In truth, the nativists thrived off the most thuggish strain of politics of the system, as those violent customs had fed heartily off ethno-cultural animosities. Nativists promised a part of the working classes political domination through violence. To be sure, the American Party attracted for a time able politicians who had been respectable leaders of previously dominant parties in the country—men like John M. Clayton and Henry Wilson. When such men, the candidates for the highest-ranking offices in the land, spoke to the public about the American Party's principles, they spoke in the impeccable language of political principle.

Other Know-Nothing speakers spoke a different language, an argot of hatred and the gutter. Thus at a Know-Nothing demonstration in New York City in November 1854 one of the resolutions passed declared that "An element foreign to our nationality" had afflicted the nation's politics, "demanding immediately the early application of the scalpel to free the body politic from the fungous, putrid excrescence."[44] The enemy identified here was "*unscrupulous demagogues* and *political tricksters,*" and the denunciations did not direct the rhetoric of putrefaction specifically to the party's ethno-cultural enemies. But the strength of the rhetorical denunciation went beyond the tone and content of the leaders' usual public statements. In a speech given the same week by Delaware's John M. Clayton, a Know-Nothing presidential hopeful, Know-Nothing "principles" were vindicated in the traditional platform language of the Constitution and political ideals. He defended their principles as "liberal and fair," noting that "religious toleration [was] in the words of the Constitution itself" and claiming "no bigotry, no proscription" in the movement's program.[45]

Know-Nothings at Pool's level did not offer mainly promises of good government. The pamphlet biography by William L. Knapp, published in late April 1855, drew lessons for the working classes from Pool's life.[46] Pool "had a right to think as he chose, express his principles when and where he chose without being molested by a gang of bigoted, ignorant, foreign hireling paupers." Knapp also contended that "Americans should not be compelled, in order to live, to take up with the crumbs dropped from an alien's table; but that, in the distribution of offices by the general government, or that employers in all kinds of business, should give, at all events, the American citizen an equal chance with those that had no kindred feeling with the institutions and republican principles of this country."[47]

"A Prominent Whig Fighting Man"

In one crucial respect, however, the *Herald* was right in its description of the history of American political parties: political thugs were an essential part of the political culture of the Second Party System in New York City.

Indeed, they appear to be among the distinguishing characteristics of that second system of parties. Political culture is variously defined, but I have always followed the historian Jean Baker's definition—with one refinement. I think it should include those political practices that are common to the major political parties of the era.[48] Shoulder hitting was, and yet not many political historians have said so. The striking feature of the murder of Bill Pool (the newspapers generally dubbed him "Bill" and also consistently misspelled his name, if his biographer Knapp is to be believed, as "Poole") is the revelation of the institutionalized violence always implicit and too often explicit in the ethno-politics from the Age of Jackson to the triumph of the Republican Party. At the time of the murder, the newspapers described the characters in New York politics who were closely associated with the protagonists. They might be described as "gang" members, but many of them also had equally valid claims to being part of a political party organization. A good example was Pool partisan Cyrus Shay. The *New York Tribune* described him as "known for some years past as a prominent Whig fighting man and . . . active in that capacity in 1844 and 1852."[49] Among the men associated with the other side of the Pool-Morrissey feud was a man named James Irving. He was, as Pool had been when he started out in adult life, a butcher. Irving did very well and eventually became the supplier of meat to major hotels in New York City. He had pockets deep enough to go bail for the more active thugs when they ran afoul of the law, which was frequently. Men like Irving did not have to have the same violent credentials as trench fighters like Pool and Morrissey and Shay. "He talks fight a great deal more than he acts fight," commented the *Tribune*.[50] The press described Irving as an "active Soft-Shell Democrat." Johnny Lyng, the man who ran the gambling house to which the murderers fled after the crime, was described by the *Tribune* as "a notorious rough-and-tumble fighter, and an active politician in his precinct in the Sixth Ward. His shell is Hard or Soft according to circumstances." Patrick McLaughlin also did political work. He was arrested on November 13, 1854, for attempting to murder one Smith Leycroft. The alleged crime occurred on the night before an election and was "caused by a dispute in reference to 'electioneering services' rendered by the accused."[51] As for the man who murdered Pool, Lewis Baker, he and Pool had once been patron and protégé, but "some election difficulty made them bitter enemies."[52]

To put it bluntly, thuggery often lay at the heart of urban American political culture in the heyday of party rule before the Civil War. That is not the way I used to conceive of it, but it stands to reason. If the ethno-cultural theory of voting is true for this period, and it has not been decisively refuted or replaced by another theory based on extensive statistical voting analysis, then violence lay very close to the essence of voting, for the violence demonstrated at Stanwix Hall and throughout Pool's political life was rooted in a heightened sense of ethnicity.

"Gained the Good Will of the Roughs"

Any political historian is eventually going to run into the phenomenon of unaccountable violent behavior making a puzzle of the record of the Second Party System and its immediate successors in the 1850s. The murder of Bill Pool came about one year after another little-known but startling event rooted in violent ideals of manliness, a near duel between two members of the House of Representatives debating the Kansas-Nebraska Act. Such salient political events of 1854–55 as near-duels and murders are bound to alter one's image of the nature of party competition in the 1850s. The near-duel was occasioned by the attempt to refer the Kansas-Nebraska Act to the Committee of the Whole rather than the Committee on Territories. The debate over that parliamentary maneuver in early 1854 led Francis Cutting of New York to challenge Kentucky's John C. Breckinridge to a duel. The two wild-eyed men headed for Bladensburg, Maryland, with rifles as chosen weapons for the affair of honor, but the intervention of Thomas Hart Benton averted the actual exchange of weapons fire, which would almost certainly have been fatal for one of the two representatives.[53] The Northerner was the challenger in this near-duel, and gender values more than sectionalism explained the behavior. Remarkably, the headlines generated by the dispute between Cutting and Breckinridge for about two weeks displaced substantive coverage of the provisions of the Kansas-Nebraska Act in the *New York Herald.* In other words, at a key period in the congressional debate over the Kansas-Nebraska Act in 1854, the large segment of the public that got its news from the *Herald* was focused on the drama of dueling and not on the sectional, political, and moral issues surrounding the Kansas-Nebraska Act.

When I read press coverage of the murder of Bill Pool, reported less than a year after the Cutting-Breckinridge affair, I could not help rethinking the place of violence in the Second Party System. It had a central place. Whigs, of course, would have said it was all the Democrats' fault. They had to imitate the successful organizational discipline of the Democrats, they complained. But was it really a matter of Democratic initiative and Whig response in kind?

No, the devices of force and fraud were institutionalized. And they may have been a feature peculiar to the Second Party System. The "tumults and riots" described in Charles S. Sydnor's classic work on voting in eighteenth-century Virginia, appear to have been grog fed and motivated by spontaneous partisan enthusiasm, not led by professional election bullies with fists for hire. Thus Election Day could be disorderly in George Washington's time, but the violence was usually a matter of overheated partisanship and rum punch. The operatives who were unique to the Second Party System were not drunk and excited partisans but cool election bullies.[54] Such bruisers seem not to have been so noticeable in later years and were perhaps relics of the past by the end of the century.[55] But in the heyday of the party system, for at least a third of the period of party dominance, violence was a part of the political culture, the common practices of the system for the parties.

In some places under the Second Party System, though we do not know how many or what kind, violence was the point of entry into the organization for some important party organizers. Showing prowess in a boxing match was a route to local political power in the rougher wards in New York City (membership in a volunteer fire department engine company and saloon ownership were usually later and higher steps). It is striking that pugilism was often the first step. Thus the historian Tyler Anbinder describes the rise of Democrat James E. Kerrigan, who would try to help Pool's murderer escape the country after the crime, as beginning with membership in a volunteer fire company after his return from service in the Mexican-American War. Then, shortly before his nomination to run for the city council, he joined a group of "short boys" (Anbinder defines that term as meaning political thugs) who went to Syracuse from the city to help city politicians gain power at the Democratic state nominating convention.[56] Kerrigan's principal rival at this time was a man named Pat Mathews, who first came to the party's attention when he helped invade a Democratic meeting in December 1852 and gave a concussion to a prominent politician by hitting him with "a large arm chair."[57] Violence came first for the career of Isaiah Rynders, the infamous Democratic politician and Buchanan appointee as federal marshal. After a career of gambling, fighting, and—maybe—murder, he institutionalized violence in the Democratic Party in New York by founding the Empire Club as a response to the hopes of the Whig Party in 1844. The Whigs had recently been invigorated by an embrace of disciplined party organizational methods in 1840. Among those methods was the use in 1842 of members of the Unionist Club, a Whig fighting club.[58] Rynders's club, formed of street bullies and boxers and bruisers, was the Democratic answer and the hope of candidate James K. Polk in the city.[59] An obvious point to be derived from Anbinder's fascinating assemblage of biographical sketches of the forgotten men of American political culture is that the first step was usually a violent one. A less obvious point is that the Whigs acted first.

Is the violence a feature only of urban political culture in the second American party system? To answer that will require much work beyond the confines of this essay, but it might be pointed out that Abraham Lincoln's start in politics came on the heels of a celebrated wrestling match. The facts left to historians of Abraham Lincoln's youth are few and far between, but one of the first important events was a fabled 1831 wrestling match with a bully who lived near New Salem named Jack Armstrong. Lincoln was twenty-two years old. Armstrong was said to be the "leader" of the Clary's Grove Boys, a group of toughs who lived in a settlement near New Salem. An employer of the promising Lincoln placed a wager that Lincoln could throw Armstrong in a wrestling match. This was sport similar to the rough-and-tumble sport at which William Pool excelled, but without urban settings or ethnic tensions. The Lincoln-Armstrong match may have ended in a draw, but accounts agree that Armstrong became Lincoln's friend and the rest of the Clary's Grove Boys became his followers. None of the descriptive language used at this point in the old settlers' recollections is specifically political: they said that Lincoln emerged a "leader," for example, but never explicitly a political leader. The language used by the foggy old settlers interviewed decades later about Lincoln's youth did include substantial agreement on some terms. James Short recalled in 1865 that by means of the wrestling match Lincoln "gained the good will of the roughs and was never disturbed by them." Lynn M. Greene said that "from that day forward the Clary Grove Boys Were always his firm friends." Robert B. Rutledge, brother of the famous Ann Rutledge, said that "after this wrestling match Jack Armstrong and his crowd became the warmest friends and staunchest supporters of Mr Lincoln." "Supporters" of Lincoln in what way? Was it political? The historian Michael Burlingame insists that support from local ruffians was essential to Lincoln's early political success on the frontier and he is likely correct.[60]

The wrestling match did immediately precede Lincoln's service in the militia in the Black Hawk War the next year. That in turn proved to be a definitely *political* first step, as the penniless Lincoln was elected captain by his men. Jack Armstrong was a sergeant in the unit. An old settler named Robert T. McNeely recollected in 1866, "I Knew Lincoln in 1831—Early—Knew he was Elected to the Captaincy of a Company in Clary's Grove under the Militia law of Ill[inoi]s—Know it was before the black Hawk war."[61] As is often the case in this early oral history, the dates were confused but the significance shines through: election, Clary's Grove, Black Hawk War. Lincoln himself never forgot the militia election. In an autobiographical statement made in 1860 for the use of a presidential campaign biographer, Lincoln, writing in the third person, recalled that he "joined a volunteer company, and to his own surprise, was elected captain of it. He says he has not since had any success in life which gave him so much satisfaction."[62] After his return from the war, Lincoln ran for the state legislature.

The differences between Lincoln's early life and Bill Pool's are as important as the parallels. James Short, the first of the witnesses to the Armstrong match quoted above, was careful in his recollections to say also that Lincoln "never played cards, nor drank, nor hunted."[63] Others bet on him, but Lincoln was not, as the notorious pugilists in New York were to a man, himself a participant in the saloon and gambling-hall culture. None of the old settlers recalled that violent methods such as were on display in the Lincoln-Armstrong match were of utility in politics. None said outright that the wrestling match was the beginning of Lincoln's political career.

But whatever the connections between the wrestling match, militia election, and candidacy for state legislature, we can say that it is not the case that Lincoln renounced violence when he became a respectable Whig candidate for important public offices.[64] The mark of violence was on Lincoln's career thereafter. He pursued respectability relentlessly, becoming a lawyer and political candidate, and escaped the hardscrabble frontier and drinking men betting their knives and whiskey on Lincoln or Armstrong to win. But the form of violence that marked the lives of men in the higher social stations was dueling rather than bare-knuckle boxing or rough-and-tumble wrestling. In 1842 Lincoln came within a hair's breadth of fighting a duel with the Democratic politician James Shields using militia cavalry swords. The two young politicians arrived on the dueling ground across the river before seconds calmed them at the very last minute. Lincoln later told his law partner, "I did not intend to hurt Shields unless I did so in perfect self-defense. I could have split him from the crown of the head to the end of his backbone."[65]

Bill Pool's world of nose-biting strife held echoes of the more respectable forms of violence, as we have seen. At one point in the affray at Stanwix Hall, one of the men present, a friend of Pool's from Albany named Suydam, asked, "Mr. Pool, will you fight Morrissey on Wednesday next at ten paces with pistols?"[66]

Violence and Models of Party

I do not know of any model of party organization for the antebellum period that includes the shoulder hitters in the organization chart. Such models, generally assumed, are difficult to find explicitly laid out by the historian. Richard McCormick puts as much emphasis on the role of organizers in the parties of the Second Party System, the Whigs and Democrats, as anyone, but he seems only to admire their organizational genius and abilities to create crowd-pleasing public ritual. He likens politics to religious ritual in Europe or spectator sports in twentieth-century America, but he has no obvious place for violence.[67] Even the most cynical of descriptions of party organization, such as that of J. Mills Thornton III, does not explain the shoulder hitters. Thornton clearly delineates candidates, who are constantly searching for a "hobby" to ride, and party workers on the beat, in whom, Thornton says, the approach of Election Day "induced a state of mind almost akin to insanity" in their dedication to party purposes. Sometimes the leaders could be silly—he has a wonderful example of them throwing spit wads in the Alabama state legislature—but they were seldom sinister or life threatening.[68]

We do not know whether, when, where, or how exactly Whigs, Democrats, or Know-Nothings engaged the services of the shoulder hitters. In sum, even at this late date in the historical consideration of the Age of Party, as Joel Silbey has dubbed it, we do not have any precise order of battle for a nineteenth-century political party. Indeed, Silbey himself, when talking about organization and party discipline, tends to idealize it as "consensus building" within the organization and largely ignores descriptions of specifics of "discipline" despite the implication of force in the very word. There is no place within such conceptions of party organization for a brute like Bill Pool. In the cities, it was notorious among the respectable newspaper editors that party conventions were often controlled by hired thugs. Yet Silbey characterizes a convention as the "high court" of the party, an image of judiciousness and law-abiding rectitude that leaves little room for the talents of Bill Pool.[69] The model of Whig imitation of Democratic political methods does not exactly fit the shoulder hitters of the Second Party System, either. Their use in primary meetings—the usage most often commented upon and condemned by the newspapers of the era and the civic reform movements—was, after all, the use of force by Whigs on Whigs (and by Democrats on Democrats). All we can say at this point with certainty is that violent political thugs were part and parcel of the political culture of the Second Party System in the city.

Recently, the brutal antics of Election Day, if not of the party conventions and organizational meetings that marked the rest of the political calendar, have begun to shock and dismay political historians. Richard Bensel's book *The American Ballot Box in the Mid-Nineteenth Century* offers a sobering view of fraud and violence practiced on Election Day on such a scale as to frustrate any ideal of the expression of the democratic will. And that is a view echoed by another steady student of the ballot box, Tracy Campbell.[70] Urban historians have proven the most comfortable with the inclusion of shoulder hitters in their descriptions of elections of the period.[71] Political historians too must make room for them.

End of an Era?

The best treatments of the phenomenon in the literature deal with it as a function of urban history. The fullest account comes from Tyler Anbinder, who studied the Five Points neighborhood in New York City in depth. He argues that the end of deferential politics in the early nineteenth century was followed by the era of violence and shoulder hitters in the antebellum period. He depicts election violence as the sign of an assertiveness on the part of the voters that overthrew the smug elite that dominated politics in the Early Republic and eventually brought Irish immigrants into public office in New York. About the time of the Civil War, the violent era ended with the advent of voter fraud rather than physical intimidation as the favored means of controlling election results from the immigrant wards. This is a brilliantly attractive scheme, but it cannot be easily extended to the nation as a whole, and parts of it are a little unsatisfactory.

First, the violence at the polls that marked the antebellum period in New York City was not exactly violence directed at old elites. What elite was Bill Pool attacking when he fought Morrissey? It was violence directed at the opposing political party or faction. As violence against faction it was often directed against other members of the lower order in society, against the other party's shoulder hitters, men recruited from the ranks of the city's butchers and firefighters. The elites previously deferred to at the polls may have been casualties also, but they were not the only ones and perhaps not the intended ones. Moreover, in the primary meetings, where, if the press of the day can be believed, the violent behavior was most prevalent, the political thugs were the hirelings of the men who wanted to become candidates for office. The violence, especially if it is generalizable beyond urban history, is best accounted for by the intense competition of the parties in the systems that followed the First Party System of the Early Republic and preceded the Progressive Era.[72]

That competition was based substantially on identity politics, and the Pool-McLaughlin violence epitomized in rawest terms the political animosities between parties, not toward elites of either party.

Second, it is not clear that voter fraud replaced violence as a new or better way of controlling election results. Violence was itself voter fraud and was sometimes provoked by the standard procedures of voter fraud, particularly attempts to steal and stuff ballot boxes.

Third, the decline of violence, at least in New York City, might more accurately be attributable to the trauma of the draft riots of July 1863. Certainly they shocked the rest of the municipalities in the country into feverish activity to raise bounties for volunteers to avoid the draft and consequent draft rioting. Their deleterious effects on the city might well have caused activists to pull back from easy employment of six-barrel pistols and Colt five-shooters. Ethno-cultural determinants of voting do not seem to have changed, and at bottom ethno-cultural conflict fueled the institution of Whig fighting clubs and Empire clubs and smart boys. It is not altogether clear why these political institutions disappeared in the Gilded Age.

But even before the shocking excesses of the draft riots in the city, a transformation does seem to have taken place. One possibility is that the unsavory Know-Nothings lay at the root of the transformation. The Know-Nothings embraced violent methods and used club-like organizations of young men called "Wide Awakes" to police or harass public rallies and the Irish Americans who turned out to jeer at the anti-Catholic street preachers. In the revolution of parties that ensued, the Republicans adopted the Wide Awake model very closely from the American Party, including the name of the organization and the use of distinctive clothing or uniforms. But the Republican Wide Awakes seem to have sublimated the original violent purpose into military drill and parading and spectacle. Meanwhile, the discrediting and downfall of the American Party must have served to tarnish its bloody methods. At any rate, the elections of the Third Party System are different, as Anbinder and others have noticed. If we look at the elections in the city during the Civil War, all of them remarked upon by the press as frantically hard fought, it is remarkable that the newspapers did not report on them ward by ward for the sake of their exemplification of violent behavior. In 1862, for example, the *New York Herald* observed of the November 4 Election Day that "Order Reigns in New York." There was "No Disturbance During the Day." Three wards retained reputations for turbulence, and political violence remained possible, but there was no longer any talk of shoulder hitters and pugilists at the polls. That proved true not only of the great national elections of November but also of the later hard-fought charter elections, that is, the elections for city offices. The local politicians took intense interest in those, and there were few ideological issues involved. They were about political organization and money and power exclusively. But the December 2, 1862, charter election was also "Wonderfully Quiet" in the opinion of the *Herald*.[73]

We do not have a satisfactory explanation of the political culture of the nineteenth century. It does seem clear that, insofar as political culture includes practices and beliefs and styles of argument common to all parties in the system, shoulder hitters were a part of the political culture of the Second Party System and of the Know-Nothings afterward. Who actually engaged these men and for what remuneration is as yet unknown. Why their revolting skills rather suddenly ceased to be in demand by newly reorganized parties is unknown as well.

"The Primogeniture of First Settlers"

The rediscovery of the importance of the Know-Nothing Party by Michael F. Holt is among the most important developments in the study of American political history in the last fifty years. This essay is only reaffirmation of that insight. I have just completed a book about American nationalism during the Civil War, and one thing that became clear as I wrote it was that many of the most important landmarks in the history of nationalism in America preceded the Civil War. One of those occurred immediately before the Civil War: the rise and fall of the Know-Nothing Party. The American Party in the 1850s mounted the most formidable movement in all of American history to identify the nation not with a set of ideals but with ethnicity. To borrow Mitchell Snay's categories of nationalism, the American Party represented the supreme attempt to establish an ethnic rather than a civic nationalism in this country.[74] Or to borrow Woden Teachout's language, nativists for a time captured the flag or came near to doing so.

Many at the time recognized the great significance of the challenge to traditional national definitions posed by the Know-Nothing Party. In the aftermath of the startlingly strong showing of the American Party in the elections in the fall of 1854, the *New York Tribune*, for example, noted the danger that lurked in that party's claim to invigorate the "enfeebled and decayed nationality" of the United States. "It seizes hold of a narrow and sectional patriotism," the editors wrote. "It maintains the primogeniture of first settlers. It arrogates the prerogatives of a certain dominant race, and calls all this

Americanism." But American nationality was "not a thing of races," insisted the *Tribune*.[75]

Understanding the prominent role in the American Party played by thugs like Bill Pool is important for characterizing the importance of the American Party. If Five Points in New York City was the most famous slum in America, as Tyler Anbinder reminds us, Baltimore, noted for its spectacles of violence at the polls, was the city with the most infamous reputation for Election Day violence. The historian Richard Bensel describes the situation there this way:

> Before the Civil War, the most violent precincts in the United States were probably located in Baltimore, Maryland. During the 1850s the American party emerged as a major force in national politics, displacing the Whigs. . . . The American party in Baltimore was supported by quasi-public clubs with names such as the "Plug Uglies," "Blood Tubs," "Black Snakes," "Little Fellows," "Stingbatts," "Rough Skins," and "Babes" (the latter were reported to be "very huge fellows"). The Plug Uglies got their name from slang for a "tough or roughneck," a term that originally referred to "a member of a city gang of rowdies active in such places as Baltimore, New York, and Philadelphia." "Plug-Uglymore," in fact, became a nickname for the city of Baltimore. The formal title of the Blood Tubs was the "Native American Association." They earned their nickname when the club drove naturalized voters from the polls in the First Ward by covering them "with blood taken from barrels or tubs." . . . When the American party was in control of the city, precincts were often situated near these clubhouses so that the gangs could operate freely in the neighborhood around the polling place.[76]

We might well see these political street gangs as the forerunners of the sinister enforcers who formed an essential part of the ultranationalist fascist parties of the next century: Brownshirts, Blackshirts, and the like. In other words, America's most successful party of ethnic nationalism included forerunners of the street violence of the twentieth century's parties of pathological nationalism.[77] Other political parties in the United States in the mid-1850s seem to have turned toward the ritualization of physical force in uniformed marching groups like the Republican Wide Awakes. But it is difficult to imagine the American Party without its squads of blood-slinging thugs to intimidate its ethnic and partisan foes. The American Party seems to have represented the real apotheosis of ruffianism. I do not know of any

Republican fighting clubs as successors of the Whig fighting clubs or their nativist and Know-Nothing successors.

The demise of the Know-Nothing Party represented a landmark in American nationalism. With the Know-Nothing Party died the greatest attempt to identify the nation with ethnicity. With that party's death, there may also have been a major blow dealt to the common use of violence in party politics. The murder of Bill Pool was a sordid signpost along that route.

Notes

1. *New York Herald,* March 12, 1855.

2. Elliott J. Gorn, *The Manly Art: Bare-Knuckle Prize Fighting in America* (Ithaca, NY: Cornell University Press, 1986), 108–13.

3. In August 1854, in the angry preliminaries to the fatal fight with Morrissey in 1855, Pool, who was a smaller man than Morrissey and at a recognizable disadvantage, had suggested a fight with knives. Morrissey said that he tried to avoid such fights, but he had to agree or back down. In turn Morrissey could suggest the place—important for evading the law—and he suggested Canada. Pool would not go there, and the fight without weapons evolved from further negotiations. Butcher knives had been Pool's tools of trade early in his life, as they had been for many of the pugilists, who often had worked as butchers in New York's big markets. *New York Times,* July 28, 1854. The general description of pugilists' encounters is based on accounts in New York newspapers of the mid-1850s, as well as on Gorn's excellent book cited in n. 2.

4. William L. Knapp, *The True Life of William Pool, Giving a Correct History of His Grandparents and His Parents with a Full Account of the Terrible Affray at Stanwix Hall, in Which He Received a Fatal Wound . . .* (New York: W. L. Knapp, 1855), 13–15.

5. *New York Tribune,* March 9, 1855.

6. William Goetzman, "The Mountain Man as Jacksonian Man," *American Quarterly* 15 (Autumn 1963): 402–15.

7. Leonard Richards, *"Gentlemen of Property and Standing": Anti-Abolition Mobs in Jacksonian America* (New York: Oxford University Press, 1970). See also the works cited in note 10.

8. See, for example, *New York Herald,* January 20, 1854.

9. Fights between fire companies are frequently documented in New York newspapers of the time. On the masculine culture of firefighters see Amy S. Greenberg's excellent book, *Cause for Alarm: The Volunteer Fire Department in the Nineteenth-Century City* (Princeton, NJ: Princeton University Press, 1998). See also "Fights, Skirmishes, and Arrests," part of the headline for a ward-by-ward description of the election of the previous day in *New York Herald,* November 9, 1853.

10. Mark E. Neely Jr., "The Kansas-Nebraska Act in American Political Culture: The Road to Bladensburg and the *Appeal of the Independent Democrats,*" in John R. Wunder and Joann M. Ross, eds., *The Nebraska-Kansas Act of 1854* (Lincoln: University of Nebraska Press, 2008), 14–23. Coverage of the Cutting-Breckinridge affair began in the *New York*

Herald on March 28, 1854. For the "Affair of Honor" between African Americans see *New York Times,* August 24, 1854.

11. *New York Tribune,* March 10, 1855.

12. *New York Tribune,* February 26, 1855.

13. *New York Tribune,* March 9, 1855.

14. Ibid.

15. *New York Herald,* December 1, 1862.

16. *New York Tribune,* March 10, 1855.

17. *New York Tribune,* November 6, 1852.

18. Knapp, *True Life of William Pool,* 11.

19. *New York Herald,* July 13, 1853. Though Woden Teachout is right to focus on the importance of the flag to nativist movements, she somewhat exaggerates their success in capturing it as their symbol. The Ancient Order of Hibernians in New York City, for example, contested the flag's meaning and looked forward to the time, which actually arrived some eight years later, when its members would prove their identification with it by military service. See Woden Teachout, *Capture the Flag: A Political History of American Patriotism* (New York: Basic Books, 2009), esp. 72.

20. Jerome Mushkat, *Fernando Wood: A Political·Biography* (Kent, OH: Kent State University Press, 1990), 34–36.

21. Ibid.

22. *New York Times,* November 9, 1854.

23. *New York Tribune,* November 6, 1852.

24. Tyler Anbinder, *Five Points: The 19th-Century New York City Neighborhood That Invented Tap Dance, Stole Elections, and Became the World's Most Notorious Slum* (New York: Free Press, 2001), 145–46.

25. *New York Times,* November 9, 1854.

26. *New York Herald,* March 9, 1855.

27. Knapp, *True Life of William Pool,* 14, 25. On Know-Nothing hats see the *New York Herald,* June 19, 1854. See also *New York Tribune,* March 10, 1855.

28. Knapp, *True Life of William Pool,* 15.

29. Ibid., 12.

30. *New York Atlas,* March 4, 11, and 18, 1855; *New York Tribune,* March 20, 1855.

31. Knapp, *True Life of William Pool,* 16.

32. *New York Atlas,* March 18, 1855.

33. *New York Tribune,* March 12, 1855.

34. *New York Herald,* March 12, 1855.

35. Ray Allen Billington, *The Protestant Crusade, 1800–1860* (1938; Chicago: Quadrangle Books, 1964), 304–9.Michael F. Holt wrote briefly about Pittsburgh's famous street preacher Joseph Barker in his first book, *Forging a Majority: The Formation of the Republican Party in Pittsburgh, 1848–1860* (New Haven, CT: Yale University Press, 1969), 111–15.

36. *New York Herald,* March 12, 1855.

37. *New York Atlas,* March 18, 1855. I cannot explain the reference to the presence of Rynders's grenadiers in the procession, as that was most likely a Democratic club.

38. *New York Tribune,* March 12, 1855; *New York Herald,* March 12, 1855; Knapp, *True Life of William Pool,* 20.

39. *New York Herald,* March 12, 1855.

40. It was published in New York by W. L. Knapp in 1855.

41. *New York Herald,* February 27, 1855.

42. *New York Herald,* March 10, 1855.

43. Ibid. For a book that emphasizes the antiparty animus of the Know-Nothings, see Mark Voss-Hubbard, *Beyond Party: Cultures of Antipartisanship in Northern Politics before the Civil War* (Baltimore: Johns Hopkins University Press, 2002).

44. *New York Times,* November 10, 1854.

45. *New York Times,* November 11, 1854.

46. *New York Herald,* April 28, 1855 (advertisement for the Knapp pamphlet).

47. Knapp, *True Life of William Pool,* 8.

48. Jean H. Baker, *Affairs of Party: The Political Culture of Northern Democrats in the Mid-Nineteenth Century* (1983; New York: Fordham University Press, 1998), esp. 11–12.

49. *New York Tribune,* March 10, 1855.

50. Ibid.

51. *New York Times,* November 14, 1854.

52. *New York Tribune,* March 10, 1855.

53. Neely, " Kansas-Nebraska Act," 14–15.

54. Charles S. Sydnor, *American Revolutionaries in the Making: Political Practices in Washington's Virginia,* (orig. pub. as *Gentlemen Freeholders,* 1952; New York: Free Press, 1965), 21–33.

55. Identifying the nineteenth century as the age of party is one of the many excellent ideas of Joel H. Silbey. See his book, *The American Political Nation, 1838–1893* (Stanford, CA: Stanford University Press, 1991). For the end of the period of party dominance and high voter participation, see Michael E. McGerr, *The Decline of Popular Politics: The American North, 1865–1928* (New York: Oxford University Press, 1986).

56. Anbinder, *Five Points,* 274–76.

57. Ibid., 276.

58. Ibid., 156.

59. Ibid., 141–44.

60. Douglas L. Wilson and Rodney O. Davis, eds., *Herndon's Informants: Letters, Interviews, and Statements about Abraham Lincoln* (Urbana: University of Illinois Press, 1998), 74, 80, 386. For extended coverage of the Lincoln-Armstrong wrestling match, see Douglas L. Wilson, *Honor's Voice: The Transformation of Abraham Lincoln* (New York: Alfred A. Knopf, 1998), 19–51. For an account with more emphasis on its possible political importance, see Michael Burlingame, *Abraham Lincoln: A Life,* 2 vols. (Baltimore: Johns Hopkins University Press, 2008), 1:62.

61. Wilson and Davis, *Herndon's Informants,* 369.

62. Roy P. Basler, ed., *Collected Works of Abraham Lincoln,* vol. 4 (New Brunswick, NJ: Rutgers University Press, 1953), 64.

63. Wilson and Davis, *Herndon's Informants,* 73. Michael Burlingame is careful to point out Lincoln's lack of participation in the Clary's Grove Boys' culture of drinking and cruelty to animals. See Burlingame, *Abraham Lincoln,* 1:62.

64. Burlingame, for one, asserts that the wrestling match was out of character for Lincoln, who was a peacemaker by nature. See Burlingame, *Abraham Lincoln,* 1:62.

65. Don E. and Virginia Fehrenbacher, eds., *Recollected Words of Abraham Lincoln* (Stanford, CA: Stanford University Press, 1996), 248–49.

66. Knapp, *True Life of William Pool*, 69.

67. Richard P. McCormick, *The Second American Party System: Party Formation in the Jacksonian Era* (Chapel Hill: University of North Carolina Press, 1966), 350–52.

68. J. Mills Thornton III, *Politics and Power in a Slave Society: Alabama, 1800–1860* (Baton Rouge: Louisiana State University Press, 1978), 71, 76, 126, 130.

69. Joel H. Silbey, *The American Political Nation, 1838–1893* (Stanford, CA: Stanford University Press, 1991), 60.

70. Tracy Campbell, *Deliver the Vote: A History of Election Fraud, an American Political Tradition—1742–2004* (New York: Carroll and Graf, 2005).

71. See for example Edwin G. Burrows and Mike Wallace, *Gotham: A History of New York City to 1898* (New York: Oxford University Press, 1999), chapter 46.

72. There is a tendency to argue the opposite: that the party system tamed and displaced violent disagreement rather than institutionalizing it.

73. *New York Herald*, November 5 and 30, December 1, 2, and 3, 1862.

74. Mitchell Snay, *Fenians, Freedmen, and Southern Whites: Race and Nationality in the Era of Reconstruction* (Baton Rouge: Louisiana State University Press, 2007).

75. *New York Tribune*, November 9, 1854.

76. Richard Franklin Bensel, *The American Ballot Box in the Mid-Nineteenth Century*, 168–70. Bensel accepts as proof of Baltimore's premier status in political violence the work of David Grimsted, *American Mobbing, 1828–1861* (New York: Oxford University Press, 1998). Grimsted's work focuses on slavery and political violence and leaves ethnic and other party considerations for a later volume. Jean H. Baker's *Ambivalent Americans: The Know-Nothing Party in Maryland* (Baltimore: Johns Hopkins University Press, 1977), like Holt's work on the period, emphasizes the political importance of the Know-Nothings, but she tends to attribute more of the electoral violence to Democrats. Her description of election conditions in Baltimore is excellent; see especially 131ff. She also points out that "for historians of the Know-Nothing party, physical intimidation challenges the use of an essential investigative tool—election returns" (134). In general, the practitioners of the New Political History, which dominated writing on the Second Party System after the mid-1960s, tended to minimize the importance of violence and fraud. The present essay is an attempt to balance that image of the politics of the period.

77. On the near-pathological nature of nationalism in the twentieth century, see Benedict Anderson, *Imagined Communities: Reflections on the Origin and Spread of Nationalism*, rev. ed. (London: Verso, 1991), 141.

Public Women and
Partisan Politics, 1840–1860

JEAN HARVEY BAKER

In the late 1960s and early 1970s a talented group of scholars turned their attention to nineteenth-century American political history. Instead of the traditional focus on presidents, state leaders, and administrative programs, these historians offered such strikingly fresh approaches to our political past that their work soon became known as the New Political History. Influenced by the emergence of an equally novel form of social history that concentrated on previously overlooked Americans, political historians ran the numbers on electoral turnouts and falloffs. Individual voters and their party preferences became the objects of their research. These young historians began employing statistical methods at a time when computers and computer programming, rather than covering only one project at a time, developed the capacity for time-sharing and handling hundreds of tasks simultaneously. Soon practitioners were constructing multivariate analyses to determine who voted for whom and why. They scavenged diverse kinds of census records—from church attendance as measured by pews and local tax records to the number of slaves owned by an individual—in order to deliver a grassroots people's political history, grounded in efforts to understand the behavior of American voters.

Necessarily the political party, previously given cursory and episodic attention, became a prime matrix for their research. Not only was democracy recognized as unthinkable without political parties, but partisan organizations were understood in their interactions as the basic institutions required for the translation of mass preferences into public policy. Moving away from specific campaigns and famous politicians to themes and patterns, sometimes the new political historians studied national parties and sometimes state organizations. Even the behavior of a single city placed under a microscope could deliver important, exportable generalizations. Frequently in the dogged pursuit of their queries, the practitioners of the new political history did not just observe single elections but used time series to deliver longitudinal views of American party preferences. And increasingly they connected parties, their policies in office, and the electorate's response. A famous example of this approach is Michael F. Holt's *Forging a Majority: The Formation of the Republican Party in Pittsburgh, 1848–1860*, published in 1969.

Through such methods the issues of elections, if not always postelection legislative outcomes, were connected to voters and partisan organizations. Soon party periods and realignments, no longer opaque, became part of the historical vocabulary. And political historians like Holt sought "an integrated and comprehensive history of American political development," which required a chronological narrative allowing room for "the impact of individual decisions, contingencies and unforeseen events." These powerful popular parties "appear to have been the dominant influence on political life in the previous century."[1]

By the twenty-first century, party politics had lost some market share in the overall output of historians, and Holt, among others, decried that "American political history had become an object of scorn." True to his original lodestar of political history as the study of parties, Holt wrote in his latest book, *The Fate of Their Country*, which was published in 2004, "What politicians did during those decades had crucial consequences."[2]

Concurrent with the New Political History, though entirely autonomous, separate, and, in the beginning, lacking credibility within an academy committed to history as past politics, was the emergence of women's history. If the devotees of a new kind of political history were focused on microelectoral history writ large, the creators of women's history sought to retrieve the macrohistorical past of previously forgotten Americans, representing over half the population. At first historians wrote biographies of women worthies such as Abigail Adams and Dolley Madison in the model of contributory history, and this framework would continue to have appeal. As time went on, however, new approaches were developed from the perspective of women's experience and culture—the American past viewed, as one textbook title offers, through women's eyes. Other perspectives focused on women as a minority group, not in numbers, of course, but rather in their position in society.

When a pioneer in the field, Gerda Lerner, defined several useful techniques for investigating women's history, she named compensatory history as one of those approaches and defined it as the process of filling in the categories of male history with women.[3] Clearly this method was the most evocative approach for historians who studied public women, and it was the eventual meeting place for the New Political History and women's history.

Yet for two decades there was little cross-fertilization between historians who studied politics and those who studied women. How could there be, for students of politics, when women throughout the nineteenth century had little public presence and when politics was still defined as dealing with formal matters of governance, policy, and leadership—the running of national, state, and local entities? Eventually it became one of the contributions of women's history to broaden what politics was and expand it beyond what is sometimes called "high politics," although as Sidney Verba has pointed out, defining the word to cover "all human relationships dealing with power or influence or domination of some by others extends the definition too far."[4]

Most American women married and thereafter became enclosed in the legal system of femme couverte. Imported from English common law and codified by the eighteenth-century English lawyer William Blackstone into what served as the applied custom of the community, a husband and wife were one person, with he the one in public affairs—as when, wrote Blackstone, "a small brooke or little river incorporates with the Thames, the poor rivulet looseth her name. It beareth no sway."[5]

Yet the civic invisibility of women did not begin with the American Revolution or the writing of the U.S. Constitution, but instead rested in what the political scientist Carole Pateman has called "the sex contract," in which men enjoyed rights in the political realm and held authority over women, who were subordinated into the private domain.[6] The static English legal traditions inherited from the Middle Ages concretely represented the sex contract through the common law of couverture. The latter covered not just domestic relations but property rights and removed women entirely from politics as the male members of a household—fathers, brothers, and husbands—represented women in all legal, civic, and economic affairs. By extension, even the unmarried and widowed femme sole could neither vote, nor hold office, nor become members of the partisan system that was the focus of the New Political History.

By the 1980s political historians had mapped out new terrain. In contrast to the seemingly unvarying status of antebellum women, there were vibrant changes in the United States that took place in the 1830s when political organizations, so feared by the founding generations for their ability to sway independent judgment, became the dominant secular institutions in public culture. For men, wrote one newspaper editor in the 1850s in a comment that summed up two decades of partisanship, "politics seemed to enter everything, and very little attention is now paid to anything unless it be mixed up in some way with the political movements of the day."[7]

By 1832 all white men, even those without property, could vote—a democratizing process that had been adopted without controversy by state after state. Legislatures reduced the colonial period's property requirements for male voting, first replacing them with simple taxpaying criteria, although even women who paid taxes could not vote. Finally all such class-based criteria for men were relaxed, though one anomaly in this process occurred in New Jersey. In that state women had briefly voted after the state's hastily drawn constitution of 1776 extended the franchise to all inhabitants of the state worth fifty pounds until a new constitution prescribed only males.

Electoral politics was henceforth gendered, a fact whose political implications did not escape Elizabeth Cady Stanton. "All men," she said to a woman's convention in Worcester, Massachusetts, in 1848, "have the same rights, however they may differ in mind, body or estate. ... We [women] should not feel so sorely grieved if no man who had not attained the full stature of a Webster, Van Buren, Clay ... could claim the elective franchise, but to have the rights of drunkards, idiots, horseracing, rum-selling rowdies, ignorant foreigners and silly boys fully recognized, when we ourselves are thrust out from the rights belonging to citizens, it is too grossly insulting to the dignity of woman to be longer quietly submitted to."[8]

There were other implications to the gendering of American politics after civic membership was accomplished through all-masculine partisan allegiances. Men expressed their patriotism and social solidarity through their participation in the rituals of politics—joining a party, marching in its parades, discussing the issues of the day in public spaces with other men, and on the appointed day going to the polls. Separating them from women, the right to vote became something that men enjoyed together, in the same way that whites shared skin color different from blacks and thereby in this similarity gained a collective sense of superiority in what has been described as a Herrenvolken mentality.

There was no place for women in the transformations of formal politics in antebellum America, and in one of the ruling prescriptions (though not always realities) of the period, white middle-class women retreated to their homes and created there a separate sphere of domesticity, graced by the essential characteristics of good women—chastity, purity, and submissiveness. True women—the especial breed of what Noah Webster called "females of worth"—prescriptively functioned in their homes as mothers and wives by transforming husbands and sons into good Americans who served a fragile new nation based on the principles of antimonarchical republicanism and a tentative democracy.

But as historians of women—and they were mostly female, just as political historians were overwhelmingly male—continued to probe their past, they applied the method of compensatory history and discovered women who had undertaken public roles as abolitionists and writers, temperance workers and organizers of charitable organizations. Such was the origin of the civic culture of American women. In this essay, using ideal types, I call these public women *benevolent activists*. Later a new phase of women's political history emerged, focusing in the antebellum period on efforts for enfranchisement and legislative changes especially in married women's property discriminations. I call the women attracted to this new wave of civil rights activism *political integrationists*. They include leaders such as Elizabeth Cady Stanton, Susan B. Anthony, and Lucy Stone. Simultaneously, a third type of public woman emerged in the scholarship of women's historians operating from a compensatory point of view. These scholars discovered women in active, though always subordinate, partisan roles during the period 1840–60. I call these women *partisan enablers*. The women in all three of these groups were public women who in different ways confronted the party system and discovered their political identities between 1840 and 1860.

Of course these classifications were permeable, and in any case much more relevant to New England, the Middle Atlantic, and the Upper Midwest than to the South, although Elizabeth Varon's 1998 *We Mean to Be Counted: White Women and Politics in Antebellum Virginia* argues that "elite and middle-class women (in Virginia) played an active, distinct and evolving role in the political life of the Old South."[9] Overall, there were only a few women who participated in these activities at a time when to be called a public woman implied promiscuity and to travel without a male escort threatened reputations.

To be sure, many of these overwhelmingly middle-class women migrated from one group to another, mostly beginning their public life in female charity organizations and moving from there toward their struggles for inclusion in the crucially important party system described by the new political historians. For example, the great suffrage leader Susan B. Anthony began as a benevolent activist working in temperance organizations, and she noted, in her first schoolteaching job away from home, that while she had heard her father talk of politics, she had never actually "seen folks electioneer before now." Later she became an integrationist dedicated to suffrage and the inclusion of women as voters and equal members of the body politic.[10]

In another instance of the lack of female access to American politics, Frances Willard, later the head of the powerful Women's Christian Temperance Union, remembered that she, her sister, and her mother stayed home when her father and brother set out from their farm outside of Janesville to vote for John Fremont, the Republican presidential candidate in 1856. And all three Willards perceived the discrimination.[11] Many women—Willard, Anthony, Stanton, and Stone—refused what they believed the exploited condition of partisan enablers.[12]

Later the leader of the American Woman Suffrage Association, Stone changed her lecturing focus from antislavery to women's rights until told by her employer, the American Antislavery Society, to save women's advocacy for the less well-attended meetings that took place on weeknights.[13]

A fourth, albeit virtual, role women played during this period has been highlighted by contemporary historians interested in semiotics: their usefulness to the political system as symbols, often as living statues dressed in white muslin and reflecting the American ideals of Liberty and Freedom in parades and on floats. In such a capacity women served as the classic expression of "the other"—the second sex, as Simone de Beauvoir has written, who, lacking any political identity of their own, performed as surrogates for the nation's highest ideals.

The gendering of American politics, when political parties were developing in the third decade of the nineteenth century, created a self-consciously masculine membership as well as citizenry. Males who did not participate were classified as effeminate "Nancy men." On the other hand, loyal enthusiasts bonded as Whigs, Democrats, Know-Nothings, and Republicans, cultivating through their gendered solidarity a fervent attachment to their parties and their rituals. Part of the attraction of organizational politics for men, like all-male colleges, taverns, and clubs, during what practitioners of the New Political History called the party period was its masculinity. And voting often took place in places associated with men such as barbershops and taverns.

Benevolent Activists

The first group of public women, classified in this essay as benevolent activists, served as trailblazers for later female participation. Serving in a variety of all-female associations and some mixed societies in the third and fourth decades of the nineteenth century, women developed, organized, and ran associations that, though previously overlooked in American history, played important roles in community life. Here local history, long considered a backwater of antiquarianism, emerged as a potent and common evidential site for both political and women's historians.

The former, intent on discovering who voted for whom and why, employed local sources to answer questions about the religious or economic background of voters. Were they members of pietist or liturgical religions? Were they commercial or local-market farmers? Studies such as those of Paul Kleppner on the Midwest attempted to provide answers. Meanwhile, using the same kinds of demographic information, women historians focused as well on the social, economic, and religious background of local activists.

For women's historians local sources such as the records of the Female Charitable Society, organized by fourteen women in Rochester, New York, in 1822 to aid "the sick poor" provided the historian Nancy Hewitt with statistical information about who these reformers were, what they did, and how they moved beyond the isolation of their homes into community life. Soon after its founding the society divided Rochester into districts and sent its members, in the role of what later generations would call public health nurses, but which in this period the society called visitors, to assess the condition of the "sick-poor" in their area. Of course, this neighborliness, like many of the initiatives of associational women, applied traditional gender-based characteristics of women in such a manner that women became the accepted moral guardians of civic life.[14] Clearly the society's initiatives sent women out of their homes into the community as public women.

In many cities women organized female "moral reform" societies that were intent, in the words of one group, "on refusing to put vice on an equal footing with virtue," work that women because of their ethical standards supposedly did better than men. Occasionally—especially in New York City—they held vigils outside of brothels, hoping to persuade prostitutes to abandon their sinful lives. The means used in these evangelical efforts to perfect communities included not only distributing biblical tracts but praying with those who might find a new path through religion. In Grafton, Massachusetts, in the late 1830s, a minister's wife initiated the call for a meeting that eventually numbered fifty-five women who wrote and voted on a constitution, decried the licentiousness of the times, read scripture, and discussed methods of raising what their generation called "moral children."

In one of the most salient techniques used by public women, the women of Grafton organized a petition drive calling for a law against the seduction of women by men, an especially timely topic when young girls had begun working in the factories at nearby Lowell. As the reformer Angelina Grimké wrote, "Petitions are an appropriate means for women to politically express themselves. They are a natural and inalienable right derived from God."[15] Requiring door-to-door canvassing, the process also taught self-confidence and assertiveness in the public sphere. The historian Susan Zaeske has found over three million of what she labels antislavery "signatures of citizenship" on petitions sent to Congress in the period 1831–63.[16]

Certainly the most studied of these antebellum associations have been the antislavery societies that black and white women, separately and together, established in Northern cities and towns. By the 1830s there were over a thousand such societies in the United States—some with both men and women, others sex-segregated, and a few racially integrated. In Massachusetts, for example, there were forty-one female antislavery societies, with white women more welcoming to black members than were white males, according to Anne Firor Scott.[17] One of the recent contributions of women's history has been to chronicle the rapid appearance in New England and in the Midwest of these all-female groups that emerged, segregated by gender partly by choice but partly as a result of opposition by men to any females as officers. In the classic example of exclusion by males, in 1840 the American Antislavery Society split over the issue of whether Abby Kelley could serve in such a prominent role as a member of its executive committee.

For such benevolent activists, the hazardous nature of antislavery activity, necessarily public in its nature, everywhere aroused hostility. But because women were defying norms that restricted them to private life and limited public speech to men, they faced a heightened level of violence. In Philadelphia a mob burned down a hall in which the Female Antislavery Society was holding a meeting. In upstate New York Susan B. Anthony was hounded during her speaking tours by antislavery mobs in a way that Henry Stanton, Elizabeth Cady Stanton's husband and an agent for an antislavery society, never faced. Stanton's friend Elizabeth Chace of the Rhode Island Female Antislavery Society noted another form of hostility in the "social ostracism, persecution, slander and insult" that came with antislavery work.[18]

The historian Julie Jeffrey in her recent book *The Great Silent Army: Ordinary Women and the Antislavery Movement* suggests that women, often overlooked in the top-heavy scholarly attention given to Frederick Douglass, William Lloyd Garrison, and the Tappan brothers, were the critical "boots on the ground" for a movement that depended on day-to-day routines. Women were accustomed to repetitiveness and routinization in their lives and so took diligently to the grassroots tasks of propaganda. Writes Jeffrey, "For more than three decades, they raised money and distributed propaganda, circulated and signed petitions, and lobbied legislatures. During the 1840s and 1850s, they helped to keep the moral content of abolitionism alive when a diluted political form of antislavery emerged."[19] Certainly women were more inclined than men to carry their own petitions, to raise their own money, and to organize the antislavery fairs that were so much a part of fund-raising, where they sold their homemade goods.

While antislavery associations have received the most attention, all-female associations—whether those supporting temperance, moral reform, or missionary work—provided an avenue for women into public life. Statistically there were never many women involved: Jeffrey concludes that out of a population of 30 million in 1860, only around 20,000, of all American men and women were members of antislavery societies. But those females who joined were trained in what Anne Gordon has called "the school of antislavery," and some of its graduates, alert to the discrimination, compared themselves to slaves.[20] But in these reform associations women did not first learn of their oppressed circumstances, which they were already aware of, but rather they absorbed how to become public women and seek various collective goals.

As the historian Anne Firor Scott explains, "Within this network women learned how to conduct business, carry on meetings, speak in public, and manage money. Experiences in small-scale voluntary associations prepared women for politics, broadly defined. By finding a way to take up public concerns, they were contributing to the expansion of American democracy."[21] In the beginning their work had little to do with the activities of political parties, and their exclusion from the two-party system resulted in the perception of party affairs as corrupt and without the leavening influence of the moral guardians of society.

Political Integrationists

In 1848 a handful of women, including some veterans of benevolent activism, organized the first civil rights campaign in American history. Meeting in Seneca Falls, New York, they indicted a generic "He" for failure to include females in the social and economic affairs of the nation. Boldly they asserted that all laws that violated the natural rights of women must be abrogated. On the second day of their meeting, having the first day indicted men for disenfranchising them, they resolved to become voters. Yet enfranchisement was only one of a series of demands, including that they be given equal wages, that they be permitted to attend the colleges and universities closed to them, and that they be allowed to control their inheritances. But despite the broad range of its complaints the "Declaration of Sentiments" that emerged from this meeting was a distinctly political document in which the women spoke, in the language of Blackstone, of being civilly dead.

Intrepidly they resolved that in a government that denied women the vote "all laws which place [women] in a position inferior to that of man are contrary to the great precept of nature and have no force or authority." While they did not specifically mention political parties and the emerging two-party electoral system in their founding document, neither had the U.S. Constitution. But what they proposed was the opposite of the glorification of the separate spheres promoted by most benevolent activists.

These political integrationists sought the vote, which would deliver membership in the powerful political parties that had overwhelmed earlier anti-party proscriptions. For the next seventy-two years, until the ratification of the suffrage amendment in 1920, with the exception of Margaret Sanger's birth-control movement, enfranchisement remained the most audacious of all the demands of women reformers. It was also the most challenging and threatening to men. "Ah Lizzie thee will make us ridiculous," Lucretia Mott cautioned her young friend Elizabeth Cady Stanton, who insisted that political equality must be their goal.[22]

The Seneca Falls Convention received notice from women historians before the emergence of the new women's history of the 1970s, notably in Eleanor Flexner's *Century of Struggle*, which was first published in 1959. To be sure, with an acute sense of how important their activism was, these founding mothers left their own records, most notably in the *History of American Suffrage*, a six-volume chronicle of the movement. Their historicism sets them apart from other activists. Yet in the last half century, the meeting at Seneca Falls, along with the women's movement's eventual focus on votes for women as the prime nineteenth-century feminist reform, has taken on new significance.

Other, pre–Seneca Falls groups have been discovered, and hence the spontaneity of Seneca Falls is suspect, suggesting that more women than previously thought supported integration into the male system of politics. In 1846, according to the historian Lori Ginzberg, a group of "ladies" in Jefferson County, New York, resolved that "by denying the female portion of the community the right of suffrage and any participation in forming the government and the laws," men were tyrants. And using a tactic well known to benevolent activists, women organized petition drives that sought their inclusion in the body politic.[23] So adept did they become that after the Civil War they were able to deliver petitions to Congress with over four hundred thousand signatures.

Thus suffrage has become one of the benchmarks for studies of women's history, and the story of the struggle has emerged as one of the few historical events mainstreamed into general American textbooks covering the pre–Civil War period. What has also emerged from this new attention is an understanding of the reasons for just how threatening the enfranchisement of women was to party men who wished no disturbance of their all-male organizations. Enfranchising women threatened men because it overturned male control not just in public arenas where exclusion from the electoral process testified to female inferiority but also in their homes, where husbands and fathers continued to rule. For men, voting enacted personal sovereignty and linked them to the essential national value of the consent of the governed. To include women, as Ellen DuBois has written, "raised the prospect of female autonomy in a way that other claims to equal rights could not."[24]

But the early leaders of the woman's movement, along with modern students of women's past, recognized, as benevolent activists and contemporary practitioners of political history generally did not, the importance of the vote as an essential tool for equality. Voting was ever a blunt instrument, but without it women understood that they had a limited public identity. Activists thus sought not just the improvement of society but also the tools for their own inclusion in the polity. They believed, even as they encouraged other reforms during the 1850s such as divorce or married-women property acts, that membership in political parties was a means of changing the policies that denied their equality. They insisted that they gain immediate admission to all the rights and privileges that belonged to them as citizens of these United States.

Voting became the essential political instrument by which women could achieve improvements in their status. If women could vote, they would end the system of granting automatic child custody to fathers. If women could vote, given their acknowledged position as moral guardians of their homes, they would reform the corrupt practices of American politics. But the leaders and participants of the women's conventions that proliferated in the 1850s and after the Civil War also saw the vote as the essential transaction in any democracy between the people and those to whom they delegate authority.

From the beginning these integrationists connected politics and potential policy outcomes.

"Man," wrote Elizabeth Cady Stanton, the intellectual sparkplug of the early women's rights movement, in September 1848, "must know the advantages of voting for they all seem very tenacious about the right. . . . Had we not a vote to give might not the office holders and seekers propose some change in woman's condition?" Stanton dismissed the argument that women were already represented by the votes of their fathers, husbands, brothers, and sons. "We have had enough of such representation," she avowed. "Most cunningly [man] entraps [woman] and then takes from her all those rights which are dearer to him than life itself."[25]

At the Seneca Falls Convention women had pledged their "zealous and untiring efforts" and had invited men to join them, though as attendance at the women's rights conventions revealed, it was overwhelmingly women who fought for their own political inclusion. They made their claim as Americans who, like the men of the Revolution, had protested to the British, "No taxation without representation." At first, female integrationists used arguments from natural-rights theory in order to establish themselves as part of humanity. Wrote Lucy Stone, the young graduate of Oberlin, "We ask only for justice and equal rights—the right to vote, the right to our own earnings to equality before the law—these are the Gibraltar of our cause."[26]

Never content with the understanding that women were different from men in their political capacity, an argument implicitly accepted by benevolent activists and partisan enablers, they argued for similarity. To her brother Daniel Anthony an aggrieved Susan B. Anthony explained, "You blunder on this question of woman's rights, just where thousands of others do. You believe woman unlike man in her nature. . . . Like the American Revolution it is the same with woman's revolution, though every law were as just to woman as to man, the principle that one class may usurp the power to legislate for another is unjust and all who are not in the struggle from the love of principle would still work on until the establishment of the grand immutable truth: all governments derive their just power from the consent of the governed."[27]

In the process of struggling for their rights, political integrationists employed tactics similar to those used by political parties and thereby learned various nondomestic skills. With the arrival of universal male suffrage, party men had developed a popular style of appealing to the mass electorate through conventions, meetings, rallies, speeches, and even newspapers. Although women rarely participated in partisan parades where men marched in costumes, they made women's rights conventions in the 1850s the centerpiece of their activities. In local and the significant annual women rights conventions—the latter held in Syracuse, Worcester, Cincinnati, Cleveland, and New York—they elected officers, gave speeches, debated issues, and rallied members, who included a few progressive men, to the cause.

Throughout the 1850s they campaigned for a multifaceted civil rights agenda. Specifically, they resolved to work for the reform of marriage laws, especially with regard to divorce and guardianship. They sought reform in inheritance laws and control of their wages. But always political action through the vote was the pinnacle of their efforts. After the Civil War and the failure of women to be included in the Fifteenth Amendment, which gave black males the vote in 1870, political inclusionists concentrated entirely on suffrage in their long crusade that ended with the ratification of the Nineteenth Amendment. And so they named their postwar organizations the National Woman Suffrage Association and the American Woman Suffrage Association.

These political integrationists vigorously applied the male tactic of lobbying, most famously for married-women property acts. When Elizabeth Cady Stanton appeared before the Senate Judiciary Committee of the New York legislature where she delivered an impassioned speech in 1854, her father threatened to disinherit her and questioned her sanity. "I passed through a terrible scourging when last at my father's," she wrote Susan B. Anthony. "I cannot tell you how deep the iron entered my soul. . . . To think that all in me of which my father would have felt a proper pride had I been a man is deeply mortifying to him because I am a woman."[28] Armed with such principles, Stanton spent little time on what she considered the distractions of volunteering in political parties and benevolent societies.

Advocates for suffrage also traveled from town to town giving speeches in the same manner that political candidates did. Especially Stone, Stanton, and Anthony rented lecture halls, created and posted their own advertisements for their forthcoming lectures, and indefatigably brought the message of women's civil rights to communities throughout the Northeast. Perhaps the most famous of these stump speakers was the young Philadelphia Quaker Anna Dickinson, whose natural talents at public persuasion were soon recognized by the Republican Party. Before the war Dickinson had crafted a successful career lecturing against slavery and, occasionally, on women's rights in her talk "A Plea for Woman." By 1863 Dickinson, earning handsome fees, became what her biographer Matthew Gallman has called "an increasingly important political player," sought by Republicans as a speaker in their local campaigns. By all accounts she was especially successful in Connecticut and

New Hampshire.[29] Besides lobbying, meeting in conventions, and lecturing, integrationists established their own press, where the female agenda, which briefly included appeals for bloomer dress, was promoted. Women like Amelia Bloomer established, financed, and ran publications like the *Lily* and the *Una*. These were counterparts to the party newspapers that flourished during the period and that eschewed the modern separation of editorial comment and news reporting.

Partisan Enablers

Using the compensatory approach to political history, by the 1980s historians had discovered women who had served in various ancillary capacities in political parties. Most of their work appeared in articles such as Jean Gould Hales on the Know-Nothings and Ronald and Mary Zboray on the Whigs. There were also a few book-length studies of women enablers that extended the time frame of such activities into the twentieth century.[30] While demonstrating that women had some limited effect on party issues and leaders, such scholarly efforts also were intended to demonstrate the interest, knowledge, and activism that women had for the great game of politics.

Using compensatory and female experience conceptualizations, some historians concentrated on the activities of women partisans during the two decades of the party period. They discovered that women listened to the speeches made by prospective candidates—indoors and outdoors. But as Elizabeth Cady Stanton learned during a campaign event in Johnstown, New York, when party leaders believed there would be a sufficient audience of males, women were required to stay home. "We do not wish to spare any room for ladies" came a similar injunction in Rochester when the third-party Free-Soil candidate John Hale was to speak during the presidential election of 1852. "We mean to cram the hall with voters," to which a dismayed Anthony responded, "I have done my best to be a voter, and it is no fault of mine if unavailable people occupy your seats. So I am determined to go and hear Hale." And so she did, along with twelve other women.[31] But at outdoor meetings there was plenty of room, and so many women listened intently to the Lincoln-Douglas debates in various small Illinois towns in 1858.

A few—for parades were usually an all-male preserve—waved handkerchiefs as their preferred candidates marched by. In a less threatening domestic behavior, other partisan enablers stayed home, illuminating their windows when their chosen marched past and darkening their kerosene lamps and candles when the opposition appeared. In this way, as one New Hampshire woman wrote, "We as woman cannot vote, but we can speak and we will do that."[32]

Besides such overt secondhand cheering for their party choice, women provided behind-the-scenes contributions. They sewed the silk banners that parties used in the ceremonies of nineteenth-century politics and often in symbolic gestures of acquiescence presented them to important public men, as Stanton did in 1860; they baked cakes and provided food for party meetings and decorated assembly rooms; they raised money (one Whig activist sold raspberry bushes), and a few wrote propaganda pamphlets for their parties. In New York in 1860, women spent hours sewing the outfits of the famous Republican Wide Awakes.

As Michael Holt has written of Whig politics, "In sharp contrast to Democrats whose demonstrations remained exclusively male and often rowdy affairs, Whigs ostentatiously invited their wives, sister and daughters to rallies to testify to the party's family-oriented responsibilities."[33] Yet even as part of the Whig family ideology and a prominent issue in the campaigns of the 1840s, the roles played by partisan enablers reveal the refusal of men to allow women as equal participants.

Not everyone approved of even these limited spectating activities, and female participation became a subject of debate. In the 1840s Democrats attacked Whigs for the high visibility of their female supporters. An anonymous critic in the *Democratic Review* complained that under the "wild infatuation of party enthusiasm, ladies forsook their home paths and appeared in public, presenting banners, making speeches, joining in hard-cider, log cabin and Tippecanoe processions and choruses until the common pursuits of duty and pleasure seemed quite dull and inane."[34]

A few women enablers served as spousal spectators, and there was no better example of this model than the very partisan Mary Todd Lincoln, who not only talked politics with her husband but gave parties in Springfield to which she invited the leading Whigs and Republicans of the community. Certainly Mary Lincoln knew the difference among Whigs, Know-Nothings, Free-Soilers, and Democrats, and thereby she displayed the political knowledge and consciousness of many enablers. When her husband was a candidate for the U.S. Senate in 1854, she watched from the galleries and was familiar enough with the partisanship of the state legislators to predict for whom they would vote. And she was disappointed when Lincoln, ahead in the voting but lacking the necessary majority to defeat a Democrat, surrendered his votes to Lyman Trumbull, the eventual winner. Six years later when Lincoln heard the returns from Pennsylvania in the presidential election, he immediately went home and his neighbors heard him call out, "Mary, Mary, *We* are elected."[35]

The existence of partisan enablers certainly rebuts one of the arguments used to challenge the suffrage movement at the end of the century when opponents argued that women did not want to vote. Clearly even before the Civil War, though disenfranchised, a few women were eager participants in the partisan system that emerged between 1840 and 1860. "Disfranchisement," writes Melanie Gustafson, "did not prevent women from participating in partisan politics. In contrast to voting, a right formally extended by governments, the parameters of nonpartisan and partisan activism were not bound by laws. . . . Parties were rather political representations of public culture."[36] Still, women's status as mere enablers shows the refusal of men to allow women into the system as equal participants and the willingness of women to accept subordinate positions.

Women also served, again in an enabling fashion, as symbols. Often dressed in white robes as Liberty or the Constitution or Freedom, they took their places on floats, not as themselves or in support of a cause that they supported, but rather in the diminished role of passive expressions of patriotism, best conveyed by handsome young females. Historian Julie Jeffrey discovered a pageant during the Kansas crisis in the early 1850s when thirty-one women dressed in white and one in black representing the beleaguered state of Kansas provided a tableau for voters.

Clearly the "party period" from 1840 to 1860 described by political historians like Michael Holt has intersected with the new women's history to provide displays of a rich tapestry of female activism demonstrated in various forms in which women found methods of influencing the public debate. Some women during the period embraced opportunities—however limited—for a citizenship yet to be defined, which as late as 1919 did not include voting. But if political history inspired some of the focus for women's history and the unraveling of a female political culture, then women's history has also suggested new definitions that go beyond electoral politics. The inclusion of women in politics—albeit their kind of politics—probably would have attenuated the academy's sharp drop of interest in political history given the growing attraction of social history in the last three decades.

Finally, from the perspective of some American women, voting was not the only way to be a public woman. While benevolent activists demonstrate the importance of lobbying and partisan enablers participated in forms of political expression that moved beyond voting, political integrationists best reveal women's long struggle for equality.

Notes

1. Michael Holt, *Political Parties and American Political Development from the Age of Jackson to the Age of Lincoln* (Baton Rouge: Louisiana State University Press, 1991), 27.

2. Michael Holt, *The Fate of Their Country: Politicians, Slavery Extension, and the Coming of the Civil War* (New York: Hill & Wang, 2004), xii, 127.

3. Gerda Lerner, "Placing Women in History: Definitions and Challenges," *Feminist Studies* 3 (Fall 1975): 5–14.

4. Sidney Verba, "Women in American Politics," in Louise Tilly and Patricia Gurin, eds., *Women, Politics, and Change* (New York: Russell Sage Foundation, 1990), 567.

5. Quoted in Jean H. Baker, *Women and the U.S. Constitution, 1776–1920* (Washington, DC: American Historical Association, 2008), 6.

6. Carole Pateman, *The Sexual Contract* (Stanford, CA: Stanford University Press, 1988).

7. Stephen Maizlish and John Kushmà, eds., *Essays in Antebellum Politics* (College Station, TX: Texas A&M University Press, 1982) 15, 39.

8. Elizabeth Cady Stanton and Susan B. Anthony, *The Selected Papers of Elizabeth Cady Stanton and Susan B. Anthony*, ed. Anne Gordon (New Brunswick, NJ: Rutgers University Press, 1997), 1:104–5.

9. Elizabeth Varon, *We Mean to Be Counted: White Women and Politics in Antebellum Virginia* (Chapel Hill: University of North Carolina Press, 1998), 1.

10. Ida Harper, *Life and Work of Susan B. Anthony*, vol. 1 (North Stratford, NH: Ayer, 1997), 58.

11. Jean H. Baker, *Sisters: The Lives of American Suffragists* (New York: Hill & Wang, 2005), 142.

12. The exception came when Stanton handed a ceremonial flag to a contingent of the Republican Party called the Wide Awakes in 1860.

13. Baker, *Sisters*, 13, 14.

14. Nancy Hewitt, *Women's Activism and Social Change: Rochester, New York, 1822–1872* (Ithaca, NY: Cornell University Press, 1981).

15. Angelina Grimké, *Appeal to the Christian Women of the South* (1836; New York: Arno Press, 1969), 26.

16. Susan Zaeske, *Signatures of Citizenship: Petitioning, Antislavery, and Women's Political Identity* (Chapel Hill: University of North Carolina Press, 2003).

17. Anne Firor Scott, *Natural Allies: Women's Associations in American History* (Urbana: University of Illinois Press, 1991), 45–51.

18. Julie Jeffrey, *The Great Silent Army: Ordinary Women in the Antislavery Movement* (Chapel Hill: University of North Carolina Press, 1998), 3.

19. Ibid., 8.

20. See, for example, Stanton and Anthony, *Selected Papers*, vol. 1, *In the School of Antislavery*.

21. Scott, *Natural Allies*, 2.

22. Baker, *Sisters*, 49.

23. Lori Ginzberg, *Untidy Origins: A Story of Woman's Rights in Antebellum New York* (Chapel Hill: University of North Carolina Press, 2005), 7–10.

24. Ellen DuBois, *Feminism and Suffrage: The Emergence of an Independent Women's Movement in America, 1848–1869* (Ithaca, NY: Cornell University Press, 1978), 46.

25. Stanton and Anthony, *Selected Papers*, 1:106.

26. Harper, *Life and Work of Susan B. Anthony*, 1:74.

27. Ibid., 1:169.

28. Baker, *Sisters*, 115.

29. Matthew Gallman, *America's Joan of Arc: The Life of Anna Dickinson* (New York: Oxford University Press, 2006), 20–21.

30. For example, Melanie Susan Gustafson, *Women and the Republican Party, 1854–1920* (Urbana: University of Illinois Press, 2001); and Rebecca Edwards, *Angels in the Machinery: Gender in American Party Politics from the Civil War to the Progressive Era* (New York: Oxford University Press, 1997).

31. Harper, *Life and Work of Susan B. Anthony*, 1:62.

32. Jeffrey, *The Great Silent Army*, 165.

33. Michael Holt, *The Rise and Fall of the American Whig Party: Jacksonian Politics and the Onset of the Civil War* (New York: Oxford University Press, 1999), 106–7.

34. Jo Freeman, *A Room at a Time: How Women Entered Politics* (New York: Rowman & Littlefield, 2000), 33.

35. Jean H. Baker, *Mary Lincoln: A Biography* (New York: W. W. Norton, 1987), 162.

36. Gustafson, *Women and the Republican Party*, 2.

II

The Politics of the Secession Crisis

The Southern Opposition
and the Crisis of the Union

DANIEL W. CROFTS

The last stand of the Upper South's Whig Party often has been overlooked. In 1859, five years after the national party disappeared, Whigs in the Upper South organized an "Opposition Party"—opposed, that is, to the Democratic Party. Most members of the so-called Southern Opposition were eager to damp down North-South acrimony. They looked askance at Southern Rights Democrats, who fanned Southern insecurities and attempted to capitalize on them. A possible counterweight to forces that soon would wreck the Union, the Southern Opposition came close to changing the partisan balance in the Upper South.[1]

A small group of ex-Whigs from the Upper South joined with Northern Democrats and Republicans in early 1858 to defeat the Lecompton Constitution, which would have made entry of the Kansas Territory into the Union contingent upon defining its status as a slave state. Anti-Lecompton Southerners thereby rejected demands by Southern Democrats for regional solidarity on a slavery-related matter. By killing Lecompton, its opponents resolved the disruptive Kansas issue and assured that Kansas ultimately would enter the Union as a free state. And with no other territory owned by the United States holding any promise for plantation slavery, the Upper South's persistent Whigs thought they spotted an opening. They aspired to regain power in the Upper South—and perhaps to build a national party—by distancing themselves from both Southern proslavery absolutists and Northern antislavery hard-liners. Kentucky senator John J. Crittenden, heir to the mantle of Henry Clay and a fixture on the national stage for four decades, repudiated President James Buchanan's administration not only for trying to drive through Lecompton but also for its extravagance, its corruption, and its inability to maintain prosperity. Crittenden attempted to reach across North-South sectional lines by emphasizing issues that all opponents of the administration could agree upon. He hoped that the sharp economic downturn of

1857–58 would prompt voters to give priority to tangible pocketbook issues rather than abstract disagreements regarding the future of slavery.[2]

The diminished profile of the Kansas issue after mid-1858 endangered the Republican Party. It had formed between 1854 and 1856, and had carried a majority of free states in the 1856 presidential election, by challenging proslavery excesses in Kansas and by opposing the spread of slavery to any other territories. In 1858 and 1859 prominent Republicans feared that anti-slavery sentiment was ebbing. They worried that the Republican organization might be absorbed by a "polyglot opposition party" and consigned "to an early grave." Between late 1858 and early 1860, the historian Michael F. Holt concluded, the threat of an opposition party confronted the Republican Party with "its sternest challenge."[3]

Holt was not the first to ponder the possibilities for a new national party led by ex-Whigs from the Upper South. The historian Allan Nevins considered the rise of the Southern Opposition a key juncture in the history of the era. In his view, it might have checked the growth of "fanaticism and disruption" while inaugurating "long-overdue attention to internal reform and development." Rather than continuing the barren quarrel over slavery in the territories, the Opposition would have promoted economic policies that had bisectional appeal—"more railways, more canals, better seaports and river ports, a fairer tax system, and free public schools." In retrospect, the Upper South's readiness to consider "moderation and reconciliation" rather than North-South polarization offered a "last hope of adjustment."[4]

This essay first explains why the Southern Opposition emerged where it did—in the Upper South. Second, the core of this essay addresses the haunting might-have-beens that hover about the Southern Opposition's brief history—how its rise stirred discussion about a united opposition that might have given shape to the slippery middle between Southern Democrats and hard-line Republicans. Finally, this essay briefly considers the interconnection between partisan politics in the Upper South in the late 1850s and the startling insurgency against secession that briefly took hold there after Abraham Lincoln's election as president in November 1860.

Let us begin with an overview of two-party politics in the late antebellum South. Our understanding of the political crisis that led to war emphasizes the South's attachment to—and domination of—the Democratic Party. By 1860 the free states outnumbered the slave states eighteen to fifteen, and the population gap was larger, approximately twenty million to twelve (slaves constituted four of the twelve million). But the South increasingly called the shots in the one remaining national political party. As the historian William W. Freehling has noted, "the minority section wielded the power base of the majority party" because "the Democratic Party was the nation's majority party, and the South was the party's majority section." Buchanan won in 1856 because he carried every slave state except one. This "barely Northern" president then selected a cabinet top-heavy with Southerners, and he routinely sided with the South.[5] Democrats also controlled the legislatures in every single slave state by the late 1850s and had governors in all but one. Their legislative supremacy enabled Southern Democrats to choose U.S. senators. The resulting contingent was both numerous and powerful. Robert M. T. Hunter, James M. Mason, James A. Bayard, Clement C. Clay, Robert Toombs, John Slidell, Judah Benjamin, Jefferson Davis, and a host of other less well-remembered Southerners assured that the minority region in the country exercised de facto majority power in the upper chamber.[6]

Because a significant increment of Northern free-soil Democrats became Republicans during the 1850s, the national Democratic Party acquired a more pronounced Southern tilt. "After 1854 the Southern wing could dictate party decisions as it had never been able to do in previous Congresses," the historian David Potter wrote.[7] This power was misused. Instead of being sobered by the heavy losses the party suffered in the North following enactment of the Kansas-Nebraska Act in 1854, Southern Democrats became more high-handed and domineering. They demanded unflinching loyalty, heedless of the way their course might weaken what remained of the party in the North. Southern Rights Democrats thus endangered the basic arrangements that gave them power in the first place. The South alone could not generate Democratic victories. Only by maintaining party strength in some of the free states could Democrats keep their party afloat. Buchanan could not have won in 1856 without support from the Lower North—New Jersey, Pennsylvania, Indiana, and Illinois.

By the mid-1850s, Democrats enjoyed a hammerlock in the Deep South. The Whig Party there had fallen into irreversible decline. The 1852 Whig presidential candidate, Winfield Scott, was routed across the Deep South, as the Whig share of the popular vote, which had been close to half in 1848, plunged below 40 percent (Scott waffled on the Compromise of 1850, which contained important concessions to the South, notably the Fugitive Slave Law). Soon the party collapsed. The American Party attempted to supplant the Whigs but failed to take root in the Deep South. An American ticket headed by former president Millard Fillmore ran a slightly more competitive campaign in 1856 than Scott had in 1852. But the American Party failed to win any state in the Deep South, and it too then disappeared.[8]

Democrats also gained in the Upper South during the 1850s. They carried every state there except Kentucky and Tennessee for presidential candidate Franklin Pierce in 1852. But Whig allegiances persisted in the Upper South, and partisan competition remained unrelenting. Some Upper South Whigs clung to their party as it collapsed elsewhere. By 1854–55, however, most flocked to the new American Party, with some notable results. Maryland's American Party pulled together a genuinely new partisan coalition that dominated the state for several years. Kentucky Whigs used the fig leaf of the American Party in 1855 to recapture the governor's seat and maintain control of the legislature. Elsewhere in the Upper South, however, the American Party failed to reach the levels of support that Whigs once enjoyed, and the new affiliation proved transitory. Fillmore's 1856 candidacy fell short everywhere except Maryland. By 1857, American parties in the Upper South—except in Maryland—were moribund, and it appeared possible that one-party politics might take hold in the Upper South, just as in the Deep South. But at that juncture the Upper South and Lower South diverged. During the late 1850s, what called itself the "Southern Opposition" or the "Opposition Party" emerged as the rival to Democrats in the Upper South.[9]

The Upper South's unwillingness to mimic the Deep South pattern of one-party Democratic rule must be seen both as a consequence—and as a cause—of the rule-or-ruin frenzy that seized Southern Democrats. When the Republican Party burst to prominence in 1856 by celebrating free labor and scapegoating slaveholders, the powerful Senate cabal of Southern Democrats demanded regional solidarity to protect the South's interests. They warred not only against Republicans but soon against Northern Democrats—especially Stephen A. Douglas of Illinois—and against any in the South who dared to question their Southern Rights agenda. Freehling shows that anxieties about the future of slavery in the Upper and Border South fueled proslavery extremism.[10] Yet the campaign to whip the Upper South into line failed. A Southern Rights platform antagonized Union Democrats and most former Whigs and American Party members. The Opposition withstood accusations that its very existence imperiled the region, and it made significant gains in 1859 and 1860. Had war been averted, the Upper South might have broken decisively with the secession-tainted Democratic Party.

There were eight states in the Upper South, but five are of particular interest here—North Carolina, Virginia, Tennessee, Kentucky, and Maryland. These five states sent twenty Opposition members to the House of Representatives in 1859 and offered the party its best chances to develop and grow.[11] In contrast to the North and the Deep South, the Upper South's Jacksonian and Whig electorates remained durable (Maryland was the exception). In rural areas especially, patterns of partisan allegiance persisted. Democrats jousted with Whigs and Whig-successor parties both for control of state governments and in national contests. Elections continued to be hotly contested, with margins of victory and defeat often narrow.[12]

North Carolina illustrates the continued salience of partisan alignments in the Upper South. Because the state was closely divided, both Democratic and Whig managers probed for ways to mobilize voters. Here and elsewhere in the Upper South, a delicate balancing act was required. Steadily increasing majorities of voters were nonslaveholders, but no party dared to antagonize slaveholders, whose wealth, education, and social position made them a power in both parties. In the early and mid-1850s, North Carolina Democrats rode the "free suffrage" issue to victory by promising to end an archaic requirement that limited voting in elections for the state senate to those who possessed fifty acres of land. By attacking a less significant aspect of the state's elitist heritage, Democrats depicted themselves as "the champions of reform and the friends of the common man." The "free suffrage" campaigns enlarged voter turnout and generated sufficient Democratic gains in the heretofore Whig-leaning western part of the state to tip the overall statewide balance between the parties. Responding to the "fever heat" of "Rail Road excitement," Democrats attempted to solidify their gains by extending westward the North Carolina Railroad.[13]

Virginia's two parties competed on less equal terms. Democrats enjoyed a persistent statewide advantage, with the result that factional struggles within the Democratic Party often tended to generate as much heat as Whig-Democratic face-offs. The state's sprawling size and bifurcated geography made it difficult for party managers to define coherent policy platforms. Parts of Virginia's Tidewater and Piedmont had concentrations of slaves characteristic of the Deep South. By contrast, the state's trans-Allegheny northwest had few slaves and was economically oriented toward Ohio and Pennsylvania, with which it shared a four-hundred-mile-long border. At mid-century Virginia's east-west strains reached a critical point. But a handful of enlightened Whig and Democratic leaders devised a plan to ameliorate western grievances at a state constitutional convention in 1850–51. For the first time Virginia enfranchised all white males without property qualifications and made county governments and the office of governor subject to popular election. The compromise also diminished, without eliminating, legislative malapportionment that favored the wealthier and high-slaveholding east. The state and its two political parties thus limped ahead into the 1850s. A conspicuously Southern Rights leadership of the Democratic Party—led by U.S. Senators Hunter and Mason—warred with insurgent Democrat Henry A. Wise, whose appeal to new voters won him the governorship in 1855. Voter turnout in Virginia increased with the removal of property qualifications, but the percentage of eligible voters participating still lagged behind that of adjacent states.[14]

Partisanship in Tennessee was intense and complex. Rivalries between its three distinct regions were central to political life in this long, narrow state. Each party struggled to create coalitions linking its east, middle, and west. All white males were eligible to vote, without property qualifications. Personalities helped to drive Tennessee partisanship. A quarter century of relentless and closely contested two-party competition in Andrew Jackson's home state elevated strong leaders and forged durable partisan loyalties in the electorate. The state's cast of major actors included two presidents (Jackson and James K. Polk), one future president (Andrew Johnson), two other major presidential candidates (Hugh Lawson White and John Bell), and one of the most outrageous and polarizing newspaper editors in the country (William G. Brownlow). An era of narrow Whig advantage stretched from the late 1830s to the early 1850s. Then in 1853, Johnson, the self-proclaimed egalitarian Democrat, was narrowly elected governor by calling for a reapportioned state legislature based on white population—a winning issue in his predominantly nonslaveholding home region of East Tennessee—and for a state constitutional amendment providing for the popular election of judges. By diminishing Whig advantages in East Tennessee, Johnson tipped the overall statewide party balance. The Volunteer State maintained high levels of voter turnout.[15]

Kentucky was Tennessee's twin. Both entered the Union in the 1790s, the first states west of the Appalachians to do so, and both stretched from the mountains to the Mississippi. The towering giant of Kentucky politics was Henry Clay, Jackson's longtime rival and founder of the Whig Party. Kentucky's Whigs therefore "prided themselves as being the nation's oldest and most loyal party members." In Kentucky as elsewhere, Clay appealed to those who welcomed economic development—transportation improvements, banks, a protective tariff, and public schools. Capable leadership and a dynamic partisan press maintained sharp partisan rivalries and spurred high voter turnouts. Kentucky's electorate was closely divided, albeit with an overall Whig advantage. Each party had regions of strength—Whigs in the prosperous bluegrass country centered around Lexington, Clay's home; Democrats in the fertile Jackson Purchase region of the southwest. As in Tennessee, Whig margins frayed in the early 1850s, but Kentucky Whigs regrouped successfully in the post-Clay era and maintained the upper hand through 1855, when the disappearance of the national Whig Party prompted Kentucky Whigs to seize control of the new American Party. Aided by a nativist surge in fast-growing Louisville, Whig-Americans won a narrow statewide victory in August 1855. For the next several years, however, Whig fortunes plummeted. The American Party was blamed, probably unfairly, for the extraordinary level of violence that marked Louisville's elections in 1855, and the party also suffered in 1856 when most Northern Know-Nothings gravitated toward the anti-Southern Republican Party. Democrats successfully depicted James Buchanan's 1856 presidential candidacy as the best way to safeguard the interests of the South. During the next two years Kentucky's Democratic advantage widened as the American Party unraveled.[16]

During the mid-1850s Maryland underwent "the most dramatic voter realignment experienced by any slave state," with parallels to the turbulent partisan upheaval in the North. Previous partisan allegiances eroded amid rapid urban growth and increased foreign immigration. In 1855 Maryland Know-Nothings gained control of the state legislature and four of the state's six seats in Congress. Know-Nothings created a strikingly new entity, the American Party, based in Baltimore and including not just former Whigs but a good many former Democrats and nonvoters. Assertively Protestant, the American Party preyed on fears that Catholic immigrants gave primary loyalty to the pope in Rome rather than to the United States. Maryland voter turnouts surged as the American Party battled Democrats. For several years the American Party controlled the state, even while losing rural formerly Whig areas on the Eastern Shore and in southern Maryland that had been settled by Catholics two centuries before. Maryland's American Party reached its high-water mark in 1857, when Thomas H. Hicks was elected governor.[17]

The Southern Opposition took shape in 1859, but its roots may be traced to the repeal of the Missouri Compromise and the passage of the Kansas-Nebraska Act five years before. Most Southern Whigs initially kept their heads down and refused to challenge the Democratic measure. Of the thirteen Southern Whigs in the Senate in 1854, only John Bell of Tennessee voted against the Kansas-Nebraska Act (three others abstained). In the House, thirteen Southern Whigs also sided with the majority, but seven swam against the Kansas-Nebraska tide, while three of the four who abstained "desired its defeat" but "dared not vote openly against it."[18]

As the Kansas controversy continued to roil national politics, growing numbers of Whigs and former Whigs from the Upper South refused to knuckle under to Democratic demands for Southern unity. They thought it futile to attempt to impose slavery on regions where Henry Clay and Daniel Webster had long insisted it never could take hold, and they complained that all efforts to do so would only backfire. Some who initially had failed to follow their better judgment—notably former North Carolina senator George E. Badger—subsequently wished to retrace their steps. Those who articulated such doubts found themselves condemned as free-soilers and abolitionists by the self-appointed political guardians of Southern interests. But the clamor for Southern unanimity never silenced the Upper South's non-Democrats.[19]

As already noted, the Kansas furor reached a dismal conclusion in 1858 when the Buchanan administration tried to get Congress to approve the so-called Lecompton Constitution, which would have admitted Kansas to the Union as a slave state. Resisting extraordinary pressure, the Southern holdouts argued that Lecompton did not reflect the wishes of Kansas settlers. They condemned Democrats for provoking the North and insisted that the resultant furor would weaken rather than strengthen the South. Lecompton's most high-profile Southern opponents were two members of the Senate—Kentucky's John J. Crittenden, a longtime Whig who claimed a seat in the upper house in 1855 under auspices of the American Party, and Tennessee Whig John Bell, who earlier had voted against the Kansas-Nebraska Act. But as in 1854, the real showdown came in the House. Although their numbers were small, a handful of dissident Southerners managed to play a decisive role. On the key vote to reject Lecompton, six "South Americans"—Henry Winter Davis, J. Morrison Harris, and James B. Ricaud of Maryland; Humphrey Marshall and Warner L. Underwood of Kentucky; and North Carolina's John A. Gilmer—tipped the balance and sealed Lecompton's narrow defeat, 120–112. They deplored the way the Lecompton debate had been used to inflame sectional hatred and warned that such recklessness could lead to civil war. By voting as they did, the Southern anti-Lecomptonites faced a barrage of criticism for siding with William H. Seward, Joshua Giddings, and the "Black Republicans."[20]

The 1859 congressional elections in the Upper South showed that Democratic demands for Southern unity were ineffectual. Overall, the Opposition Party's Upper South contingent in the House expanded to twenty seats in 1859—seven in Tennessee (a gain of four), five in Kentucky (a gain of three), four in North Carolina (three more than in 1857), one in Virginia (a gain), while holding its three in Maryland. Its numbers more than doubled from the previous House in the five states considered here. The Opposition secured a majority of the House delegation in Tennessee, while dividing evenly the delegations from Kentucky, Maryland, and North Carolina. With a presidential election upcoming in which the outcome could well have been thrown into the House, the Opposition thus denied Democrats control of four slave states. Opposition gains in Tennessee and Kentucky resulted in part from gerrymanders engineered earlier in the decade when Whigs still controlled those states.[21] But even if the 1859 results slightly exaggerated Opposition strength in Tennessee and Kentucky, the results in Virginia were deceptive for opposite reasons: the Virginia Opposition failed to challenge Southern Rights Democrats in five districts narrowly carried by the Opposition candidate for governor, while at the same time, Union Democrats carried three Virginia House seats. In the judgment of the historian William Link, the 1859 elections in Virginia demonstrated "a popular backlash against southern extremism."[22] On balance, the mid-decade advantage enjoyed by Upper South Democrats had eroded, and the partisan balance in each state had become close.

The House also incubated the Opposition's next generation of national leadership. The two aging U.S. senators, Crittenden and Bell, provided the most visible national faces for the Opposition in 1858. But because Democrats had gained control of the legislatures in both Tennessee and Kentucky, Bell would not return to the Senate, and Crittenden's term had only two more years to run. Without doubt, Henry Winter Davis of Maryland was the most polished member of the Opposition in the House. Wealthy and charismatic, he was praised as "the most eloquent and promising member of his party." Davis impressed one newcomer as "the greatest man in Congress." But he had moved so close to the Republican Party, with which he would eventually affiliate, as to call his Southern allegiances into question. John A. Gilmer of North Carolina, who had stood with Davis to block Lecompton, therefore became the spokesman for his party in the House. Gilmer won reelection to his seat from the North Carolina Piedmont by an increased majority, defeating both a Democrat and a former Whig, both of whom spent the campaign "bitterly denouncing" Gilmer's vote against Lecompton. Gilmer's success in overcoming proslavery smears thrilled the embattled remnant of North Carolina emancipationists, one of whom rejoiced that "the people are now standing with their eyes almost open." Davis, who lauded Gilmer's "great personal popularity and ability," orchestrated his advancement.[23]

Also notable in the House's Opposition ranks were two Tennesseans,

Emerson Etheridge and Robert Hatton, and a North Carolinian, Zebulon Vance. Etheridge, who had voted against the Kansas-Nebraska Act, made a political comeback, narrowly defeating the popular J. D. C. Atkins. Although routinely denounced as a "Southern Black Republican," Etheridge gave as good as he got and was hailed by his friends as a "true patriot of the Clay and Webster school." Hatton, a moderate on North-South issues, had sacrificed himself as the fast-fading American Party's candidate for governor in 1857. He entered Congress for the first time in 1859 when the Opposition in his Middle Tennessee district dumped the incumbent, Charles Ready, who had voted for Lecompton. Ready ran for reelection with Democratic support but lost to young Hatton, a rising star. In western North Carolina, young Zebulon Vance—who would have a long future political career—won an upset victory in an 1858 special election for a House seat that earlier had been held by a Southern Rights Whig turned Democrat, Thomas Clingman. In 1859 Vance breezed to reelection.[24]

But the Opposition's core message was blurred. Both in Virginia and Kentucky, it taunted Democrats for being insufficiently Southern and charged that Northern Democrats would dictate party policy and deny the South its rights. This sort of partisan one-upmanship, which the historian William Cooper has aptly labeled "the politics of slavery," had been going on since the 1830s. In part, the Opposition hammered away at Democrats by pointing out that proslavery excesses had boomeranged—that the South had been weakened and made more vulnerable by Kansas-Nebraska and Lecompton. This was a legitimate point, not Southern Rights grandstanding. But the Opposition's Virginia and Kentucky campaigns in 1859 severely compromised its claims to sectional moderation. The Virginia Opposition's candidate for governor, William Goggin, attacked Democrat John Letcher as an emancipationist—exactly the sort of accusation that Opposition candidates elsewhere, notably Gilmer in North Carolina, had to fend off. Goggin campaigned strenuously in high-slaveholding areas east of the Blue Ridge. The *National Era* denounced the Virginia Opposition for "the folly of trying to underbid the Sham Democracy for the support of the slaveholding interest" and interpreted Goggin's narrow loss as evidence that the tide of "Slavery fanaticism" had "begun to recede." Meanwhile, the Opposition's candidate for governor of Kentucky, Joshua Bell, announced that he favored congressional protection for slavery in the territories—the hobbyhorse of Deep South extremists. "He was fool enough to try to outbid the Locos [Democrats] on the negro question," huffed Maryland's Henry Winter Davis. "I prefer his defeat to his success on such grounds." As soon as the election took place—and Bell lost—the erratic Kentucky Opposition abandoned "protection" and warned that Democrats were closet secessionists.[25]

The 1859 Opposition campaign in Tennessee, by contrast, steered clear of proslavery one-upmanship. Instead, its platform opposed both a slave code for the territories and the reopening of the African slave trade, while favoring a protective tariff. It condemned Democrats for attempting to salvage power through "a complete sectionalization of the country." John Netherland, the Opposition candidate for governor, rejected Democratic alarms about imaginary dangers to slavery. Democrats responded by blasting Netherland as a dupe of "Black Republicans" and abolitionists. Although Netherland ran a strong race, he lost narrowly. "The Tennessee Opposition borrowed no thunder from their opponents," noted the *New York Times*. "No attempt was made by them to out-Herod Herod, in the advocacy of Southern ultraisms. On the contrary the ground which they chose to occupy, is a ground upon which the Conservative Northern Opposition can equally stand and fight in the approaching Presidential canvass." The Washington correspondent for the *Philadelphia North American* likewise heralded the Tennessee Opposition for having built "a moral breakwater against the fanaticism of Southern extremists." Its platform was one that "any Northern state might accept."[26]

North Carolina's Opposition picked up half the state's seats in Congress in 1859 by condemning the extravagance and corruption of the Buchanan administration. Opposition spokesmen spurned Democratic accusations that they were allies of Republicans and abolitionists. Smears of this sort were a *"decoy* cry" designed to distract attention from "the *true issue*." The Opposition further distanced itself from Deep South bitter-enders in North Carolina's gubernatorial and legislative elections, held one year later in the summer of 1860. Under Democratic governors during the 1850s, state taxes had more than tripled, largely to finance costly railroad construction. The Opposition Party made a bold departure in its campaign for governor in 1860 with a plan to readjust property assessments. It proposed taxing slaves at fair market value, so as to end a tax exemption enjoyed by slaveholders. Democrats complained that ad valorem taxation would array nonslaveholders against slaveholders at a time when the entire South was under attack from "Black Republicans." The Opposition countered, however, by claiming slavery would rest on a firmer base, and enjoy more hearty support from nonslaveholders, if slaveholders paid their fair share of taxes. Although the ad valorem campaign distressed some "old conservative Whigs," it appeared to energize nonslaveholders and came close to success. Democrats narrowly prevailed, but over 47 percent of the state electorate was apparently satisfied by Opposition assurances. Voter turnout exceeded 80 percent, the highest level in twenty years.[27]

Maryland's American Party celebrated its support for the Union, which was, it warned, endangered by "Southern fire-eaters." They clung to power, charged Henry Winter Davis, by raising false alarms about the safety of slavery. While brushing aside accusations that he was a Republican in disguise, Davis made no secret of his wish that the Opposition both North and South might unite to defeat Southern extremists. But Democrats received an unexpected boost several weeks before Maryland's November 1859 state elections, when John Brown crossed the river from Maryland to attack Harpers Ferry. Democrats blasted the American Party as proto-Republicans who refused to confront the abolitionist menace. Davis acknowledged privately that the "Harpers Ferry tragedy" had been the "turning point" that placed his party on the defensive. Maryland's Opposition was also tarnished by election violence in Baltimore, which became more scandalous between 1855 and 1859. Although Know-Nothing "plug uglies" were blamed for the situation, both Democratic and American clubs practiced intimidation, under the guise of preventing illegal voters. In November 1859, an urban Democratic "reform" movement allied with newly Democratic rural regions to narrowly wrest control of the legislature away from Maryland's American Party. The latter continued, however, to hold three of the state's six house seats and the governorship.[28]

Southern Democrats tended to run poorly in cities, especially border-state cities where slavery was in decline. Urban non-Democrats there successfully depicted themselves as the champions of free white labor. Baltimore Know-Nothings, who provided the backbone for Maryland's American Party, pledged to restrict immigration and raise the tariff. They would thereby "protect the jobs of native-born workmen," who allegedly were threatened by cheap foreign-born labor and cheap European goods. Louisville, like Baltimore, also demonstrated the appeal of nativism to workingmen, as the American Party won big victories in 1854 and 1855. Non-Democrats in St. Louis blasted Democrats for putting the interests of slaveholders ahead of the interests of white workingmen. In the latter part of the decade, St. Louis free-soilers and German immigrants audaciously claimed the Republican label and depicted slavery as an impediment to economic growth.[29]

Baltimore, Louisville, and St. Louis provided proslavery standpatters with a horrifying glimpse of a future in which white nonslaveholders might turn against slavery. If the four border states—Delaware, Maryland, Kentucky, and Missouri—moved toward emancipation, the total number of slave states might shrink to eleven. It might then become possible to imagine passage of an antislavery constitutional amendment. Already, most Delaware blacks and close to half of those in Maryland were free. Although few blacks in the two western border states were free, large parts of Kentucky and Missouri had scant commitment to slavery. Kentucky had five times as many white nonslaveholding families as slaveholding families, and Missouri had six times as many.[30]

On balance, the rise of the Opposition in 1859 suggested that proslavery politics in the Upper South had come close to a dead end. Even though Democrats hammered away at the Opposition as fifth-column "Black Republicans" and abolitionists, the Opposition hit back, wrapping itself in the mantle of the Union and warning that Democrats were giving aid and comfort to those who plotted secession. Almost all Opposition leaders proclaimed their loyalty to slavery and the slave system, but they blamed Democrats for having intensified Northern antislavery sentiment. By decade's end, the Democratic advantage in the Upper South had become tenuous. A shared partisan affiliation with Deep South militants placed Upper South Democrats at risk.

Let us turn now to consider the relationship between the Southern Opposition and the movement to create a national "United Opposition." If there ultimately was no fire, there certainly was plenty of smoke. In January 1859 "a number of gentlemen from all sections of the country" gathered in Washington to try to forestall a presidential election in 1860 that would pit a pro-Southern Democrat against an anti-Southern Republican. They hoped instead to define some "intermediate ground upon which all entertaining national and conservative opinions might stand together." The time had come, noted the longtime North Carolina Whig William A. Graham, for leaders from both North and South to end disputes about slavery in "distant territories." Kentucky's Crittenden, joined by a scattering of diehard Northern Whigs and conservative Republicans, worked to organize a "United Opposition" across sectional lines. They hoped to rebuild a new national party that might ride to power on a wave of popular disgust with the Buchanan administration. John Minor Botts of Virginia, an outspoken veteran Whig and former congressman, let it be known that he was ready to head the ticket for a united opposition—or even to take the Republican nomination if that party would tone down its antislavery message. Discussions along these lines increased during the summer of 1859, as the Opposition posted gains in the Upper South's elections. It was at this juncture, in Holt's view, that Republicans faced their "sternest challenge."[31]

The challenge was made especially acute because a number of Republicans, notably Horace Greeley, editor of the *New York Tribune,* doubted whether their party alone could carry a national election. "I *know* the country is not Anti-Slavery," Greeley reasoned. "It will only swallow a little Anti-Slavery in a great deal of sweetening. An Anti-Slavery man *per se* cannot be elected, but a Tariff, River-and-Harbor, Pacific Railroad, Free Homestead man *may* succeed *although* he is Anti-Slavery." Republican success might require running as part of a united opposition. The *New York Times* likewise announced that "it is as a national opposition, not as a sectional organization, that the Republicans must look for victory in 1860, if they are to win at all." The issues that had dominated the 1856 campaign had become obsolete. "The admission of Kansas as a Free State is now a foregone conclusion," the *Times* observed, and no other territory was similarly endangered. "Where is the territory to be threatened as Kansas was with the armed establishment of the institution of slavery?" Washington Hunt, a former Whig governor of New York, thought that "further extension [of slavery] had become impossible." The time had come to "drive Republicans from a sectional into a national position" and make it so that "it can carry some of the Southern States."[32]

The political logic underpinning the concept of a united opposition made sense—up to a point. Members of the Southern Opposition were eager to regain a national party affiliation. The demise of the Whig Party and then the American Party had left them with no national political home. But most of their presumed Northern allies were "Black Republicans." Even if Republicans chose to muffle their opposition to any new slave territory and agreed to drop their anti–Slave Power rhetoric, it would have been a tough sell to persuade Southern voters to favor a united opposition that was so dependent on support from non-Southerners, many of whom had an anti-Southern track record. Alternatively, the Southern Opposition might have allied with Union Democrats to form a united opposition. Stephen A. Douglas had led the charge against Lecompton, and in so doing he had deeply impressed Crittenden. "The position taken by him, was full of sacrafice [*sic*], and full of hazard, yet he took it, and he defended it, *like a Man*," Crittenden explained to Abraham Lincoln. Douglas enjoyed broad popular support in the North plus pockets of support in the South. But a large reservoir of partisan distrust separated the Southern Opposition from Union Democrats. Issues such as redistricting made it difficult to overcome traditional party allegiances.[33]

Yet some would-be architects of the united opposition stood ready to enlist Northern allies. Henry Winter Davis hated all Democrats but wanted to join hands with Northern non-Democrats. He hoped that Republicans and Opposition representatives in Congress would vote together on issues such as the tariff, the transcontinental railroad, and agricultural colleges, so that "a sense of community of interest" would displace "the old standing line of division which the predominance of the slavery contest has made the boundary of party relations." A united opposition would marginalize both "the antislavery interest" and the "aggressive pro-slavery movement." It could agree to prevent renewal of the African slave trade or the acquisition of new territory suitable for slavery, and it could stifle secession. When the time came, the united opposition could agree to run a single presidential candidate—perhaps John Bell, Thomas Corwin, or Edward Bates—without a platform.[34] The *Louisville Journal*, edited by George Prentice, was the long-standing newspaper of record for Kentucky's Whigs-turned-Opposition. Like Davis, the *Journal* contended that a shared interest in protective tariffs and internal improvements could lead to a working arrangement between Republicans and the Southern Opposition, and that both would oppose the African slave trade. It suggested that the two groupings unite to select a new Speaker of the House—such as Thomas Corwin, the former Whig and now conservative Republican from Ohio, or Tennessee's Emerson Etheridge, who had just regained his seat. The new House could then turn its attention to investigating the Buchanan administration's corrupt dealings.[35]

Speculation about a united opposition alarmed orthodox Republicans. Between May and September 1859, Abraham Lincoln wrote more about this topic than any other. Repeatedly he warned his correspondents against lowering the "Republican Standard" in order to accommodate "the southern opposition element" or the supporters of Douglas. Republicans had come together to stop the nationalization of slavery, and if they were to backtrack, Lincoln fumed, "it would gain nothing in the South, and lose every thing in the North." He estimated that fifty thousand former Democrats in Illinois who had joined Republican ranks to bar slavery from the territories would never support a united opposition pledged only to opposing renewal of the African slave trade. The only path to victory in 1860, Lincoln insisted, lay in uniting the North behind the Republican Party.[36]

Many other Republicans agreed. A "distinguished" Wisconsin Republican complained that any alliance with the American Party "would certainly ruin us in all the northwestern states." The *National Era* condemned the constant effort by some "timid conservatives and short-sighted skeptics" to drag down the Republican Party "into one of mere opposition to the Administration, and to evade the Slavery Issue." It scorned the decision by the Virginia Opposition in 1859 to run upon a platform "as thoroughly Pro-slavery as that of the Black Democracy" and dismissed as "ridiculous" the thought that the Republicans "might harmonize with such an 'Opposition.'" The *National Era* also pointed out that "even the most liberal" of "Southern oppositionists" had spurned the advances of Republicans such as Greeley. The Opposition insisted, instead, that Republicans "crawl upon their bellies" and "abandon their party organization and name, and fall into rank as private soldiers, under the lead of old conservative Whigs." In short, the drive for a united national opposition was simply a scheme "for dividing and breaking up the Republican party."[37]

John Brown then struck a grievous blow against the chrysalid united opposition. However inept Brown's plan to ignite a slave rebellion, his assault on Harpers Ferry in October 1859 had a pronounced political impact. It poisoned partisan discourse, as many Southerners blamed Republicans for having established a climate of opinion within which the raid had taken place. Some in the South even pretended that Brown was a Republican agent. Crittenden, probably the leading would-be architect of a united opposition, observed in January 1860 that he could not carry a single Southern state if he ran as a Republican and that his presence on such a ticket would doom it in the North. As the historian Richard H. Sewell has noted, the Brown raid meant that "henceforth all talk of an intersectional coalition was just so much hot air."[38]

In other ways, however, the Brown raid put the Southern Opposition even more in the spotlight. As Congress assembled in December, immediately after Brown was hanged, it became apparent that the Southern Opposition, with twenty-three seats, held the balance of power in the House of Representatives. Republicans stood a few votes short of a majority and could not elect a speaker on their own. Democrats, most of whom came from the South, held twenty seats fewer than Republicans. Democrats insisted that electing any Republican would be an intolerable insult to the South. For two months, the stalemate persisted. The Opposition put forward North Carolina's John A. Gilmer. At one point he won a dozen additional votes from conservative Republicans but none from Democrats. His supporters then taunted Democrats as insincere hypocrites—they claimed to care only about defeating a Republican but then refused to elect Gilmer, a non-Republican and a Southern slaveholder. In the end, the most outspoken maverick among the Opposition, Baltimore's Henry Winter Davis, played a decisive role. Davis, who believed that Democrats were "the only party which is really dangerous to the country," urged his friends to throw their support to a moderate Republican. He privately deplored the Opposition's "weakness" and "vacillation": "Oh! The folly of timidity in the face of the democrats—sure to beat us *in detail* if we remain divided: and if we unite, we have forces on the field enough to overwhelm them—and our people are afraid to beat them!!" When Republican managers brought forward William Pennington, elected on a Whig-American "People's Party" ticket in New Jersey, Davis was put to the test. His vote delivered control of the House to a coalition of Republicans, anti-Lecompton Democrats, and Opposition Whig-Americans. Several committee chairmanships went to Davis's hesitant Southern friends. It could thus be said that a very attenuated united opposition had emerged, in spite of all the forbidding circumstances weighing against it.[39]

Davis was the exception. None of the other Southern Opposition men in the House dared to ally openly with Republicans. Instead, the Southern Opposition decided to run its own presidential candidate. The aged Crittenden declined the honor, so the nomination went instead to John Bell, who was slightly Crittenden's junior. Bell's candidacy was purportedly national rather than regional, so its managers entitled their project the "Constitutional Union Party" and enlisted Edward Everett of Massachusetts, a respected former Whig, to run for vice president. But the ticket had scant appeal in the free states, so Bell's hopes centered on the Upper South. His candidacy therefore may appear to have offered no hope of victory. But the Electoral College beckoned. In 1856 the presidential election had come close to ending up in the House. Slender Democratic margins in Kentucky, Tennessee, and Louisiana had saved the day for James Buchanan. The Southern Opposition expected to do better than Millard Fillmore had in 1856. Its prospects were enhanced by a poisonous Democratic split, in which Douglas held the regular party nomination but John C. Breckinridge of Kentucky, the incumbent vice president, was the standard-bearer for insurgent Southern Rights Democrats. The Opposition aspired to hold the balance of power and claim a potential kingmaker's role—or perhaps even the great prize itself. Had the presidential election been thrown into the House, each state would have had a single vote. There were thirty-three states in the Union, so that seventeen would have been required to choose. Neither Democrats nor Republicans would have had a majority. The Southern Opposition thus had some slender basis for hoping that its presidential candidate just might emerge as a compromise winner.[40]

For the election to end up in the House, Republicans would have had to lose several key states in the Lower North. And the only person who could defeat them there was Douglas. Accordingly, Opposition spokesmen in the Upper South quietly encouraged the few Bell supporters in states such as Pennsylvania, Indiana, and Illinois to vote instead for Douglas, because Bell had no chance there. "The severity of the national crisis," the historian Harry Volz has written, forced "an *entente cordiale*" between the Bell and Douglas campaigns. The historian Robert W. Johannsen, Douglas's biographer, likewise noted the "element of compatibility" linking the Douglas and Bell forces.[41]

The final segment of this essay surveys the startling and fateful sequel to the 1860 election. Viewed narrowly, the Southern Opposition's performance in the presidential race was successful. Bell managed to carry three states—his home state of Tennessee, plus Kentucky and Virginia. Although he did not win an outright majority in any state, the division of the Democratic vote between Douglas and Breckinridge allowed Bell to claim the three plurality victories. His thirty-nine electoral votes thereby qualified him to contend, had the contest ended up in the House of Representatives. But that did not happen. Abraham Lincoln swept the free states and thereby compiled more than enough electoral votes to claim the presidency.[42]

The 1860 election triggered the most dangerous crisis the country ever had faced. The Deep South, led by South Carolina, refused to accept Lincoln's victory and plunged ahead to create a new nation, the Confederate States of America. The Lower South's rash course confronted the Upper South with a complex dilemma. Lincoln had won only a few scattered votes along the border, and his victory was widely deplored across the Upper South. But those who considered his election a justification for secession found themselves decisively outnumbered in the Upper South. A coalition of antisecessionists, or Unionists, suddenly took shape there. Fearful that war might erupt at any moment, Unionists worked desperately to defuse the impasse, preserve the peace, and implore the Lower South to reconsider. They insisted that disunionists endangered the very thing they claimed to treasure. Slavery was secure and enjoyed ample constitutional guarantees, Unionists asserted. Lincoln's election was a cause for regret, not for suicidal overreaction.

Having experienced a modest renaissance in 1859 and 1860, the Opposition suddenly found in early 1861 that its stance against secession converged with majority sentiment in the Upper South. For several months, the drive to create an independent South stalled. States containing two-thirds of the South's white population spurned the Confederate nation. Several states in the Upper South held elections that provided a referendum on secession, and Unionists swept every contest decisively. Most Unionists were former Opposition voters. A significant increment of nonslaveholding Democrats and previous nonvoters also opposed secession. What resulted was something new. To a far greater extent than ever before in each state, slaveholders tended to vote one way and nonslaveholders the other, with nonslaveholders overwhelmingly opposed to secession. Union victories could easily have been achieved in all three states without the vote of a single slaveholder.[43]

Unionist victories stunned Upper South Democrats. Lincoln had won the presidency without Southern support. Then the Unionist groundswell in the Upper South jeopardized the power of Democrats at home, just as Lincoln had jeopardized their power in the nation. The secession stigma threatened to upend the long-standing arrangements that made Southern Rights Democrats powerful. But Unionists knew that their advantage in the Upper South might be no more than transitory. They keenly appreciated that they were held hostage by events they could not control—that war could sweep them away in an instant. They therefore labored to prevent any armed collision between secessionists and the federal government.[44]

Unionists affiliated with the Southern Opposition were in the thick of the struggles to enact a Union-saving compromise in Congress and to avert hostilities. A closely related high-stakes drama played out behind closed doors. The defeated Republican presidential aspirant, William Henry Seward, and his alter ego, Thurlow Weed, persuaded Lincoln to offer a cabinet slot to North Carolina's John A. Gilmer. Henry Winter Davis, who would have been more receptive to the offer, told Lincoln that Gilmer was the man for the job. His appointment would be the best way to hold the Upper South in the Union and to set in motion a sober second thought in the Deep South. But for the plan to work, Davis realized, it was imperative to keep the peace. "Gilmer will be very useful in organizing support in the South," Davis wrote confidentially to a friend, so long as the revolution did not spread to North Carolina. But "in that event he would I fear be too timid to remain or to act. Still he is very important to *begin with*." Lincoln had qualms about including in the cabinet someone who had opposed his election and who did not accept the key ideas that defined the Republican Party, but he knew that Gilmer had dared to stand up against proslavery dogmatists on Lecompton. For two key months in early 1861, a cabinet post was Gilmer's for the taking.[45]

In the end, Gilmer decided against joining Lincoln's cabinet. He wanted assurances, which he could not get, that Lincoln would forswear the use of armed force. At the last minute, Opposition leaders attempted to secure the post for Davis, but Lincoln rebuffed them. He selected instead Montgomery Blair, an avowed Republican with powerful family connections in both Maryland and Missouri. Ironically, Blair thought a show of force would nip secession in the bud. But Gilmer knew better and kept sending advice back to Washington from North Carolina in March, pleading with the new administration to keep the peace and relinquish Fort Sumter in the harbor of Charleston, South Carolina. Gilmer described the nervous impetuousness among Upper South secessionists, who were desperate to maintain their flagging revolution. Their "only hope," he noted, was a "collision of arms" between federal and state forces. They would "give a kingdom for a fight." Would Gilmer therefore acquiesce in disunion? In the short term, yes, but in the longer run, no. If things were allowed "quietly to settle down," the Upper South would develop a more unconditional attachment to the Union, he predicted, while Deep South secessionists would find that the Upper South was beyond their reach. A counterrevolution against secession ultimately would build in the Deep South. Because we know how events played out, we may find such advice naïve. And yet it offered the only possible hope for peaceful reunion. Lincoln's secretary of state, Seward, worked with Lincoln's longtime Illinois rival, Douglas, to persuade Lincoln to pull back from Fort Sumter and give Gilmer's approach a chance.[46]

Lincoln decided, however, that time was not on the side of the Union. He feared that the Lower South would never voluntarily return. So he decided to try to hold Sumter. That gave Confederates the pretext to fire the first shot—and to rouse tribal allegiances not only in the Deep South but also in the Upper South, once Lincoln moved to meet force with force. The Upper South had warned that it could not tolerate coercion of the Lower South. As the historian David Potter memorably observed: "Was not the upper South rather more in a position similar to that of a moderate and powerful nation which has made an unlimited alliance to protect a weak but belligerent neighbor, and which has thus placed its own peace at the discretion of its trigger-happy ally?"[47]

However formidable the barrier against extremism posed by the Opposition and its many newfound allies, ultimately the Upper South's two-party system could not weather the storm when war forced everyone to choose sides. In places where slaveholdings were significant, antisecession sentiment atrophied, and a mad rush out of the Union followed the outbreak of war. As Gilmer observed in March: "The only thing that now gives the secessionists the advantage of the conservatives is the cry of coercion—that the whipping of a slave state, is the whipping of slavery." If fighting were to start, he warned, the "conservative Union men" in the Upper South would be "swept away in a torrent of madness." And that is what happened—the torrent swept Gilmer himself away. But things played out differently in northwestern Virginia and East Tennessee. There, as in most of the Border South, the presence of relatively few slaves and slaveholders produced Union rather than Confederate outcomes, especially when pro-Union political leadership persisted. Party affiliation did matter—Whig-Opposition loyalties made it more likely that someone in the Upper South initially would reject secession, and low-slaveholding Whig counties emphatically rejected the Confederacy and often sent soldiers to the Union army—but when push came to shove and one had to choose sides in a war, then slavery trumped party.[48]

It is a sad but fascinating story. And it continues to attract fresh scrutiny from historians. Edward L. Ayers looks at Pennsylvanians and Virginians who, "if left to themselves," would never have gone to war, but who, when forced to choose sides, did so "with a startling passion." No book better depicts the rival nationalisms that suddenly took shape in April 1861, recasting identities and transforming "deep structures of interest and belief." William W. Freehling shows how a militant secessionist minority imposed its will on larger numbers of white Southerners to create an outcome that few either welcomed or expected. Like Ayers, Freehling makes a powerful case that slavery was the deciding element in determining Upper South allegiances. Most of what he terms the Middle South—Virginia, North Carolina, Tennessee, and Arkansas—could not tolerate the use of force against the Deep South. Nelson Lankford describes how a fault line "zigzagged" across Virginia and Maryland with "lightning speed," dividing the region into rival nations. Lankford and Ayers both recapture the nearly universal sense of astonishment that events played out as they did. Russell McClintock revisits Northern decision making during the secession winter. He rehabilitates the efforts by Seward and Douglas to preserve the peace. Lincoln too "leaned as far toward conciliation as he could without sacrificing federal authority," McClintock writes, but ultimately the new president concluded that he must risk war rather than appear to acquiesce in secession.[49]

These fine recent studies call our attention to the profound uncertainties that permeated the last years and months of peace. Because we know how the future unfolded, we are bound to marginalize other possible outcomes. But if we are to comprehend how the national political situation appeared to decision makers at the time, and why many thought the ultimate showdown could be averted, then the brief history of the Southern Opposition Party deserves notice.

Notes

1. Michael F. Holt's masterwork, *The Rise and Fall of the American Whig Party: Jacksonian Politics and the Onset of the Civil War* (New York: Oxford University Press, 1999), undergirds this essay. Holt's *The Political Crisis of the 1850s* (New York: Wiley, 1978) contends that the Upper South's persistent two-party system served as a bulwark to repel Southern Rights extremism. This fertile insight has since been validated by several scholars, and it informs the discussion here. See Marc W. Kruman, *Parties and Politics in North Carolina, 1836–1865* (Baton Rouge: Louisiana State University Press, 1983); Harry A. Volz III, "Party, State, and Nation: Kentucky and the Coming of the American Civil War" (Ph.D. diss., University of Virginia, 1982); Jonathan M. Atkins, *Parties, Politics, and the Sectional Conflict in Tennessee, 1832–1861* (Knoxville: University of Tennessee Press, 1997); Daniel W. Crofts, *Reluctant Confederates: Upper South Unionists in the Secession Crisis* (Chapel Hill: University of North Carolina Press, 1989). Throughout his career, Holt has insisted that we cannot understand the North-South sectional conflict and the outbreak of war unless we pay close attention to party leaders and the crucible of party politics.

2. Albert D. Kirwan, *John J. Crittenden: The Struggle for the Union* (Lexington: University of Kentucky Press, 1962), 322–35, 346–49; Holt, *Political Crisis of the 1850s*, 207–8.

3. Holt, *Political Crisis of the 1850s*, 208–9.

4. Allan Nevins, *The Emergence of Lincoln*, vol. 2, *Prologue to Civil War 1859–1861* (New York: Scribner's, 1950), 58–69.

5. William W. Freehling, *The Road to Disunion*, vol. 2, *Secessionists Triumphant, 1854–1861* (New York: Oxford University Press, 2007), 14, 105, 139.

6. Southern-oriented Democratic senators also represented several free states—New Jersey, Indiana, California, and Oregon.

7. David M. Potter, *The Impending Crisis, 1848–1861*, completed and edited by Don E. Fehrenbacher (New York: Harper & Row, 1976), 239.

8. Holt, *American Whig Party*, 756–60; Holt, *Political Crisis of the 1850s*, 230–36; Potter, *Impending Crisis*, 234–35. Fillmore's loss in Louisiana was narrow.

9. Holt, *American Whig Party*, 756–60, 934–37; Crofts, *Reluctant Confederates*, 130–94, esp. 193–94.

10. Freehling, *Road to Disunion*, 2:15, 71.

11. Delaware, which had more in common with Pennsylvania than it did with the rest of the South, had difficulty sustaining a successful Opposition party because many of its ex-Whigs became Republicans. As in New Jersey and Pennsylvania, Delaware's Opposition attempted to coalesce into a "People's Party," but in 1860 they divided their presidential votes—half voted for former Whig John Bell and half for Abraham Lincoln. George P. Fisher, "at heart a Republican," was narrowly elected to Congress on a People's ticket. Harold Bell Hancock, *Delaware during the Civil War: A Political History* (Wilmington: Historical Society of Delaware, 1961), 35–37. Ferocious Democratic factionalism in Missouri pitted supporters of free-soiler Thomas Hart Benton against those of proslavery David Atchison. Whigs therefore could play balance-of-power politics. But by the late 1850s, a significant segment of Missouri's potential Opposition party—German Americans led by Francis P. Blair Jr.—had become Republicans, creating a situation with parallels to Delaware. John Vollmer Mering, *The Whig Party in Missouri* (Columbia: University of

Missouri Press, 1967); Holt, *American Whig Party*, 850–52; Freehling, *Road to Disunion*, 2:61–79, 249–50. Arkansas was by far the most Democratic state in the Upper South, and the inability of Arkansas Whigs to show more than a token presence appeared to mirror trends in the Lower South. But secession temporarily divided the state in early 1861, as low-slaveholding uplands in the north and west temporarily blocked the initial push for alliance with the Deep South. James M. Woods, *Rebellion and Realignment: Arkansas's Road to Secession* (Fayetteville: University of Arkansas Press, 1987).

12. Daniel W. Crofts, *Old Southampton: Politics and Society in a Virginia County, 1834–1869* (Charlottesville: University Press of Virginia, 1992), offers a detailed case in point.

13. Thomas E. Jeffrey, "'Free Suffrage' Revisited: Party Politics and Constitutional Reform in Antebellum North Carolina," *North Carolina Historical Review* 59 (Winter 1982): 28, 40; Paul D. Escott, *Many Excellent People: Power and Privilege in North Carolina, 1850–1900* (Chapel Hill: University of North Carolina Press, 1985), 27–31; John Gray Bynum to David S. Reid, January 25, 1855, in Lindley S. Butler, ed., *The Papers of David Settle Reid*, vol. 2, *1853–1913* (Raleigh: North Carolina Division of Archives and History, 1997), 109–10; Crofts, *Reluctant Confederates*, 60–62.

14. William G. Shade, *Democratizing the Old Dominion: Virginia and the Second American Party System, 1824–1861* (Charlottesville: University Press of Virginia, 1996); Daniel W. Crofts, "Late Antebellum Virginia Reconsidered," *Virginia Magazine of History and Biography* 107 (Summer 1999): 253–86; Crofts, *Reluctant Confederates*, 56–60; Holt, *American Whig Party*, 622–23, 925–29.

15. Atkins, *Parties, Politics;* Paul Bergeron, *Antebellum Politics in Tennessee* (Lexington: University Press of Kentucky, 1982); Holt, *American Whig Party*, 793–95; Crofts, *Reluctant Confederates*, 62–64.

16. Holt, *American Whig Party*, 630–32, 793, 799, 932–33, 935–37, quotation on 935; Volz, "Kentucky and the Coming of the American Civil War."

17. Maryland's unique course, a classic instance of what the political scientist Walter Dean Burnham has called a "critical realignment," is ably analyzed in Jean H. Baker, *Ambivalent Americans: The Know-Nothing Party in Maryland* (Baltimore: Johns Hopkins University Press, 1977), esp. 145–51; and Holt, *American Whig Party*, 934–35, quotation on 935. See Walter Dean Burnham, *Critical Elections and the Mainsprings of American Politics* (New York: W. W. Norton, 1970). Baker's *Ambivalent Americans* provides the fullest assessment of the American Party's spectacular rise in Maryland.

18. The Kansas-Nebraska Act would have passed the Senate even if all thirteen Southern Whigs had voted against it. But the House vote was closer—the act passed by the narrow margin of 113–100—so Southern Whigs potentially could have defeated it. Holt, *American Whig Party*, 819–21.

19. Holt, *American Whig Party*, 815–21; Crofts, *Reluctant Confederates*, 67. Badger lost his Senate seat in 1855.

20. *New York Times*, March 12, April 2, 1858; *Congressional Globe*, 35th Cong., 1st Sess., A 282–85; Freehling, *Road to Disunion*, 2:140–42; Allan Nevins, *The Emergence of Lincoln*, vol. 1, *Douglas, Buchanan, and Party Chaos, 1857–1859* (New York: Scribner's, 1950), 293–301; Crofts, *Reluctant Confederates*, 67–68.

21. Atkins, *Parties, Politics*, 181, 216; Volz, "Kentucky and the Coming of the American Civil War," 346–49. At this time states in the Upper South held their midterm congressional

elections between May and November in odd-numbered years, before the new Congress would meet in December.

22. John Millson from Norfolk and Sherrard Clemens from Wheeling in the far northwest won reelection as Union Democrats. John T. Harris, an independent Union Democrat, defeated the regular Democrat, James H. Skinner, for an open seat in the Shenandoah valley. The one House seat carried by the Opposition, also in the Shenandoah valley, went to Alexander R. Boteler, who defeated the well-known Southern Rights Democrat Charles J. Faulkner. William A. Link, *Roots of Secession: Slavery and Politics in Antebellum Virginia* (Chapel Hill: University of North Carolina Press, 2003), 175; Crofts, *Reluctant Confederates*, 68, 139; *National Era*, July 21, 1859; *Nashville Weekly Patriot*, April 7, 1859.

23. Robert Hatton, diary, December 22, 1859, in James Vaulx Drake, *Life of General Robert Hatton* (Nashville: Marshall and Bruce, 1867), 184; John A. Gilmer to William A. Graham, February 23, 1858, in J. G. deRoulhac Hamilton and Max R. Williams, eds., *The Papers of William Alexander Graham*, 7 vols. to date (Raleigh: North Carolina State Department of Archives and History, 1957–), 5:37–39; Gerald S. Henig, *Henry Winter Davis, Antebellum and Civil War Congressman from Maryland* (New York: Twayne, 1973), 94; Crofts, *Reluctant Confederates*, 34–36, 68; *New York Times*, August 25, 1859; "From North Carolina," August 25, 1859, in *National Era*, September 8, 1859; Henry Winter Davis to David Davis, January 5, 1861, photocopy, David Davis Papers, Chicago Historical Society.

24. Charles Faulkner Bryan Jr., "Robert Hatton of Tennessee" (M.A. thesis, University of Georgia, 1971), 61–72; Drake, *Life of General Robert Hatton*; *Nashville Weekly Patriot*, April 14, 1859; Atkins, *Parties, Politics*, 212, 216; Bergeron, *Antebellum Politics in Tennessee*, 129–34; Gordon B. McKinney, *Zeb Vance: North Carolina's Civil War Governor and Gilded Age Political Leader* (Chapel Hill: University of North Carolina Press, 2004), 49–64; Crofts, *Reluctant Confederates*, 2, 31–34, 68.

25. William S. Hitchcock, "The Limits of Southern Unionism: Virginia Conservatives and the Gubernatorial Election of 1859," *Journal of Southern History* 47 (February 1981): 57–72; Link, *Roots of Secession*, 168–75; Volz, "Kentucky and the Coming of the American Civil War," 312–51; Crofts, *Reluctant Confederates*, 58–59; William J. Cooper, *The South and the Politics of Slavery, 1828–1856* (Baton Rouge: Louisiana State University Press, 1978); *National Era*, June 9, 1859; Henry Winter Davis to Samuel F. Du Pont, August 10, 1859, Samuel F. Du Pont Papers, Eleutherian Mills Historical Library, Greenville, DE. The Virginia campaign in 1859 had parallels to 1855, when the American Party attacked Democrat Henry A. Wise as an unsafe demagogue—in much the same manner as Wise was depicted by Southern Rights Democrats, his intraparty enemies. The 1859 Opposition campaigns in Virginia and Kentucky were both motivated, in part, by a wish to exacerbate divisions between Democratic factions. Both states had some Union Democrats friendly to Stephen A. Douglas. The Opposition hoped to depress the turnout of Union Democrats by transforming the campaign into a Southern Rights shouting match. Volz, "Kentucky and the Coming of the American Civil War," 327–48.

26. Bergeron, *Antebellum Politics in Tennessee*, 130–34; *Nashville Weekly Patriot*, April 14, 1859; *New York Times*, 1, 9 Aug. 1859.

27. Kruman, *Parties and Politics in North Carolina*, 184–96; *(Wadesboro) North Carolina Argus* May 12, 1859, quoted in ibid., 186; Bartholomew F. Moore to William A. Graham, July 26, 1860, in Hamilton and Williams, *Papers of William Alexander Graham*, 5:169–70;

Thomas E. Jeffery, *State Parties and National Politics: North Carolina, 1815–1861* (Athens: University of Georgia Press, 1989), 269–80; Crofts, *Reluctant Confederates*, 60–62.

28. Baker, *Ambivalent Americans*, 49–50 (on Maryland's increased Unionist stance), 129–34 (on the responsibility of both political parties for Baltimore's election abuses). See also William J. Evitts, *A Matter of Allegiances: Maryland from 1850 to 1861* (Baltimore: Johns Hopkins University Press, 1974), 123–28; and Henig, *Henry Winter Davis*, 113–19; *New York Times*, September 8, 1859; Henry Winter Davis to Samuel F. Du Pont, November 11, 1859, Du Pont Papers.

29. Baker, *Ambivalent Americans*, 48; Frank Towers, *The Urban South and the Coming of the Civil War* (Charlottesville: University of Virginia Press, 2004); Freehling, *Road to Disunion*, 2:77–79, 327–29. The smaller city of Wheeling, Virginia, also witnessed the rise of a homegrown Republican Party, with parallels to the situation in St. Louis.

30. Freehling, *Road to Disunion*, 2:14.

31. *National Intelligencer*, in *National Era*, January 6, 1859; William A. Graham to New York Whig Committee, February 21, 1859, in Hamilton and Williams, *Papers of William Alexander Graham*, 5:90–94; Freehling, *Road to Disunion*, 2:324–26; *New York Times*, August 24, September 2, 1859; Holt, *Political Crisis of the 1850s*, 209.

32. Richard H. Sewell, *Ballots for Freedom: Antislavery Politics in the United States, 1837–1860* (New York: W. W. Norton, 1976), 348–54; Horace Greeley to Mrs. R. M. Whipple, April 1860, Horace Greeley Papers, Library of Congress, quoted in Jeter Allen Isely, *Horace Greeley and the Republican Party, 1853–1861: A Study of the "New York Tribune"* (Princeton, NJ: Princeton University Press, 1947), 266; *New York Times*, March 29, August 22, 1859.

33. Freehling, *Road to Disunion*, 2:323–26; John J. Crittenden to Abraham Lincoln, July 29, 1858, Abraham Lincoln Papers, Library of Congress; Crofts, *Reluctant Confederates*, 68–69; Volz, "Kentucky and the Coming of the American Civil War," 366–75. Some of the would-be architects of the united opposition contemplated absolute silence on sectionally divisive issues; others thought it could safely oppose reopening the African slave trade while reaching out to Douglas Democrats with a "popular sovereignty" platform that would empower settlers in new territories to decide whether or not they wanted slavery. Crittenden's letter deeply disappointed Lincoln, who always thought of himself as a Henry Clay Whig. Crittenden's support for Douglas in the closely contested 1858 Senate race in Illinois may well have been decisive. Michael Burlingame, *Abraham Lincoln: A Life*, 2 vols. (Baltimore: Johns Hopkins University Press, 2008), 1:542–44, 548–49.

34. Henry Winter Davis to Amos A. Lawrence, December 1858, Amos A. Lawrence Papers, Massachusetts Historical Society, quoted in Henig, *Henry Winter Davis*, 108–9.

35. Volz, "Kentucky and the Coming of the American Civil War," 348–53. Prentice promptly repented his party's ill-advised stance in the 1859 campaign, when it called for Congress to protect slavery in the territories.

36. Abraham Lincoln to Mark W. Delahay, May 14, 1859, and to Nathan Sargent, June 23, 1859, in Roy P. Basler, ed., *The Collected Works of Abraham Lincoln*, 9 vols. (New Brunswick, NJ: Rutgers University Press, 1953–55), 3:378–79, 387–88. Crittenden's endorsement of Douglas in the 1858 Illinois Senate race likely also soured Lincoln on his erstwhile Whig allies in the Upper South. Burlingame, *Abraham Lincoln*, 1:542–44, 548–49.

37. *National Era*, January 6, 20, 27, March 17, June 9, August 25, 1859.

38. Crofts, *Reluctant Confederates*, 70–72; Sewell, *Ballots for Freedom*, 355.

39. Crofts, *Reluctant Confederates*, 72–75; Henry Winter Davis to Samuel F. Du Pont, November 28, December 20, 1859, January 19, 1860, Du Pont Papers. Davis and his Maryland colleague J. Morrison Harris each had a stake in rebuffing Democratic contestants for their congressional seats. They saw to it that their Opposition colleague John A. Gilmer was selected to head the Committee on Elections.

40. Potter, *Impending Crisis*, 264n83, 416–17, 438. The House of Representatives chooses a president from among the top three recipients of electoral votes when no candidate has a majority of electoral votes, and each state gets a single vote. In 1860 Republicans controlled fifteen free states, while Democrats controlled fourteen states (eleven slave states plus Illinois, Oregon, and California). As we have seen, the Southern Opposition held the single slave state of Tennessee, but three slave states were deadlocked between Democrats and the Opposition (Maryland, Kentucky, North Carolina). Davis pointed out the flaw in the Opposition strategy. He predicted that the House would fail to decide, so that the Democratic-controlled Senate would designate a vice president to serve as president—and the Senate would select a Democrat. Davis therefore wanted the election decided by the people, and he cheerfully accepted—at least in private—that Lincoln was the only non-Democrat with a chance to win an outright electoral majority. Henry Winter Davis to Samuel F. Du Pont, June 24(?), July (?—date uncertain), August 15, 1860, Du Pont Papers; *New York Times*, September 29, 1860.

41. *Louisville Journal*, September 20, 1860, in Volz, "Kentucky and the Coming of the American Civil War," 388–89; *Nashville Weekly Patriot*, October 8, 1860; Robert W. Johannsen, *Stephen A. Douglas* (New York: Oxford University Press, 1973), 760–61.

42. Bell did just as well in Maryland and North Carolina as in the three states that he did carry, but the Democratic vote in those states was less divided, so that Breckinridge won both. Bell lost Missouri narrowly to Douglas, who compiled far more votes there than in any other slave state. In Missouri, Maryland, and Delaware, Bell's chances were dashed by incremental support for Lincoln, which divided the anti-Democratic vote. See totals in Ollinger Crenshaw, *The Slave States in the Presidential Election of 1860* (Baltimore: Johns Hopkins University Press, 1945), 197.

43. Crofts, *Reluctant Confederates*, 130–94. The Upper South's antebellum political parties—Democrats, Whigs, American, and Opposition—were all coalitions of slaveholders and nonslaveholders. Those who owned slaves had no uniform party preference, though in North Carolina slaveholders were somewhat more likely to be Democrats. Crofts, *Reluctant Confederates*, 46–48.

44. Crofts, *Reluctant Confederates*, 193–94.

45. Henry Winter Davis to David Davis, January 5, 1861, photocopy, David Davis Papers, Chicago Historical Society; Henry Winter Davis to Samuel F. Du Pont, February 20, 26(?), March 1, 1861, Du Pont Papers; Crofts, *Reluctant Confederates*, 36, 196–205, 221–29.

46. John A. Gilmer to William H. Seward, March 7, 8, 9, 12, 1861, all in the William Henry Seward Papers, University of Rochester, except the one on March 9, which is in the Abraham Lincoln Papers, Library of Congress; John A. Gilmer to Stephen A. Douglas, March 8, 10, 1861, Stephen A. Douglas Papers, University of Chicago Library; Crofts, *Reluctant Confederates*, 229, 245–47, 257–59.

47. Potter, *Impending Crisis*, 512; Crofts, *Reluctant Confederates*, 355–58.

48. John A. Gilmer to William H. Seward, March 7, 8, 1861, Seward Papers, University of Rochester; Freehling, *Road to Disunion*, 2:527–31; Crofts, *Reluctant Confederates*, 258, 340–42, 350.

49. Edward L. Ayers, *In the Presence of Mine Enemies: War in the Heart of America, 1859–1863* (New York: W. W. Norton, 2003), 187, 415; Freehling, *Road to Disunion*, 2:527–31; Nelson Lankford, *Cry Havoc! The Crooked Road to Civil War, 1861* (New York: Viking Penguin, 2007), 6–7; Russell McClintock, *Lincoln and the Decision for War: The Northern Response to Secession* (Chapel Hill: University of North Carolina Press, 2008), 248. McClintock surprised himself by discovering that he had to focus on leadership rather than constituencies to write credibly about his topic. Ibid., 5–7.

Reviving State Rights

Before his tragically premature death, the historian William E. Gienapp joined Michael F. Holt in disputing a current conventional wisdom about the causes of the Civil War. Both historians denied that contention over *black* slavery *suffices* to explain why the war came.[1] *Black* and *suffices* define the crucial issue, in their work and in this essay. I agree that without black slavery there would probably have been no American Civil War (and certainly not in 1861) and that without Northern moral outrage at black slavery, there would probably have been no Republican Party (and certainly not in the party's victorious 1860 form). The question is whether disputes over the fate of sheerly *black* slavery suffices to explain why secession and war took the forms they did, when they did. The answer is that anxiety over supposed *white* slavery has to be stirred into the analytical mix, before the formula that "slavery caused the Civil War" suffices. And in the antebellum South, the now overly derided issue of state rights must also be added, to understand why many whites felt that their own enslavement loomed intolerably.

Bill Gienapp emphasized the Yankee parallel to this Southern anxiety. For a quarter century before the mid-1850s, the national Democratic and Whig Parties dominated the Union's politics. Both parties harbored powerful factions in each section. Both partisan organizations bridged sectional differences between their followers.

Then in the North, the Whig bridge disintegrated. In the mid-1850s, a non-bridge, the almost exclusively Northern Republican Party, replaced the Whig national coalition. Northern opposition to *black* slavery, while crucial, does not sufficiently explain this long stride toward national dissolution. In the early 1850s, so-called Know-Nothing strife over proposals to disenfranchise white emigrants also sometimes dominated Northern politics. Know-

Nothings urged that foreign voters, unless disenfranchised, would slavishly follow the pope. Alleged white slaves of the Holy Father, by wielding the decisive swing voters in close Northern elections, would subject American government to the Vatican's tyrannical commands. That specter of papal enslavement supplemented specters of black slavery's expansion in drawing increasing numbers of Northern Whigs away from their old party's economic issues and toward a new northern political alignment.

Thereafter, Gienapp and Holt believed, another increasing apprehension about Northern whites' subjection helped draw more Whigs toward the emerging Republican Party. For two decades, Northern Whigs had charged that a so-called Slave Power minority enslaved the federal majority. According to this Whig analysis, the minority of Southern slaveholders used their unequalled strength in the national majority party, the Democrats, as leverage to dictate law to the national majority. The Democrats' proslavery national dictations included congressional gag rules on antislavery petitions, Texas annexation, fugitive slave edicts, and the Kansas-Nebraska disaster.

Yankee fury at the Slave Power involved more than the explosive charge that the minority imposed laws on the majority. Republicans also urged that these Slave Power edicts slapped tyrannical shackles on whites. Congressional gag rules strangled debate on constituents' petitions to their congressmen. Texas annexation allowed the one state of Texas to swell its domain to five states and ten congressmen. The Fugitive Slave Law coerced citizens into slave-nabbing gangs. The Kansas-Nebraska Act led to repression of free speech in Kansas (just as Southern states usually repressed free debate on slavery). Thus did Southerners, to consolidate slavery over blacks, fasten handcuffs on citizens. As the string of proslavery laws lengthened and thickened during the 1850s, many ex-Whigs urged that *whites'* emancipation from the Slave Power had become the cardinal national necessity.

By claiming that first the pope, then the Slave Power enslaved Northern whites, Republicans denied that enslavement had to include owning, buying, or selling humans. Equal citizens endured degrading dictatorship whenever subjected to illegitimate sway. Anyone suffering illicit control over their willpower writhed under a despot.

This notion of slavery without ownership—of free citizens squirming under dictators' thumbs—rings strange to modern ears. But for centuries, *slavery* had been a code word for many forms of *white* bondage. Drunkards were "slaves" to liquor. Wives were "slaves" to husbands. The American colonies were "slaves" of King George. Citizens were "slaves" of monster banks. Wage earners were "slaves" of employers—"slaves without masters," in the Virginia proslavery writer George Fitzhugh's memorable phrase. To an Anglo-American republican, blacks' enslaved condition was only the extreme of the powerlessness that best defined enslavement.

Attacks on white enslavement supplemented drives to end black slavery in the Republicans' 1860 campaign. Most Northern whites—and many Republicans—were racists who shunned abolitionist pleas. These Republican voters were vital. Lincoln's election to the presidency was a close affair; a few thousand voters, by switching away from the Republicans, would have thrown the election into the House of Representatives. Abraham Lincoln's antislavery moral rhetoric stirred tens of thousands Republicans. But for the tens of thousands of Republicans immune to color-blind antislavery appeals, the call to slap the Slave Power's hands off white majorities—off *them*—became a powerful reason to vote Republican. In that combination of Republicans' color-blind and racist appeals, seeking to end black and white forms of enslavement, lies the best explanation of how Abraham Lincoln secured the presidency in 1860.

Bill Gienapp's career was cut short before he could apply this logic to the Southern side of the causes of the Civil War. So here I want to add that just as Northern outrage at black slavery does not suffice to explain enough voters' support of Lincoln in 1860, so Southern desire to protect black slavery does not suffice to explain enough rebels' support of the Southern Confederacy. Just as the more conservative Republicans' rage that the Slave Power enslaved *them* had to supplement the more radical Republicans' desire to free blacks, before Lincoln could be elected president, so the more moderate Southerners' conviction that Lincoln enslaved *them* had to supplement the more fiery Southerners' conviction that Lincoln would free blacks, before enough Southern states left the Union. To understand how Southerners' images of white enslavement added the necessary supplementary support for disunion, one must step gingerly on explosive terrain: a reconsideration of state rights as one cause of the Civil War.

The terrain is treacherous because, for a century after the war, Southerners falsely insisted that state rights, not slavery, most explained disunion. This exaggeration of the importance of state rights especially flourished inside hidebound Southern bastions of segregation and disenfranchisement. White Southerners wished to remember no reactionary crusade to keep four million blacks enchained. Instead, they wished to celebrate a progressive mission to keep Big Government from enchaining white citizens. By enshrining state rights as their ancestors' holy cause, latter-day Southerners justified their own weapons against outsiders' supposed meddling with their racial order.

As white Southerners' twentieth-century fight for their postslavery racial order slowly became as lost a cause as slavery and the Confederacy, liberal Southerners still sought some glorious Civil War memory. Their ancestors, they still wished to believe, had not died for anything so doomed and discredited as slavery. Instead, Southerners had fought for a republic based on state rights localism, viable beyond racial issues.

Mid-twentieth-century Northerners also needed an honorable and politically useful past. The Southern state rights conception blocked their double mission: to convict the South, past and present, of sins against blacks and to anoint Yankee crusaders, present and past, as America's redeemers. Their forbearers had risen up against black slavery, they needed to believe, just as they now rose up against black inequality.

Fortunately for Yankee crusaders' dismissal of state rights, the facts largely sustained their argument. During the last half of the twentieth century, a massive rereading of the sources established the massive impact of the pre–Civil War slavery issue. The native Virginian Charles Dew, for example, still relished his family's state rights mythology about the causes of the Civil War, despite decades of New England residence and his own objective studies of the slavery system. To reestablish the old truth, Professor Dew studied an important group of Southerners, to see why they precipitated disunion. He fastened on a key moment, when the Lower South had left the Union and the Upper South had yet to embrace disunion. While Upper South leaders wavered, Lower South states appointed commissioners to visit and convert the wavering. Dew studied the commissioners' private and public papers to see how they defined and spread their disunion mission.

Expecting to find many sermons on state rights, Dew found not a syllable. Expecting to find nothing about slavery, he found that commissioners' every word embraced the peculiar institution, particularly as a bulwark of racial control. His report on his findings, contained in a pithy book with confirming documents in the appendix, leaves no room for calling defense of state rights the initial secessionists' motivation.[2]

The latest scholarship leaves equally little room for state rights as the slave South's most important cause. Conventional wisdom once called tariffs, internal improvements, and banks more important to prewar Southerners than slavery issues. Furthermore, historians once contended that state rights had been a peculiarly Southern weapon, in economic contests against Yankee nationalists.

The pre-1860 facts undermine this exaltation of state rights. During the period 1825–45, when economic rather than slavery issues dominated national political debate, the South only incrementally moved toward disunion. The one exception during the period of predominately economic politics, the Nullification Controversy of 1832–33, was the classic exception that proved the rule.[3] The South Carolina Nullifiers assaulted more foes than national high tariffs. National antislavery possibilities also provoked extremist South Carolinians' assertion of their state's right to nullify national laws.

Beyond South Carolina, Southerners rejected a state's right to nullify national law. But in the name of national compromise, they secured lower tariff rates. Thereafter, still lower tariffs diminished this economic concern as a source of Southern secession.

Just as Southern economic contentions over tariffs seldom threatened the postnullification Union, so the economic side of state rights never swept the South. Whig economic nationalism vied with Jacksonian state rights in fairly equal contests everywhere in the nation, North and South alike. Whig nationalists saw nothing anti-Southern in their campaigns to build national instruments of trade, banking, and transportation. Large slaveholders, dependent on a national commercial system to market their staples, voted Whig as often as Democrat. The Whigs' most important national leader, Kentucky's Henry Clay, owned many slaves. The party's two elected presidents, William Henry Harrison and Zachary Taylor, were both Southern born and bred, and Louisiana's Taylor was another large slaveholder. State rights were as Southern as slavery? Not at all until the period between 1845 and 1860, when slavery issues overshadowed economic issues, and not without nationalistic Whig economic principles remaining highly competitive in the upper half of the South.[4]

Even as civil war approached and slavery issues became predominant, Northerners had no monopoly on pursuit of nationalistic edicts, and Southerners possessed no monopoly on state rights opposition to nationalistic laws. In the slavery contentions of the 1850s, slaveholders often claimed a national state's protections, and Northerners often countered with state rights negations.[5] Thus the national Fugitive Slave Law of 1850 required federal commissioners to judge runaway slaves and required Northern citizens to help capture alleged fugitives. Northerners responded with so-called personal property laws, deploying state court nullifications of national fugitive slave laws. Southerners responded by using federal courts to negate the state nullifiers.

Again, when Northern Republicans sought to use national power to abolish slavery in U.S. territories, Southerners claimed instead that a national slave code, if necessary, must protect territorial slavery. With neither Southerners nor Northerners claiming to be state righters for the territories, with only Northerners claiming the state rights mantle on fugitives, and with both sections harboring hundreds of thousands of ex-Whig economic nationalists, what supports the claim that state rights crusades pitched the South into secession?[6]

Not much, until a corner of the state rights persuasion assumed religious fervor during the secession crisis. Even at this late date, concerns about black slavery retained far more causal force. But for understanding how the most ardent secessionists hurdled their most towering obstacle and why the most reluctant Confederates became passionate rebels, the most holy fraction of the state rights faith is indispensable.[7]

This compelling corner of the ideology had nothing to do with laws for or against tariffs or banks or slavery—indeed had nothing to do with lawmaking. The secession crisis fragment of state rights instead drew on the most basic American republican conception: the sacred distinction between supreme constitution-making and subordinate lawmaking. When citizens made or unmade constitutions, they bestowed or withdrew the republican basis of a lawmaker's legitimacy: their natural right to consent to be governed. When the governed withdrew their consent to be ruled by a government, declared disunionists, that government's law-enforcing became enslaving.

But if all those governed had the natural right to withdraw consent, why did only a state have that right? Why couldn't a section, or a city, or a neighborhood, or a street, or a household, or even an individual exercise citizens' natural right to withdraw consent? Here state righters descended from the clouds of universal natural rights to the mandate of particular historical experience. State areas always had been the locale of citizens' claim to switch their consent to federal governance. Colonies had shifted the consent of their citizens from English governance to the Articles of Confederation. States had switched the consent of their citizens from the Articles of Confederation to the U.S. Constitution. These precedents supposedly dictated that only a state could withdraw its citizens' consent to the Union. After the state's withdrawal of consent, the delegitimatized federal government would allegedly enslave the withdrawing state's citizens if it coerced them.

Instead of crediting this powerful natural-rights bit of state rights, too many historians dismiss the secessionists' rationale for disunion as a narrowly constitutional argument. They are right that some secessionists urged only that since states ratified the Constitution, only states could repeal the ratification. These atypical legalistic arguments usually omitted any reference to a right of revolution. But far more often, disunionists based a state's right to secede on the extraconstitutional natural right to withdraw consent to be governed.

The secessionists here made a shrewd polemical decision. The narrowly constitutional and suffocating legalist justification was drier than dust and no more convincing than the nationalistic countervailing argument. In contrast, the natural and nonconstitutional right of revolution argument provoked a seductive call for freedom. The polemic founded its natural right of revolution on a stirring definition of slavery: government without the consent of the governed. Whites coerced after they legitimately withdrew consent from a government bore intolerable relation to the nonconsenting black slave.

The historical facts also propelled a state's natural (and nonconstitutional) right of revolution beyond legalistic polemics. Where the legalistic defense relied on the crabbed truth that the states came before the Constitution, the natural-rights analysis depended on the expansive fact that Americans' consent to government preceded all U.S. constitutions. This American natural-rights argument originated not with the ratification of the Constitution of 1787 but with the fount of American republicanism—the Revolution of 1776. Jefferson Davis summed up this bedrock secessionist justification in his February 18, 1861, presidential inaugural address. "Our present political position," proclaimed President Davis, "illustrates the American idea that governments rest on the consent of the governed, and that it is the right of the people to alter or abolish them." In seceding, the Confederate states had "merely asserted the right which the Declaration of Independence of July 4, 1776, defined to be 'inalienable.'"[8]

Justifications of a state's natural (and, again, not merely constitutional) right to secede usually came saturated with parallels to 1776. Charles Edward Hooker, commissioner from Mississippi to South Carolina, exalted in "the right of the people to alter, to change, to amend, aye, to abolish the form of government, whenever they deem proper."[9] P. G. T. Beauregard of Louisiana scoffed that "to deny in the 19th century the right of a people to select its own form of government is to deny the light of the sun." Beauregard called "the worst and most tyrannical of governments . . . the one *imposed* on a people."[10] Professor James Holcombe of the University of Virginia School of Law, speaking to the Virginia secession convention, added that he felt "no obligation . . . to vindicate either the right of secession; or what approaches closely to an equivalent to it, the right of revolution, "meaning" the right of the people to change their government, peacefully, when ever they become dissatisfied with it."[11]

So how did a natural right of revolution, universal to all mankind, justify a right of revolution, held *only* by a state? To the Southerners, that "only" placed the crucial fence around natural rights. A slaveholding culture could hardly abide its slaves' natural right to revolt. With a state's natural right, and only a *state's* right, to revolt, the Southerner became both a legitimate fancier of the upheaval of 1776 and a legitimate coercer of Nat Turner's slave rebels. If a revolting state suffered repression, its people became Turner-like slaves, akin to colonists' degradation if King George had won the American Revolutionary War.

The charismatic invocation of the spirit of 1776 compelled many a Southerner, although doubting the expediency of secession, to respect a state's natural right to secede. Yankees who violated a people's right to consent to a different government turned free whites into degraded blacks. The horror of Southern brothers' prospective enslavement gave this special bit of state rights a leverage that more normal state rights never bestowed on its proponents.

The widespread Southern conception of a state's right to withdraw its citizens' consent established disunionists' ground rules for secession. Only a state could depart the Union. Once the state had departed, dissenting citizens had to go with their state. Furthermore, no other state (and especially the national state) could enslave the departed. These state rights rules gave the initial secessionists their escape from their crippling predicament.

The myth about secession hides that predicament. Supposedly, the South spontaneously rose in revolution against a menacing Lincoln presidency. Actually, no more than a third of Southerners initially thought that Lincoln's immediate menace justified disunion.

An initial third for revolution may be an exaggeration, in view of the halting way secession evolved. The four Border South states—Maryland, Delaware, Missouri, and Kentucky—never seceded, even after the Civil War started. The four Middle South states—Virginia, North Carolina, Tennessee, and Arkansas—never departed until the Civil War commenced. Two out of every three Southern voters resided in these eight Upper South states.

Nor did many of the seven Lower South states strike for revolution the moment they heard that a Republican would be president. Louisiana and Georgia recorded extremely close votes on secession. The Mississippi, Texas, and Alabama governors initially sought a Southern convention before any single state seceded.

The governors' strategy of a section-wide convention, to decide for the Southern majority, alarmed the initial secessionists. In November-December 1860, disunionists knew that they would lose in a Southern convention. They saw that most Southerners doubted Lincoln's menace to slavery. They realized that a gamble on disunion could end slavery faster than any other Southern policy if the Confederacy lost a civil war. Secession would also destroy a Union that most Southerners revered.

Against these powerful deterrents to rebellion, Charles Dew's commissioners urged that, without secession, Lincoln would menace slavery and thus racial order. Most Southerners, however, found the commissioners' case alarmist. Unless the Lower South seceded, they pointed out, Lincoln would assume the presidency without a Republican Party majority in the House or Senate or Supreme Court. As for the supposedly menacing president-elect, he supported an unamendable thirteenth constitutional amendment, forever barring Congress from touching slavery in the states. Lincoln also affirmed his constitutional obligation to enforce the fugitive slave laws. If, despite all his pledges and powerlessness, he threatened slavery, the South could *then* secede. Against that solid common sense, how could the secessionists win a section-wide majority?

The state rights ground rules saved secessionists from answering. Disunionists only had to convince one state's majority to withdraw consent to be governed. Then if the federal government coerced secessionists' lone ranger, the issue in the other fourteen Southern states would no longer be only the expediency of secession to save black slavery. The question would also become the Union's right to enslave whites who had exercised their natural right to withdraw consent to be governed. Or to put it the decisive way, the issue would be not only whether the federal government might tomorrow menace black slavery but also whether federal coercers had today violated whites' natural rights.

First James Buchanan, then Abraham Lincoln helped the initial secessionists thus redefine the issue. The two Yankee presidents, like most Northerners, believed that states must not desecrate America's holy mission. The Union must remain a City on a Hill, proving that majoritarian republicanism would endure. If any state's majority withdrew its citizens' consent, presidents must enforce a national majority's laws. This looming collision of state rights and national Union augured an uncompromiseable confrontation over supposed enslavement of whites.

After Lincoln's election, South Carolina precipitated that deadly issue. Once South Carolina dared to secede first (unanimously, on December 20), James Buchanan finalized the state rights script that gave one disunionist state the leverage to move fourteen doubting others. Before the month of December was out (and before any other Southern state had decided on the expediency of secession), the president ordered a federal ship, the *Star of the West*, to reinforce the handful of federal soldiers huddled in Fort Sumter, located in the center of Charleston's harbor. Buchanan would thus provide the coercive weapons, as many Southerners saw it, to enslave South Carolina citizens who no longer consented to federal governance.[12]

South Carolinians in Washington heard that Buchanan's supposedly despotic ship was sailing. They shot home telegrams, warning about Buchanan's looming alleged tyranny. For all anyone knew, the president was dispatching enslaving weapons not only to Fort Sumter but also to every federal military installation in the Lower South. Telegraph wires instantly distributed that (falsely) supposed added possibility throughout the Lower South states. Then the wires became the means of spreading an early January secret conspiracy of Lower South governors to seize federal forts in their states before Buchanan's allegedly enslaving ships could arrive—and before citizens had voted to secede.

In early January, Lower South voters took with them to the polls newspapers with screaming headlines, boasting that their brave boys had captured their states' federal forts before the tyrant's reinforcements could be delivered. The news shifted what had sometimes been uncertain elections on the expediency of secession into Lower South landslides for citizens' natural right to resist enslavement. By the first of February, all seven Lower South states had withdrawn their citizens' consent to the Union.

That left the epic to be played out in the eight Upper South states. This part of the drama remained crucial. Two-thirds of the South's peoples and almost all of its industries thrived above the Lower South. If this majority of

Southerners stayed in the Union, the rebels' chances, in war or peace, would sink.[13]

Unlike in the Lower South, a Northern president's decision for coercion, and thus more Southerners' conversion to secession, came slowly in other Southern states. After the *Star of the West's* mission failed, President Buchanan wished President-elect Lincoln to make the next decision on reinforcing federal forts in seceding states. Lincoln was not inaugurated until March 4. Then the new president waited another month to decide whether to reinforce Charleston's Fort Sumter.

The delay helped establish that Lincoln's alleged menace to black slavery did not suffice to explain this crucial part of the Southern revolution. For months, Upper South citizens discussed whether Lincoln's supposed antislavery plans demanded disunion. The discussion especially convulsed Virginia, where a state convention debated the alleged necessity of disunion for two months.[14]

Three of Charles Dew's Lower South commissioners spoke to the Virginia convention. Per the Dew model, none of them emphasized peril to state rights. All of them stressed Lincoln's danger to black slavery and racial control.[15] Each found allies in the Virginia convention.

The commissioners' Upper South compatriots, compared with their Lower South partners earlier, more easily argued for Lincoln's menace.[16] After Lower South congressmen left the U.S. House and Senate, Lincoln gained what he had earlier lacked: a Republican congressional majority. Now his Congress could menace slavery if Republicans wished.

Yet the commissioners' argument for danger to slavery still floundered. A radical disconnect separated what the commissioners said and how convention delegates reacted. The Virginia majority still believed that any Lincoln menace to black slavery might be contained inside the Union. As late as April 4, eight days before Fort Sumter's cannon boomed, the convention majority rejected disunion by a two-to-one margin.

As in the Lower South, peril to whites' natural right to withdraw consent then decimated the Unionists. When Lincoln sent ships to reinforce Fort Sumter and war erupted in Charleston on April 12–13, Virginia still did not secede. Delegates prayed that the Charleston cannon fire would not be repeated. Only after the president issued his April 15 proclamation, calling up 75,000 state troops (including 2,460 Virginians) to subdue the rebels, did Virginia fly from the Union. Most Virginians would never help to enslave fellow Southerners who had withdrawn their consent to be governed. The 2,460

Virginians, marching down to South Carolina to coerce fellow whites, would become the essence of enslavers.

After Virginia had withdrawn its citizens' consent to be governed by an enslaving Union, most previous Virginia Unionists went with their state. Robert E. Lee, to take the classic example, had some doubts about black slavery and many qualms about secession. But whatever the expediency of disunion, after Virginia seceded, his state's natural right to withdraw consent predominated. Subsequently, when a Union invader asked a Confederate soldier why he fought, the rebel shot back, "Because you are here" (and the zealot did not need to add "Because you have no right to be here").

True, many Upper South rebels fought, in Charles Dew's commissioners' style, for the honor and safety of enslaving blacks. But many others, while unconvinced by the Lower South's agents, would not tolerate their own enslavement. As John Hughes, a Unionist delegate in the Virginia convention, explained his conversion to secessionism, "I am opposed to making any more propositions to a tyrannical and overbearing foe that desires to make slaves of me and you." When President Lincoln demanded "Virginia's quota of troops to make war upon the Southern States," concluded Hughes, only slaves could tolerate a "declaration of war upon our people."[17]

The three other Middle South states, North Carolina, Tennessee, and Arkansas, quickly followed Virginia's lead. Only the Border South's four states shunned the Confederacy. Their significance, in giving the Union a very hard-fought victory, underscored the importance of the Middle South's conversion. Unless John Hughes–style persuasiveness on menace to white liberty had overcome the Confederate commissioners' lack of persuasiveness on menace to black slavery, the Middle South would have left the Lower South in a precarious position much earlier than 1865.

So must we now roll back the clock and again call state rights, not slavery, the cause of the Civil War? Certainly not. Despite the explosiveness of a fragment of state rights persuasion, contention over *black* slavery principally shattered the Union. The point here is that the principle cause was not a sufficient cause, that contention over *white* slavery supplied a necessary supplemental cause, both North and South, and that in the South a fraction of the state rights persuasion came to be lethally entangled with detested white enslavement.

That fatal entanglement reemphasizes the overriding importance of slavery properly understood—which means not understood as only black slavery. True, the enslavement issue, when spilling beyond coercing blacks, became only a supplementary cause of national disaster, not the major cause. But supplementary causes demand emphasis when the primary cause is insufficient to bring off a disaster. Just as Republicans' moral outrage at black slavery, however important, was not sufficient to elect Lincoln, so fear of Republican emancipators, however important, was not sufficient to sweep eleven slave states out of the Union. Just as Northern thoughts of an enslaving pope and Slave Power enabled Lincoln to lure sufficient voters, so images of enslaved seceding citizens enabled the initial disunionists to rally sufficient allies. Throughout the dissolving national republic, after apprehensions of white enslavement joined anxieties about black enslavement, slavery, in all its provocative American forms, indeed sufficed to cause the Civil War.

Notes

1. Michael F. Holt, *The Political Crisis of the 1850s* (New York: Wiley, 1978); William E. Gienapp, "The Republican Party and the Slave Power," in Robert H. Abzug and Stephen E. Maizlish, eds., *New Perspectives on Race and Slavery in America* (Lexington: University Press of Kentucky, 1986), 51–78; Gienapp, *The Crisis of the Republican Party, 1852–1856* (New York, 1987).

2. Charles Dew, *Apostles of Disunion: Southern Secession Commissioners and the Causes of the Civil War* (Charlottesville: University of Virginia Press, 2001).

3. William W. Freehling, *Prelude to Civil War: The Nullification Controversy in South Carolina, 1816–1836* (New York: Harper & Row, 1966).

4. Michael F. Holt, *The Rise and Fall of the American Whig Party: Jacksonian Politics and the Onset of the Civil War* (New York: Oxford University Press, 1999).

5. A subject brilliantly elucidated in Arthur Bestor, "State Sovereignty and Slavery: A Reinterpretation of Proslavery Constitutional Doctrine," *Illinois Historical Society Journal* 64 (1961): 117–80.

6. William W. Freehling, *The Road to Disunion*, 2 vols. (New York: Oxford University Press, 1990–2007), 2:343–531.

7. Ibid., 2:345–51.

8. James D. Richardson, ed., *A Compilation of the Messages and Papers of the Confederacy*, 2 vols. (Nashville: United States Publishing, 1905), 1:32–36.

9. *Charleston Courier*, December 19, 1860.

10. P. G. T. Beauregard to J. G. Barnard, March 18, 1861, Beauregard Letterbook, March to May 1861, P. G. T. Beauregard Papers, Library of Congress.

11. George H. Reese, ed., *Proceedings of the Virginia State Convention of 1861*, 4 vols. (Richmond: Virginia State Library, 1965), 2:77.

12. For the tale of Buchanan's decision and the ensuing Lower South fort seizures, see Freehling, *Road to Disunion*, 2:482–98.

13. For the tale of Upper South procrastination, see ibid., 2:499–530, and the superb

Daniel W. Crofts, *Reluctant Confederates: Upper South Unionists in the Secession Crisis* (Chapel Hill: University of North Carolina Press, 1989).

14. For the full debate, see Reese, *Proceedings*. For an abridged, more accessible one-volume edition, see William W. Freehling and Craig M. Simpson, eds., *Showdown in Virginia: The 1861 Convention and the Fate of the Union* (Charlottesville: University of Virginia Press, 2010).

15. Reese, *Proceedings*, 1:50–93.

16. See, for example, James Holcombe's speech in ibid., 2:75–101.

17. Ibid., 4:106–8.

Where Was Henry Clay?

President-Elect Abraham Lincoln and
the Crisis of the Union, 1860–1861

WILLIAM J. COOPER

Abraham Lincoln occupies a secure place in the pantheon of great U.S. presidents. Even among that select group, in the view of many, professional historians as well as the general public, he is primus inter pares—the savior of the Union and the great emancipator. Recently, numerous Lincoln students seem to be in a contest to extol his greatness. I have no intention of challenging the overwhelming consensus, for I, too, agree that he ranks in the very top tier of our presidents and that he has no equal as a war leader. This widespread agreement focuses, however, on the Civil War. Lincoln's performance in that cauldron forms the foundation for his glowing reputation, a renown that has only brightened in the past two decades.[1]

Rather than Lincoln as a war leader, in this essay my subject is the prewar Lincoln. In fact, I concentrate on a quite narrow time frame, the few months between his election to the presidency on November 6, 1860, and his inauguration as the sixteenth president on March 4, 1861. Even more pointedly, I have a single overriding interest. Why in the great crisis of the Union during the winter of 1860–61 did the self-proclaimed admirer and apostle of the great pacificator, Henry Clay, work actively and successfully against any serious compromise designed to defuse, perhaps even settle, the explosive situation? Not only had Clay gained fame as a compromiser, but since the Constitutional Convention, compromise had enjoyed a hallowed place in the American political tradition.

Of course, I am not the first historian to address this question. Several current Lincoln scholars have looked at it, at least in part. Still, none in my judgment has provided a satisfactory explanation. Their analyses fall into two basic camps. The first does not really perceive a serious issue, praising the president-elect for his steadfast loyalty to the Republican platform, his strategy of public silence, and his rejection of any general settlement of the crisis. That outlook is surely a possibility, but it seems to me to come at the study of history backwards. A war resulted, a war in which Lincoln prevailed, with the Union intact and slavery abolished. But no one in the winter of 1860–61, not even Lincoln, could read the future, much less that precise future. The second camp, though not fixated on a post-1865 perspective, devotes more attention to the efforts at compromise, including the reaction of Republicans and the divisions within the party. This discussion places Lincoln squarely in the no-compromise column while detailing his determination to derail any plan for adjustment. These writers even note problems in Lincoln's position, such as his delay in taking the secession movement seriously. Yet even here no one has treated systematically why Lincoln remained so inflexible regarding meaningful compromise.[2]

Going back to Lincoln and Henry Clay, I want to underscore two facts that are well known but too little emphasized. First, I want to note Clay's prominence as the great pacificator or the great compromiser. During his lifetime, and after his death in 1852, tens of thousands of Americans praised the Kentuckian for his central role in settling with compromise sectional crises over Missouri in 1820–21, over Nullification in 1832–33, and over the Mexican Cession in 1850. Second, although Lincoln always praised Clay extravagantly, declaring him "my beau ideal of a statesman," the president-elect spurned compromise in 1860–61.[3]

Perhaps Lincoln's most well-known remarks on Clay came in a eulogy he delivered in Springfield on July 6, 1852, only a week after Clay's death. In it, Lincoln praised the Kentucky statesman for "his leading and most conspicuous part" in devising sectional compromise. At the same time, Lincoln underscored that "as a politician or statesman no one was so habitually careful [as Clay] to avoid all sectional ground. Whatever he did he did for the country." Showering adulation on Clay for his willingness and his ability to work with political opponents as well as allies, Lincoln highlighted his main point that Clay "engaged his whole energies" on behalf of the Union. As late as February 1861 Lincoln professed, "During my whole political life, I have loved and revered [Clay] as a teacher and leader."[4]

In the acclamation at Springfield, Lincoln also noted Clay's opposition to slavery. For Lincoln, that antislavery stance was vital, for as a sincere opponent of slavery, he could never embrace as his hero any man identified as proslavery. Several times thereafter Lincoln took care to point to Clay's detestation of slavery and particularly his opposition to the institution's spread. Although Lincoln did not invent an antislavery Clay, he overlooked or downplayed his paladin's willingness to moderate his stance.[5]

Without doubt Clay did detest slavery, even striving unsuccessfully for

Kentucky to adopt gradual emancipation. Clay also said he could never support forcing slavery into any area where it had not previously existed. Yet in 1850, referring specifically to the Mexican Cession, he declared that if the citizens there placed slavery in their constitution, he would honor their choice. And Clay did back the Compromise of 1850, which left open the possibility of slavery in the New Mexico and Utah Territories. For Clay, no other political or moral issue, slavery included, matched in importance the maintenance of the Union.[6]

Lincoln, too, spoke about compromise, and initially did not turn from it. By his own account he treasured the Missouri Compromise, and he publicly stood for the Compromise of 1850. In fact, in his first major address attacking the Kansas-Nebraska Act for overturning the Missouri Compromise, Lincoln sounded very much like Henry Clay himself. "I too, go for saving the Union," he declared, but went on to explain, "Much as I hate slavery, I would consent to the extension of it rather than see the Union dissolved, just as I would consent to any Great evil, to avoid a Greater one." In the late 1850s, however, such declarations disappeared, though as late as 1858 he indicated his acquiescence in the Compromise of 1850.[7]

Positions on major sectional compromise, either in the past or possibly in the future, were certainly not central in the selection of a Republican presidential candidate in 1860. After all, before the nominating convention met in May, nothing had occurred that occasioned calls for compromise or for the party to declare its stance on one. Without question, however, all leading contenders for the nomination accepted what had become almost an article of faith for Republicans—no slavery in any territory.

The convention did not act as most observers thought it would. The leading Republican contender, Senator William Henry Seward of New York, famous for his announcements of a "higher law" than the Constitution and of an "irrepressible conflict" between North and South, between freedom and slavery, was set aside. Seward lost because many Republican politicians feared he could not win the presidential election. Specifically, they worried that voters in the lower portion of states like Illinois, Indiana, and Pennsylvania—states essential for Republican victory—would reject Seward as being too radical. The convention delegates eventually chose Abraham Lincoln, a man widely seen as less radical than Seward and thus more electable.

Yet a closer look, even by Republicans in 1860, would have cast considerable doubt on any assumption that Lincoln was more conservative than Seward. In his widely distributed "House Divided" speech, Lincoln had explicitly pronounced that the country "cannot endure permanently half *slave* and half *free*." In substance, the notion of the "house divided" and the irre- pressibility of conflict meshed perfectly; they were synonymous. One great difference did exist, however. Far more prominent in 1860 than Lincoln, Seward had been the eminent spokesman of antislavery politics for a decade. As far back as 1850 condemning any territorial compromise, he had called on a higher law than the Constitution. For Republicans hungering for victory, Seward had simply been in the public eye for too long. He was passed over.[8]

The Republican decision to jettison Seward and go with Lincoln might well have been the major reason for the party's triumph in the presidential election. Lincoln carried all the critical states on the way to a virtual sweep of the free states, only failing in New Jersey, where he shared the electoral vote. In the nation, he won 180 electoral votes, a clear majority, though he received none in any of the fifteen slave states. But the popular vote was another mat- ter. He managed only 39.8 percent. In ten slave states he received no votes at all. Since the widespread adoption of popular voting in Andrew Jackson's time, no previous president had gone into office with such a small percentage of the popular vote.

The basic outline of President-Elect Lincoln's position on secession and compromise is well known. Initially, he rejected secession as a serious pos- sibility. One who saw him in Springfield reported that Lincoln considered the secession movement as "a sort of game of bluff." Another visitor wrote, "The threats of secession do not alarm him." To his law partner William H. Hern- don, Lincoln confided he "could not in his heart believe the South designed the overthrow of the government." Underscoring his miscalculation, he even defined the military preparation in some Deep South states as positive, for it would enable "the people the more easily to suppress any uprisings there."[9]

At the same time that Lincoln misread the danger of secession, he missed few opportunities to proclaim his steadfast, unyielding opposition to any compromise of the most contentious and vexing question, slavery in the ter- ritories. Almost without exception, Southerners maintained that the Con- stitution empowered them to take slave property into any territory, a right affirmed by the U.S. Supreme Court in the Dred Scott decision of 1857. Even so, many Southerners indicated a willingness to accept division of the na- tional domain, with part open to slavery and part closed. In contrast, the Republican platform pronounced no slavery in the territories Republican gospel. Lincoln made clear his devotion; he would "never consent to the *low- ering of the Republican Standard in the least.*" He voiced identical professions to President James Buchanan's unofficial emissary and to Republicans in Congress and out, including Thurlow Weed, the influential New York editor and confidant of Seward. To Weed's suggestion that Republicans entertain compromise, Lincoln responded, "I will be inflexible on the territorial question." As he instructed others, the president-elect had made up his mind to "hold firm, as with a chain of steel."[10]

No matter Lincoln's opinion, secession became neither theory nor threat on December 20, 1860, when South Carolina solemnly left the Union. By the end of the next month, five more Deep South states had seceded, with a sixth, Texas, far down that road. Yet this actual breaking up of the Union did not move Lincoln, nor did the creation in February 1861 of the Confederate States of America. He simply iterated and reiterated that the Union remained whole. On that point he left no doubt: "I hold that in contemplation of universal law and the Constitution, the Union of these States is perpetual."[11]

While Lincoln remained unequivocal in opposing compromise even as the Union came apart, his reasons for doing so have not been clearly delineated. To my mind, the evidence leads to three central causes: his ignorance of the South, his vigorous partisanship, and his visceral antislavery commitment. This list has no rank order, for in my judgment the record does not warrant such a ranking. Yet it does appear to me that Lincoln's lack of understanding about the South was formative.

Dismissing the seriousness of secession and looking on it as a conspiracy plotted by a small band of radicals soon to be put down by sensible Union men like himself, Lincoln found no other explanation possible. As he saw it, the drive for secession certainly had nothing to do with anything he or his party had done or said. That conclusion leads inescapably to two observations. First, he clearly rationalized his "house divided" declaration, for in it he bluntly told Southerners that the Union of the future had no place for their major economic and social institution. Moreover, the irrepressible conflict scenario embraced by many Republicans did likewise. Could Lincoln have been tone deaf to how Southerners would hear such assertions? He must have been, for he told a conservative Kentuckian that neither he nor any other "prominent Republican had justly made himself obnoxious to the South by anything he had said or done."[12]

Lincoln evidently never stopped to think how he would have reacted to a responsible Southern political leader publicly maintaining that the free states had no place in a future Union. Yet he did react forcefully to what he claimed was a plot to nationalize slavery. In his rhetoric, that goal was part of a Slave Power conspiracy. Even though Lincoln struck out on the stump against this specter, even suggesting that the U.S. Supreme Court intended to make Illinois a slave state, no important Southern politician ever advocated such a cause.[13]

Second, it appears indisputable that he assumed such a stance because he knew so little about the South. Yes, at nineteen and twenty-two he had taken brief trips down the Ohio and Mississippi Rivers to New Orleans. Also, he was born in Kentucky, and his wife came from a slave-owning family in that state, as did his best friend, Joshua Speed. But that part of the Border South was all that he knew. After his two youthful journeys to New Orleans in 1828 and 1831, he never traveled in the South beyond Kentucky. Aside from a few Kentuckians, he really did not know any Southerners, certainly not any Southern politicians. He had in the late 1840s served one term in the U.S. House of Representatives, where he surely met Southerners and was friendly with a few. But that was almost a decade and a half before the crisis of 1860–61. In the interim, he had kept up with none of those men. Fundamentally, he had no friends who could educate him about the South and Southern politics.[14]

The record indicates that Lincoln's image of the slave South basically matched the common abolitionist and fervent antislavery depictions. In this South, rich planters dominated society and politics, in 1860–61 agitating for secession and cowing nonslaveholding whites. He appears to have had no understanding either of the widespread ownership of slaves among whites or how deeply slavery had become embedded in Southern society. Instead of comprehending that the overwhelming majority of Southern whites were committed to their slave society, it appears that Lincoln thought of them as conservative Unionists with little attachment to slavery. In other words, they were like him, though probably without the moral outrage at slavery. Perhaps the mass of Southern whites could not or would not act against slavery, but he could imagine them neither proslave nor on their own acting against the Union. A South where nonplanters and even nonslaveholders had an influential political voice, feared Republicans, and actively supported secession was both foreign and unknown to Lincoln. When a visitor in early November urged Lincoln to reassure Southerners honestly alarmed by a Republican triumph, his reply spoke volumes: "There are no such men."[15]

In light of the famous epistolary exchange between Lincoln and Alexander H. Stephens of Georgia in November and December 1860, historians have often described the two men as friends. Such a definition is surely an exaggeration, for they had only seen each other during the sessions of the Thirtieth Congress and had not been in contact since Lincoln left Washington in early 1849. In his request on November 30, 1860, for a copy of Stephens's address to the Georgia legislature, Lincoln indicated he had seen newspaper accounts. Responding, Stephens said they were substantially correct.[16]

I wonder how carefully Lincoln read the speech. Yes, Stephens did deplore the rush to secession just because Lincoln had been elected. At the same time, however, Stephens left no doubt about his opinion of the Republican Party. "If the policy of Mr. Lincoln and his Republican associates shall be carried out," he announced, "no man in Georgia will be more willing or ready than myself to defend our rights, interest, and honor at every hazard and to the last extremity." Defining that policy, Stephens gave primary importance to a congressional prohibition of slavery from the common territory. Of course, for Lincoln, that restriction was the primary Republican mission. Stephens urged Georgia to delay, not because he found the Republican program acceptable or because he would acquiesce in it, but because he argued the Congress controlled by Democrats along with the federal judiciary would thwart Lincoln. He predicted an enfeebled Lincoln presidency that could do the South no harm.

The four letters the men exchanged certainly have a civility about them, with each man assuring the other of his respect. Stephens drew empathetic attention to Lincoln's massive burden, telling him that "no man ever had heavier or greater responsibility resting upon him than you have in the present momentous crisis." Trying to be conciliatory and reassuring, Lincoln, on December 22 in a letter marked "For your eyes only," stated that he "appreciate[d] the present peril." He also told Stephens that the South had nothing to fear from him or a Republican administration. Word even came to Stephens indirectly that Lincoln called him "a great man." Still, Lincoln did recognize that he and Stephens differed on the "right" and "wrong" of slavery.

In his second letter, dated December 30, Stephens declared, "Personally, I am not your enemy—far from it." He then called on Lincoln to do what he could "to save our common country." But Stephens was also pointed. Southerners worried, he wrote, that the Republicans' "leading object seems to be simply, and wantonly, if you please, to put the Institutions of nearly half the states under the ban of public opinion and national condemnation." He connected that object to "the influence of fanaticisms," which he saw influencing the Republican Party. Yet the Georgian concluded that "a word fitly spoken by you now would be like 'apples of gold in pictures of silver.'" To this entreaty Lincoln did not reply.

With no firsthand knowledge of the South and no friends or even serious acquaintances among Southern politicians, Lincoln unsurprisingly did not acknowledge distinctions between fire-eaters, the zealous advocates of secession, and men like Stephens and even Jefferson Davis who were fundamentally conservative with no relish for disunion. Lincoln gave no awareness that he understood the political force pressed by the radicals on Southern conservatives and regulars.

The extent of popular support for immediate secession in the Deep South, still a vexing issue, is not my subject here. Even so, no conspiracy took those states out of the Union. The fire-eaters surely pushed, and they drove for haste, but no secret cabal manipulated events from South Carolina to Texas. Every one of those states held a popular vote for delegates to conventions that would decide on secession.[17]

While Lincoln's ignorance of the South powerfully influenced his adamant opposition to compromise, his actions also make clear that he approached the crisis not as president-elect of the United States but as leader of the Republican Party. Moreover, he had in November 1860 but a few months as party chief. That brief tenure left him unsure about the security of his leadership and anxious about party unity. During the crisis many Republicans and non-Republicans alike urged him to make a public statement addressing the issues in which he would reassure Southerners of their rights and his determination to be president of all Americans, Southerners as well as Northerners. Time and time again Lincoln adamantly refused.[18]

Responding to this cascade of requests, Lincoln embraced a mantra: "I could say nothing which I have not already said, and which is in print, and open to inspection to all." *"Repetition"* as he phrased it, could only do harm to his political position. Three observations seem pertinent. First, to repeat a point I made earlier, he seemed not to fathom that some of his most vigorous rhetoric could terrify the South. Second, never did he acknowledge that every one of those statements had been made as a Republican partisan, not as the forthcoming president of a country. Furthermore, none of those declarations had been made when the country faced a monumental crisis.[19]

Lincoln never stepped forward in an effort to conciliate alarmed Southerners. Given his unmatched gift for crafting the befitting phrases for a given political moment, one might imagine his theme, if not his words. Such an address could have noted his recognition that he was not one of them and that he represented a party perceived by the multitude of Southerners as their enemy. Yet, he would have quickly countered, we are all still Americans, and during his presidency neither he nor his party would in any way try to harm the South. Not once did Lincoln ever say publicly that he would be president of all Americans. In wedding himself to the Republican platform and claiming he could never deviate from it, he acted like a partisan's partisan, not the leader of a country.

The critical question focuses on the *why* underlying his rigidity. The evidence strongly suggests that he feared alienating his party's most fervent antislavery zealots, or in modern parlance, its left wing. Lincoln constantly expressed concern that any serious compromise would fracture the party—in other words, drive off the left. If that segment bolted because of a sectional compromise, Lincoln worried the Republican Party would disintegrate. That group did not, of course, encompass the Republican Party. Undoubtedly, it was a minority, albeit an articulate, vigorous minority. Although precision about numbers is impossible, in a party whose adherents ranged from radicals like Charles Sumner to conservatives like Edward Bates to supreme pragmatists like Thurlow Weed, the hard-line left wing could not have been a majority. The closest students of the party during the crisis underscore the divergence of opinion within its ranks and emphasize the strength of a great middle.[20]

A suggestive approach to assess Lincoln's course concentrates on William H. Seward, the preeminent Republican prior to Lincoln's nomination. For that nomination, Seward had been turned aside for being too radical, but in the aftermath of the election he and his political partner, Thurlow Weed, moved sharply toward the center. During this period many Republicans still looked to Seward as their chief, believing Lincoln untried and dubious about his ability. The party needed "to see in the lead the only person who can give the country confidence," Massachusetts congressman Charles Francis Adams wrote Seward.[21]

Evidence abounds that Seward was willing to grasp a serious sectional compromise, one that included the territorial issue. In his *Albany Evening Journal,* Weed specifically proposed reviving and extending the Missouri Compromise line westward. The two men tried to keep Seward's name apart from that proposal until the political landscape became clearer. Yet the longtime closeness between them and the conversations they had after the election leave little doubt that they agreed. What is indisputable is that a number of Republicans indicated a willingness to take that road. Republican newspapers in cities like New York, Cincinnati, Pittsburgh, and Detroit saw merit in Weed's proposition. Likewise, businessmen in New York City who had voted for Lincoln lined up behind Weed. Additionally, many Republican politicians signaled their willingness to sign on for compromise.[22]

Although it is impossible to quantify precisely the compromise-inclined

Republicans, they surely provided a substantial base for a leader who wanted to guide the party in that direction. Had the party done so, might secession have been thwarted? That is a complex question and not my concern here. But secessionists across the South prayed for Republican intransigence, dreading that a Republican commitment to compromise would torpedo their plans. In my judgment they had a legitimate worry, a worry that Seward recognized. As I read the evidence, Republican backing in November and December for anything resembling Weed's ideas might very well have stymied the fire-eaters everywhere but in South Carolina. Then the Nullification Crisis of 1832–33 would have been repeated—South Carolina alone confronting the United States.[23]

My concern here, however, is Seward and why he looked favorably on compromise. In my view he did so for at least three reasons. Early on, certainly by mid-November, he perceived the Union in mortal danger. Above all, he wanted to prevent its dissolution if at all possible. Having been in Washington for the entire decade of the 1850s and knowing many Southern politicians, he had a much better grasp than Lincoln of the political force of secession and the political reality facing the more moderate men in the Deep South. Then, he and Weed believed the territorial issue had done its work, elected a Republican president. To them it was chiefly a political matter. With all the territory controlled by the United States in 1860 already covered by existing law, they thought any chance of adding new land remote and certainly not taking place without Republican concurrence. As Weed put it in a letter to Seward's senatorial colleague from New York, "There is no political temptation in all the territory belonging to us. The fight is over."[24]

Additionally Seward and Weed saw the Republican victory in no small part as a result of Democratic division. Because they judged that "the normal proclivities of the American people are Democratic" and that "the issues of the late campaign are obsolete," they regarded new issues as necessary to keep the Republicans in power. In 1864, a reunited Democratic Party would cause trouble for the Republicans unless the party could expand. Seward wanted to reach out to Unionists in the South, especially in the upper and border slave states. To him, bringing them into the Republican tent was both possible and essential. Without question a number of them, overwhelmingly former Whigs, made clear their willingness to come into a party that focused on the Union, not sectional antagonism. No evidence suggests that Lincoln at the time conceived of a Republican future beyond the borders of the 1860 party.[25]

As for the unity of the newly triumphant Republican Party, Seward occupied different ground than Lincoln. Since the inception of the party and even before that as the major spokesman for antislavery Northern Whigs, Seward had been the evangelist of the irrepressible conflict. He had the standing to withstand an assault from the Republican left, which would surely have come. Moreover, if a party opting for sectional compromise really distressed the zealots, where could they go? But even if the most radical bolted, the adherence of Southern Unionists would offset their loss. Thus, for Seward the Republican Party would become the great Union party, with a solid presence in the slave states, particularly in the Upper and Border South. Lincoln did turn to the Union party idea, but only during the war. Before hostilities, he absolutely rejected such an initiative.

Although the record is not so clear as one would like, important Southern leaders hoped that Seward would prevail in bringing his party to the compromise standard. This interpretation helps explain the timing of the Southern reaction to the Senate Committee of Thirteen created to search for a sectional compromise. Initially, senators from the Deep South, like Jefferson Davis, spurned the committee, but then they reconsidered, agreeing to serve. Davis also made clear his willingness to support any measure the committee adopted similar to the Missouri Compromise admitting Southern rights in the territories. Another committee member, the avowed secessionist Robert Toombs of Georgia, stated that if the committee agreed on that kind of arrangement, he would accept it despite his lack of enthusiasm, because it would satisfy his state.[26]

In Washington, Seward remained publicly quiet, "mum as an oyster" in the colorful image of one Republican congressman. On December 14 Seward left the capital for home; at the same time Thurlow Weed headed west for a meeting with the president-elect in Springfield. In his newspaper Weed repeated the call for compromise. But he found Lincoln still steadfastly opposed to anything resembling an extension of the Missouri Compromise line. Lincoln underlined to Weed what he had been telling others: no territorial compromise. Party policy on that point was granite. Upon his return to New York State, Weed met with Seward. When the senator returned to Washington, he voted with his fellow Republicans on the committee to refuse any serious territorial compromise. The Committee of Thirteen failed; the Deep South marched out of the Union.[27]

Seward was unwilling to cross the new party leader. And without question Seward's acquiescence in Lincoln's directive signaled that Lincoln was not only president-elect but also unquestionably the Republican chieftain. This is not the place to discuss why Seward bowed to Lincoln, but I want to note that even though Seward acceded to Lincoln's wishes, he kept trying to push the new leader to the right, all the way to Fort Sumter.[28]

In my view a third fundamental underlay Lincoln's rejection of compromise. I am persuaded that he had a much deeper, more visceral hatred of slavery than did Seward. Seward did abhor slavery, never giving it equal billing with freedom. Convinced, however, that the rapid geographic expansion along with the burgeoning economic power of the free states would naturally overpower slavery, he was willing to let the institution and the Southern political strength based on it become casualties of America's inevitable progress. Thus, after the territorial issue had accomplished its political task in 1860, Seward was quite willing to shelve it.

Not so Lincoln—to him the territorial issue was never just about politics. To him it spoke about the nation, even if primarily as symbol. That conviction informed his Cooper Union speech of February 1860, which made him a viable presidential possibility to eastern Republicans. In that address Lincoln, concentrating on a discrete group of men, insisted that the Founding Fathers had intended an antislavery future for the new republic. In Lincoln's version of history, that noble goal had somehow been shunted aside. The duty of Republicans was to restore its primacy. On that February evening in New York City, Lincoln's remarks were brilliant as a partisan cry and legal brief, but one-sided as history. For three decades after the ratification of the Constitution, slavery and freedom had marched westward side by side. That simultaneous movement had occurred with powerful support from leading members of the Founding Fathers. New territories open to slavery had been acquired or organized under every president from George Washington to James Monroe.[29]

Those facts did not deter Lincoln. For him the venerated Fathers simply could not have countenanced the extension of the great evil of the country. Thus for Lincoln, to accept any compromise that even theoretically permitted the possibility of expanding slavery meant turning from a vision he cherished both of past and future. Even if only symbolic, territorial compromise signified a moral blot. Accordingly, for Lincoln, the Union as a good in itself was less powerful than an antislavery Union. To Alexander Stephens, he put it starkly: slavery was "wrong." As a result, Lincoln was willing to risk the Union of the Fathers to get his antislavery Union. Yet in the winter of 1860–61, he could not imagine the price of his gamble.[30]

To return to my initial query about Lincoln and Henry Clay, in this essay I have advanced my views about why despite his words Lincoln in the great crisis of the Union did not look to Henry Clay. In those momentous weeks

Seward demonstrated himself much more than Lincoln a man of national outlook. In the winter of 1860–61 the New Yorker acted like the disciple of Clay. In this instance, Seward had legitimate claim to the mantle of Henry Clay.

Notes

1. Notable recent Lincoln books include Michael Burlingame, *Abraham Lincoln: A Life*, 2 vols. (Baltimore: Johns Hopkins University Press, 2008); George M. Fredrickson, *Big Enough to Be Inconsistent: Abraham Lincoln Confronts Race and Slavery* (Cambridge, MA: Harvard University Press, 2008); William C. Harris, *Lincoln's Rise to the Presidency* (Lawrence, KS: University Press of Kansas, 2007); Harold Holzer, *Lincoln President-Elect: Abraham Lincoln and the Great Secession, Winter 1860–1861* (New York: Simon & Schuster, 2008); James M. McPherson, *Tried by War: Abraham Lincoln as Commander in Chief* (New York: Penguin, 2008); William Lee Miller, *President Lincoln: The Duty of a Statesman* (New York: Alfred A. Knopf, 2008); Craig L. Symonds, *Lincoln and His Admirals* (New York: Oxford University Press, 2008); and Ronald C. White Jr., *A. Lincoln: A Biography* (New York: Random House, 2009).

2. The classic account, which still retains great value, is David M. Potter, *Lincoln and His Party in the Secession Crisis* (1942; Baton Rouge: Louisiana State University Press, 1995). It is in the second camp along with Patrick Michael Sowle, "The Conciliatory Republicans during the Winter of Secession" (Ph.D. diss., Duke University, 1963); and Russell McClintock, *Lincoln and the Decision for War: The Northern Response to Secession* (Chapel Hill: University of North Carolina Press, 2008). For the first, see Burlingame, *Abraham Lincoln*, vol. 1, chap. 17; and Holzer, *Lincoln President-Elect*. A balanced treatment is Harris, *Lincoln's Rise*.

3. Roy P. Basler et al., eds., *The Collected Works of Abraham Lincoln*, 8 vols. (New Brunswick, NJ: Rutgers University Press, 1953–55), 3:29, hereafter cited as *CWL*. The best biography of Clay is Robert V. Remini, *Henry Clay: Statesman for the Union* (New York: W. W. Norton, 1991).

4. *CWL*, 2:121–32, quotations on 125, 126, 129; Lincoln to Daniel Ullman, February 1, 1861, ibid., 4:184.

5. Ibid., 2:130–31 and 3:29, 89, 300–305.

6. Robert Seager et al., eds., *The Papers of Henry Clay*, 10 vols. and supp. (Lexington: University Press of Kentucky, 1959–92), 10:658, 664. For Clay and the Compromise consult Remini, *Clay*, chap. 40.

7. *CWL*, 2:232–33, 241–42, 270 (quotation), 272, 3:119–20.

8. Ibid., 2:461. Still best on the 1850s is David M. Potter, *The Impending Crisis, 1848–1861*, completed by Don E. Fehrenbacher (New York: Harper & Row, 1976), which has considerable material on Seward.

9. *CWL*, 4:142, on military preparation; Donn Piatt, *Memories of the Men Who Saved the Union* (New York and Chicago: Belford, Clarke, 1887), 30 (first quotation); Lincoln to Peter H. Silvester, December 22, 1860, *CWL*, 4:160 (second quotation); Don E. Fehrenbacher and Virginia Fehrenbacher, comps. and eds., *Recollected Words of Abraham Lincoln*

(Stanford, CA: Stanford University Press, 1996), 253 (third quotation), hereafter cited as *Words*.

10. Hawkins Layton to John Allison, December 21, 1860, Abraham Lincoln Papers, Library of Congress (hereafter LC) (first quotation); Lincoln to Lyman Trumbull, December 17, 1860, to Elihu Washburne, December 13, 1860 (third quotation), to Thurlow Weed, December 17, 1860 (second quotation), *CWL*, 4:149–50, 151, 154; *Words*, 253; Duff Green to James Buchanan, December 28, 1860, James Buchanan Papers, Historical Society of Pennsylvania; Harold G. Villard and Oswald Garrison Villard, eds., *Lincoln on the Eve of '61: A Journalist's Story by Henry Villard* (New York: Alfred A. Knopf, 1941), 23; Carl Schurz to his wife, February 9, 1861, in Joseph Schafer, trans. and ed., *Intimate Letters of Carl Schurz* (Madison: State Historical Society of Wisconsin, 1928), 247.

11. *CWL*, 4:264.

12. *Words*, 341.

13. See his "House Divided" speech, *CWL*, 2:461–69.

14. Biographies of Lincoln such as those by Burlingame and White cited in n. 1 cover this material. No Lincoln scholar has uncovered any serious contact; neither have I.

15. *Words*, 341.

16. Lincoln to Stephens, November 30, December 22, 1860, *CWL*, 4:146, 160; Stephens to Lincoln, December 14, 1860, Lincoln Papers, LC; Stephens to Lincoln, December 30, 1860, in Stephens, *A Constitutional View of the Late War between the States . . .* , 2 vols. (Philadelphia: National, 1868), 2:267–70. Stephens's speech is printed in William W. Freehling and Craig M. Simpson, eds., *Secession Debated: Georgia's Showdown in 1860* (New York: Oxford University Press, 1992), 51–79, quotation on 69. For Lincoln's calling Stephens a great man, Linton Stephens to Alexander Stephens, February 8, 1861, Alexander H. Stephens Papers, Manhattanville College.

17. The most recent study as well as the best is William W. Freehling, *The Road to Disunion*, vol. 2, *Secessionists Triumphant, 1854–1861* (New York: Oxford University Press, 2007).

18. For example, see N. Paschall to Lincoln, November 18, 1860, John Gilmer to Lincoln, December 11, 1860, and Montgomery Blair to Lincoln, December 14, 1860, all in Lincoln Papers, LC; and Thomas J. McCormack, ed., *Memoirs of Gustave Koerner, 1809–1896*, 2 vols. (Cedar Rapids, IA: Torch, 1909), 2:104–5, 109.

19. Lincoln to Truman Smith, November 10, 1860 (first quotation), and to N. Paschall, November 16, 1860 (second quotation), *CWL*, 4:138, 140.

20. Especially consult McClintock, *Lincoln and the Decision for War*; Potter, *Lincoln and His Party*; and Sowle, "The Conciliatory Republicans."

21. Adams to Seward, November 11, 1860, William Henry Seward Papers, Rush Rhees Library, University of Rochester (hereafter UR). For suggestive introductions to Seward's activities, see Daniel W. Crofts, *Reluctant Confederates: Upper South Unionists in the Secession Crisis* (Chapel Hill: University of North Carolina Press, 1989), chapters 8–9; and Michael Robinson, "William Henry Seward, Compromise, and the Sectional Crisis, November–December 1860," unpublished seminar paper, Louisiana State University, 2007.

22. *Albany Evening Journal*, November 24, December 17 and 24, 1860; Sowle, "Conciliatory Republicans," 50, 84–86; Phillip S. Foner, *Business & Slavery: New York Merchants & the Irrepressible Conflict* (Chapel Hill: University of North Carolina Press, 1941), 235; J.

Watson Webb to Lincoln, December 1, 1860, Lincoln Papers, LC; James Dixon to Gideon Welles, January 2, 1861, Gideon Welles Papers, LC; W. S. Gelman to Lyman Trumbull, December 11, 1860, Lyman Trumbull Papers, LC; George D. Morgan to Thurlow Weed December 8, 1860, Thurlow Weed Papers, UR.

23. For examples, see *Charleston Mercury*, January 22, 1861; J. L. Pugh to William Miles, January 24, 1861, William P. Miles Papers, Southern Historical Collection, University of North Carolina, Chapel Hill; Robert Toombs to E. B. Pullin and others, December 13, 1860, and to People of Georgia, December 23, 1860, in Ulrich Bonnell Phillips, ed., *The Correspondence of Robert Toombs, Alexander H. Stephens, and Howell Cobb* (Washington, DC: Government Printing Office, 1913), 519–22, 525. Seward noted the fire-eater hope in a letter to Hamilton Fish, December 11, 1860, Hamilton Fish Papers, LC.

24. Weed to Preston King, December 10, 1860, in Thurlow Weed Barnes and Harriet A. Weed, eds., *The Life of Thurlow Weed . . .*, 2 vols. (Boston: Houghton, Mifflin, 1883–84), 2:309 (quotation); J. H. McKee to Lincoln, December 12, 1860, and Henry Winter Davis to Lincoln, February 1861, Lincoln Papers, LC; John P. Kennedy to George S. Bryan, December 27, 1860, Letterbook, John Pendleton Kennedy Papers, Enoch Pratt Free Library, Baltimore; H. R. Riddle to Thurlow Weed, December 24, 1860, Weed Papers, UR; J. M. Taylor to Seward, January 21, 1861, J. R. Bailey to Seward, February 11, 1861, H. Fountleroy to Seward, February 12, 1861, all in Seward Papers, UR; Thomas Fitnam to Seward, February 19, 1861, and M. J. Crawford to Robert Toombs, March 8, 1861, in Frederic Bancroft, *The Life of William H. Seward*, 2 vols. (New York: Harper & Brothers, 1900), 2:537, 109–10n.

25. Weed to Preston King, December 10, 1860, in Barnes and Weed, *Thurlow Weed*, 2:309.

26. Davis to Frank H. Alfriend, August 17, 1867, in William J. Cooper Jr., ed., *Jefferson Davis: The Essential Writings* (New York: Modern Library, 2003), 393–97; Samuel S. Cox, *Union-Disunion-Reunion: Three Decades of Federal Legislation, 1855–1885 . . .* (1885; Freeport, NY: Books for Libraries, 1970), 77; Ulrich Bonnell Phillips, *The Life of Robert Toombs* (New York: Macmillan, 1913), 206–8.

27. George C. Fogg to Lincoln, December 19, 1860, Lincoln Papers, LC; *Albany Evening Journal*, December 17, 1860.

28. There is no other persuasive explanation for Seward's striving to get Lincoln to conciliate the Upper and Border South, moderate his inaugural address, and evacuate Fort Sumter.

29. Harold Holzer in his *Lincoln at Cooper Union: The Speech That Made Abraham Lincoln President* (New York: Simon & Schuster, 2004) agrees with Lincoln's interpretation.

30. Lincoln to Stephens, December 22, 1860, *CWL*, 4:160.

III

Parties and Federalism
in the Era of the Civil War
and Reconstruction

"Come Weal, Come Woe, I Am with the Anti-Slavery Party"

Federalism and the Formation of the Pennsylvania Union Party, 1860–1864

SEAN NALTY

In early June 1864, a strange assemblage of Republicans, Democrats who endorsed President Lincoln and the war, and border-state Southerners gathered in Baltimore to formally nominate the incumbent for a second term. Just four years before, Republicans had denounced Southern Democrats as part of a "slave oligarchy," but here were Northern Democrats and loyal slaveholding politicians pledging their support to the same candidate who had earlier won on an expressly anti-Democratic, anti-Southern platform. Why did Republicans and even some non-Republicans embrace the new party? For many at the convention, the war had convinced them that old party questions paled in comparison to the goal of preserving the Union. Indeed, Republicans referred to their party in 1864 as the National Union Party, which represented a kind of wartime fusion among proadministration political groups.[1]

Historians have long considered why the Republican Party underwent a metamorphosis into the National Union Party. James McPherson, for instance, describes the 1864 National Union Party Convention as a Republican ploy "to attract War Democrats and southern unionists who might flinch at the name Republican." In his estimation, the party gained these additional adherents at little cost to traditional Republican principles. Even while demanding the unconditional surrender of the Confederate armies and the abolition of slavery, the platform adopted in 1864 entirely ignored the "divisive reconstruction issue." Thus the National Union Party emerged with the paramount objective of simply dealing with the exigencies of war, with little consideration given to its future beyond the war's end.[2]

In contrast to McPherson's depiction of the Union Party as a change of name by Republicans to cultivate a sense of wartime unity, Michael Holt advances a different understanding of the significance of the National Union Party. In exploring the contrast between President Lincoln's conciliatory policies toward the South and harsher measures favored by Republican majorities in Congress, Holt focuses on the electoral strategy of Lincoln in pursuing his reelection for 1864. The president, according to Holt, "set out to destroy the Republican party as it existed in 1860 . . . an exclusively northern party whose sole basis of cohesion was hostility toward the South and the Democratic party." The new, bisectional National Union Party would replace anti-Southernism and condemnations of the Slave Power with a more conciliatory treatment of Southerners as outlined in Lincoln's "Ten-Percent Plan."[3]

Common to both these interpretations is an emphasis on the emergence of the National Union Party as a national party during the 1864 campaign. Precious little has been done to explore why various Northern states embraced the Union labels well before the 1864 election. By examining how Republicans and non-Republicans responded to the formation of a Union Party in Pennsylvania, I hope to shed light on the practice of federalism amid the stresses of civil war.

This essay first reconsiders the importance of the original Constitutional Union or John Bell supporters of 1860 to the wartime political scene in Pennsylvania. I argue that, far from representing a feeble, antiquated set of principles as depicted in some historical accounts, Bell supporters like Philadelphian Henry Charles Lea were instrumental in helping to reorient the Pennsylvania People's (i.e., Republican) Party ideology from its original emphasis on free labor and anti-Southernism toward an ideology of antiparty nationalism. These "Bell and Everett" men of 1860 also brought a reformist impulse into their new political homes. The inclusion of these men in the Union Party after 1860 generated an important tension within the wartime Union Party between the "wire-pulling" political practices of Pennsylvania Republican political leaders and the antipolitical sentiments of the former Bell voters. This tension would persist until the emergence of the Progressive movement and the corresponding rise of the ideal of the independent, issue-oriented (as opposed to party-oriented) voter.

Second, this essay examines how advocacy of the Union Party among Pennsylvania's leaders, such as Governor Andrew Curtin, helps to explain the governor's conflict with the Lincoln administration over federal recruitment policies throughout the war. In particular, Curtin consciously tried to build support for the Pennsylvania Union Party among non-Republicans through his efforts to reduce the federally imposed quota for Pennsylvania enlistments. Through this electoral strategy of incorporating non-Republicans into a new Union Party, Curtin and his political allies in Pennsylvania exacerbated their long-standing factional rivalries with Simon Cameron's wing of the Republican Party and risked alienating the War Department in

Washington. I further show how the decision to embrace the Union Party idea by some political leaders in Pennsylvania helps to explain the difficult relationship William Blair has observed between Curtin and the authorities in Washington. In so doing, this essay invites a reconsideration of the role that the development of state Union parties played in the relationships among officials across different levels of government.[4]

The election of 1860 did not guarantee the Republican Party permanence in the political landscape of the time. The realignment of the 1850s had proven such a disorienting experience to many politicians that few could predict with any certainty where political alignments would ultimately settle. This seemed especially true of the victorious Republican Party, whose members had come together primarily in opposition to a Democratic Party that had generally protected Southern slaveholding interests. Yet this assemblage of former Democrats and Whigs could little agree on anything beyond a refusal to allow the further extension of slavery into the federal territories. This seemingly ad hoc Republican coalition appeared to outsiders as doomed to failure, for winning was the easy part—governance was much harder. Herschel Johnson, the running mate of Stephen Douglas on the Democratic ticket in 1860, expressed a rather common belief among non-Republicans that the party would crumble under its own weight. "The Republican Party must fall to pieces," he argued. "Besides, who does not know, that there are two distinct wings of the party," representing an "ultra rabid" and a "conservative" wing. If Lincoln tried to win over the one wing through patronage, "the other would instantly make war upon his administration." Johnson perceptively identified the chief problem for Republicans: how to keep their coalition from splintering as the party transitioned from opposition to control of the White House. This process only became more difficult with the secession of South Carolina and six other Deep South states from December 1860 to February 1861. Faced with the need for unity against a Southern rebellion, the incoming Lincoln administration would have to decide how far it was willing to go to secure the support of those voters who had shunned the party in 1860.[5]

One of those groups in the North who had fought the Republicans was the Constitutional Union Party. These men looked upon the emergence of a sectional antislavery party with great revulsion, despite the affinity these Bell voters of 1860 had with the economic program of the Whig-dominated Republican Party. Despite their paucity in numbers, this group of conservative nationalists in the Constitutional Union Party seemed important allies for Republicans in the fight against secession. It is true that this group only managed to yield a paltry 2.5 percent of Pennsylvania's vote for president.

Nevertheless, interest in attracting such self-described "conservative" Constitutional Unionists to their respective parties made Democrats and Republicans eager to appeal to this small but socially prominent demographic. Representing a wide range of professional men, from the Philadelphia medievalist Henry Charles Lea to the Pottsville medical doctor, black colonization pamphleteer, and local organizer Jacob Dewees, these men did not simply give up and abandon public life once the results of the November election became known. Instead, these Constitutional Unionists eagerly contributed their time and money to influence the state's politics during the course of the war.

While Lea would go on to join the newly formed Union Party and Dewees would endorse the Democrats, both men exhibited what the historian Adam I. P. Smith has properly characterized as a revulsion against politics as usual. The corresponding decline in the potency of old economic issues in the 1850s had left many former Constitutional Unionists convinced that party strife reflected little more than a contest for spoils. According to Lea, political "reform must begin at the beginning," that is, at the local level, so local reform became their primary objective. Using the operations of the federal system to their own advantage, these Unionists worked to implement their principles at the municipal and state levels. In so doing, they looked to prevent the recurrence of the kind of wire-pulling, office-seeking politics that they believed had dangerously brought the country to the brink of ruin. This focus would significantly continue well beyond the war, as Progressives eventually waged a successful battle against party leaders and their machine-style politics at century's end.[6]

The political scene after the firing on Fort Sumter in April 1861 seemed to contemporaries to portend a complete break up of prewar political coalitions, leaving observers to imagine new parties emerging out of the wreckage. Republicans throughout the North also sensed an opportunity to incorporate non-Republican voters into their prowar coalition. To that end, local elections in the fall of 1861 saw the creation of bipartisan "People's Union" tickets in states like New York and Ohio. In Pennsylvania, where the main opposition to the Democrats ran as the "People's Party" rather than under the name "Republican" in order to avoid charges of antislavery extremism, a serious discussion ensued over whether to establish a "Union" organization across traditional party lines. Some Pennsylvania Republicans, such as the Snyder County newspaperman Israel Gutelius, believed that Republicans needed to extend the hand of political friendship to Douglas Democrats and Constitutional Unionists and therefore urged the creation of a state Union Party. Writing to Pennsylvania's secretary of the commonwealth Eli Slifer, Gutelius underscored the importance of creating this new party while party lines in the state remained in flux, for "if any thing is to be don[e] to Save us it must be don[e] soon." Saving the country from the ruin brought on by the policies of radical antislavery men in the Republican Party, according to Gutelius, required an embrace of non-Republicans by nominating them for local and state offices.[7]

The initial response to the idea of a new "Union Party" among non-Republicans was extremely positive. Some Democrats anticipated such a move from the start. One Douglas Democrat who had recently joined the Second Pennsylvania told former Philadelphia mayor Richard Vaux that the "talk in the army is of a great National party formed of the Douglas Democracy and those men who were driven out" by the radicalism of certain antislavery leaders in the Republican Party. Recognizing the great popularity of the patriotic zeal for unity, even former president James Buchanan advised Bucks County Democrats to cater to the public desires. Democrats, he urged, should sustain various pro-Union resolutions put forth by some Republicans and Democrats, since "this is the course of expediency & what is of infinitely more importance is the course of our highest duty to our country." The records of the members of the Fifteenth Ward Bell and Everett Association in Philadelphia provided evidence of the receptivity of Constitutional Union Party members to a broad-based Union Party. In resolutions probably written in 1861, this group indicated its opposition to any "unconstitutional" legislation to abolish slavery and further declared that in "A. Lincoln our worthy president we find a man for the times . . . in whom we place full confidence, a conservative man & who will receive our full support." Little-known men like twenty-six-year-old Constitutional Unionist Joseph G. Rosengarten, forty-year-old Democrat (and former Constitutional Unionist) Thomas S. Stewart, and Douglas Democrat Thomas Greenbank sought nominations for state legislature from both major parties. Both "Union Democrats and Union Republicans," as one Philadelphia newspaper pointed out to its readers, worked together to elect the incumbent Republican state treasurer at the beginning of 1862.[8]

Some Pennsylvania Republicans scarcely hid their revulsion at the idea of becoming a kind of broad-tent organization, especially if it might weaken or sacrifice those antislavery principles that had animated the founding of the Republican Party. A major problem with establishing a Union Party in

Pennsylvania was the long-running rivalry between Governor Andrew Curtin and Lincoln's secretary of war, Simon Cameron. Each man had sought to outmaneuver the other politically in the past, with Cameron, a former Democrat, generally taking a far more advanced position against slavery than his rival. The inchoate nature of the early Republican Party made Cameron and his allies deeply suspicious of the ease with which the former Whig Curtin and his followers embraced the idea of a Union Party.

Were Curtin and his allies looking to build up a coalition for the purpose of excluding Cameron and other strongly antislavery Republicans? Cameron supporters seemed to think so. They believed Curtin wanted to attract Democrats and other non-Republicans into a pro-Lincoln coalition that would greatly diminish their own power and influence. One Republican in Lewisburg acknowledged the existence of "a kind of 'Union Movement' here, got up by the Democrats, though the call is signed by republicans without much reflection I suppose." Opposing the efforts of men like Israel Gutelius to fuse Republicans and non-Republicans into a new party, this Republican counseled state leaders to limit the spread of this movement as far as practicable. If too many Democrats and other non-Republicans were placed in "Judgeships, Congress, & [the] Legislature," he reasoned, "they will soon crawl to the throat of the administration." Cameron himself received a similar warning from a Philadelphia Republican, who predicted that "there will be a new howl against you . . . the conservative, Old-Line Pro-Slavery Whigs, Negro-driving Democrats, & weak-kneed Republicans" uniting against pro-Cameron Republicans. Thus it was far better, according to the pro-Cameron faction, to concentrate the party's efforts on retaining the loyalty of good Republicans instead of trying to win over former rivals.[9]

Even as Republicans, Democrats, and Constitutional Unionists began to come together during the first year of the war, discussions over the future of slavery threatened to derail this fusion of the old parties. Among the more radical Cameron men, criticism of Lincoln's handling of both the war and the issue of slavery grew steadily once the president began to countermand the antislavery edicts of some of his commanders. Amid repeated clashes between Confederate and Union forces outside Richmond, Republican members in Congress during June 1862 prodded Lincoln to move toward a more aggressive stance on slavery and adopted a bill calling for the confiscation of all rebel-held property, including slaves. Some Democrats took advantage of this congressional push and rallied fellow Democrats against further support of the Lincoln administration. A committed opponent of the war, Berks County Democrat J. Glancy Jones had been in Europe when the war came.

When he arrived back in Pennsylvania in the spring of 1862, however, he found many of his fellow Democrats "committed to the war." Hoping to reverse this situation, Jones spoke out against the Lincoln administration and charged it with deluding the masses into fighting a war not to preserve the Union but to abolish slavery. Given this shift, he argued, the "democracy now [is] discharged from all obligation or promises to sustain it." A Pennsylvania Republican criticized the president from the other direction. The only way Unionists could fail to win in the state elections, this Pennsylvanian wrote to Cameron, "will be because this war has not been prosecuted with sufficient vigour by the President." The problem lay in Lincoln's refusal to address emancipation, "the measure, which I hope he will address now."[10]

Lincoln did address the issue in July 1862, surprising his cabinet with his intention to pursue emancipation as a military measure after the failure of McClellan's campaign on the Peninsula. Delayed until the conclusion of the fighting at Antietam, the president's more strident position on emancipation generated an electoral backlash in the Keystone State. Racial anxieties had combined with dissatisfaction over the general conduct of the war to reduce sharply the popular enchantment with the war in Pennsylvania. Correctly foreseeing a difficult campaign ahead, Republicans and non-Republicans had formed themselves into a state Union Party at Harrisburg on July 17, 1862. Their platform "invite[d] the cooperation of all loyal men who love their country" and expressed "continued confidence" in the leadership of the president and Governor Curtin. The document produced in Harrisburg also pointed out that no issue engendered political conflict among the people of the United States beyond the question of loyalty to the Union. Conspicuously absent among the planks of the Union Party's statement of principles, though, was any position on confiscation or the eventual demise of slavery.[11]

The final results of the fall state and congressional elections in Pennsylvania gave Democrats reasonable hope for winning back deserters from their party in the future. Democrats regained control of the state house of representatives, obtaining a ten-seat majority over their opponents. In the state senate, the Union men continued to hold power, 21–12, but Democrats had also managed to pick up four seats there as well. Of equal importance, the Democratic opposition now evenly split with the Union coalition at twelve seats for each party, with the Democrats even managing to take down the current house Speaker, Galusha Grow. Despite this recent triumph, William J. Woodward undoubtedly spoke for many Pennsylvania Democrats who believed their party had yet to capture the most important state prize, the governor's chair, for only "*then* some respect will be shown for popular sentiment" by the anti-Democratic opposition.

The socially prominent Philadelphia diarist Sidney George Fisher recorded a conversation he had with Philadelphia newspaperman Morton McMichael at a private gathering where the discussion turned upon the outcome of the state and congressional races. The editor of the *North American and United States Gazette,* Fisher reported, "thinks the victories of the Democrats mean dissatisfaction with the manner in which the war is conducted, the inactivity, delay, want of ability, extravagant expenditure, & corruption, not with the war itself." The dismissal of Cameron as secretary of war earlier in the year amid charges of corruption and malfeasance with war contracts hurt the cause of the Union Party in Pennsylvania. Fisher had earlier blamed the disappointing results of state contests in October upon the absence of most Union men for service in the army, a position with which the Unionist J. W. Blackburn agreed. The absence of campaign workers, in the estimation of Blackburn, only contributed to the dearth of Union men necessary "to arouse our folks to the importance of turning out." The perception that the Lincoln administration's policies on slavery and recruitment of soldiers had cost Pennsylvania Republicans a victory placed Governor Curtin and his supporters in a bind. They wanted to continue to win over non-Republicans to join a Union Party but faced popular dissatisfaction with Lincoln's war policies as well as Cameron's actions while a member of the administration.[12]

Despite the staunch antislavery sentiment of the more radical pro-Cameron elements of the Union coalition, loyal Pennsylvania Democrats and some Republicans tried to get assurances from Cameron and his allies that they would not press the emancipation issue too far, given the recent election. One loyal Democrat complained to Pennsylvania congressman Edward McPherson that the decision to free and arm slaves through national legislation would result in mass desertions among common soldiers. More importantly, the letter implored Republicans like McPherson to remember, "If the country is going to be saved you must conciliate the loyal democrats, and yield something to the prejudices of the border state men." Finally, the present times required that "loyal men of all parties *unite* in the adoption of measures for the preservation of government." This Pennsylvanian feared "for the consequences of what must be regarded as purely *party* legislation" if Republicans in Congress succeeded in arming freed slaves to fight alongside white soldiers. Similarly, another Pennsylvanian wished Cameron and the Lincoln administration not to press too quickly such divisive racial issues given the extremely fragile nature of the Union coalition in Pennsylvania and throughout the North. It was important for Lincoln *"to remember that nothing but the attack on Fort Sumpter [sic] has afforded him an opportunity to save the Union."* Moreover, "it was this master folly, nothing else," this writer explained, that "raised the north to a full knowledge of its extreme danger." If political leaders did not manage matters delicately, these Unionists argued, the existence of the Pennsylvania Union Party would drive a permanent wedge between the Curtin and Cameron factions.[13]

As the war progressed into its third year, Republicans still managed to reaffirm their alliance with certain Democrats and Constitutional Unionists in order to win elections, and the war remained crucial. Mark Neely has offered a cogent critique of the ways in which political patronage hindered the war effort. Nevertheless, he unduly minimizes the ways in which the promise of office or military commission cemented non-Republicans to the Lincoln administration and its prosecution of the war. Despite the earlier warnings of some Republicans, political leaders at both the national and state levels tended to look beyond party and favor the appointments of any "loyal, Union loving man." Pennsylvanians did not distinguish between the political and nonpolitical effects of appointments. For instance, one Morristown resident tried to help John F. Hartranft obtain a promotion to brigadier general at the beginning of 1863. "He was in times past," according to this recommendation, "under old organizations, a Democrat, but now repudiates all party ties & recognizes only the one great paramount duty of standing by the Union & the National Adm[inistratio]n in its affairs to save it." Party patronage helped cement the loyalty of War Democrats who had previously demonstrated their devotion to the Union cause through military service.[14]

Flush from their victories in the fall congressional campaign, a number of Pennsylvania Democrats had begun to seek the party nomination for governor. Though the list of possible candidates included John Cessna, a War Democrat who had increasingly opposed Curtin's call for more troops, some Democrats began to eye state supreme court justice George W. Woodward for the prize. Democrat Thomas Morris explained the rationale for choosing a man like Woodward, "a gentleman . . . who possesses more than ordinary talent, and a man of experience, and of reputation both at home and abroad." Woodward's impeccably conservative credentials would attract not only errant Democrats in the Union Party but also those ex-Whigs who supported the Constitutional Union Party of 1860. Indeed, the times seemed to demand, in the minds of Democrats like Morris, someone like Woodward to awaken the party from its doldrums. He wrote, "I have taken no active part in politics for the last 10 or 15 years but I consider the time has arrived when we also should put our shoulders to the wheel for it is the time that is trying mens souls." Agreeing with Morris, Democrats began to rally around Woodward as the best hope for breaking up the Union coalition in their bid to improve upon their 1862 performance.[15]

By late spring, Woodward felt compelled to stand as a candidate. Though he had his own doubts about Democratic success in the fall, Woodward confided to a friend, "I have no personal aspirations. . . . I only want an honest, bold, true, and competent democrat—one who will stand by the few state rights that are left, and not surrender them to any usurper." As a state judge, Woodward insisted that his "tastes were more judicial than executive. I have no desire to quit the bench for the Governor's chair." That said, he continued, "If the democratic people think proper, without solicitation on my part, to make me their Governor I will do my best to administer the constitution & laws as they are written." Like other Democrats, Woodward could not help noticing how times had changed with a war and the national and state government under the control of the opposition. He remarked to Lewis Coryell, "Did you ever expect to see such times as these? You are the only remaining link between the present generation & a class of men who I learned to revere and love in my youth." The campaign was now underway.[16]

Prior to the summer of 1863, Governor Curtin's ill health coupled with his announced intention to retire prompted other pro-Cameron men to throw their hats into the ring. One of the most eager to win the nomination was former U.S. congressman John Covode, best known as "Honest John" for his exposure of corruption within the Buchanan administration. He and his main backer, the newspaperman Uriah Painter, undertook a campaign to line up delegates before the Union Party state convention in June. When news reached friends of the governor that Painter had embarked on a trip to Chester County to obtain pledges from the delegates there, the pro-Curtin men worked behind the scenes to hold the nomination for their man as the best way to promote their alliance with non-Republicans and curb Cameron's influence over the party. Pro-Curtin local activist Israel Gutelius told friends of the governor that he had sought to include a fair number of "loyal Democrats" among the conferees who chose delegates to the upcoming state convention.[17]

Complicating the efforts of the pro-Curtain men, however, was the presence of the Army of Northern Virginia. As General Robert E. Lee moved northward after getting approval in May for a plan to invade the North, the issue of state and local defense suddenly took on real importance. A close ally of Curtin's, Alexander K. McClure, expected little help from Washington with raising troops for the defense of Pennsylvania. Secretary of War Stanton, McClure wrote, "is so bitterly against him [Curtin] that he will interfere against any movement the Governor may desire. He seems to be actuated all the time by the impression that Gov Curtin is only seeking popularity in all these efforts; and he does not particularly desire him to be popular." The acrimonious relationship between the governor and the secretary of war resulted from Stanton's belief that Curtin had purposely hindered recruitment during the fall of 1862. To Stanton, the Pennsylvania governor appeared hesitant to raise regiments for service whose enlistments went beyond a nine-month term, preferring instead to ask the War Department if he could include nine-month men in his state's quota. Furthermore, the personal desire of the governor to appoint a number of Democrats to recruiting offices contrary to the wishes of the War Department made Stanton question the nature of Curtin's commitment to support the Lincoln administration.[18]

Faced with resistance from Washington to ease the standards of recruitment, Governor Curtin requested men and material to turn back the rebels, only to find that Philadelphia's mayor, Alexander Henry, did not believe that he could entice men to enlist. The problem centered on the six-month requirement for service in the militia that had accompanied President Lincoln's original call for troops in April 1861. Mayor Henry, however, reported that he had "consulted many intelligent citizens this morning, and all agree that except as volunteers for the immediate and present defence of the State, troops cannot be obtained *at call* from this City." No doubt exasperated with this reply and less sensitive to the local needs of the mayor in a time of crisis, Curtin accepted the possibility from Henry that three regiments in Beverly, New Jersey, whose enlistments were about to expire might be encouraged to join for the six months. Henry had another idea, to use eighty-three "colored" volunteers to meet the governor's call; however, General Darius Couch supposedly would not accept them unless the volunteers pledged themselves for enlistments of three years or for the duration of the war. Later, Curtin admitted that Couch had refused the men on the basis that he "had no authority to muster them into service of the U.S. & I had no authority to take them in any other way as the call was from the U.S.A. [U.S. Army]." In the end, Curtin promised to suspend the six-month requirement and sent a telegram to Henry and other local leaders to "give us the men."[19]

What had seemed like a complete debacle in preparing to defend the state was not lost on the politicians. With the Union and Democratic nominating conventions coming up, the Democrat Woodward anticipated a gubernatorial victory for the Democrats as a result of Curtin's "proposition that no man should be suffered to aid in our defence unless he should in advance enlist for six months in the United States Army, involved a stretch of insolence and imprudence that was sublime." Although he was clearly angling for the position of governor, John Covode believed many angry Republicans in the Union Party would refrain from giving support to "the State and National Authorities for letting the State be invaded." In fact, "many of them" believed New York Democratic governor Horatio Seymour "has done more than our own Republican Governor." The despondency seemed to pervade the ranks of the Unionists. Talking with Sidney George Fisher, the newspaperman Morton McMichael hoped that the Susquehanna River might serve as a natural barrier to a Confederate advance toward Philadelphia, but then he quickly added, "If they did [cross it] there was nothing to prevent them from coming here." A surgeon attached to the 109th Pennsylvania Regiment, James Langstaff Dunn, also pointed to evidence of civilian disaffection within southern Pennsylvania over the invasion, though he blamed the local "*Dutch Ignoramuses* that know nothing but to make a Dollar & vote for *Genl [Andrew] Jackson.*" The Army of Northern Virginia could not have picked a better time to throw Pennsylvania politics into confusion.[20]

Armed with strong indications that popular anger over the Confederate invasion would oust the incumbent, Democratic leaders understandably believed they had a compelling state issue in Curtin's mismanagement of the defense of the commonwealth. Still, the Union victory at Gettysburg combined with the exertions of the pro-Curtin men (and the decision to postpone the convention to August 5 to deal with the emergency of the Confederate invasion) signaled the end to Covode's challenge, leaving the former Pittsburgh congressman and his supporters relegated to professions of support for the party standard-bearer.[21]

The urgency of defending the state made the allies of the governor push to continue to organize the Union Party throughout Pennsylvania. Local activists worked to outmaneuver their rivals within the Republican element of the Union coalition and get non-Republicans a place at the state convention. In Snyder County, an effort was made "in a quiet way preparing the people to take a Stand to organise a union party and the union party to elect conferees to elect Delegates to the State Convention." The success of such a movement, one activist informed Secretary of the Commonwealth Eli Slifer, would be "a grade triompe [great triumph] for you over a faction [i.e., anti-Curtin Republicans and Democrats] who are determined to keep you down." A little more than a week after giving this assurance, War Democrats joined with other pro-Lincoln politicians in Snyder County to elect delegates to the state convention. One of those Democrats who spoke for two hours on behalf of his group was the lawyer Clinton Lloyd, who, according to one account, "sustaned [*sic*] the [Lincoln] Administration in all its meshers [measures]" and "made a strong appele [*sic*] to the true Democrats to do as he has don[e] to leve [*sic*] the corupt [*sic*] foul Disunion party &c."[22]

Despite the worry in some parts of their party over Curtin's performance during the rebel invasion, Unionist politicians touted the Union victory in July and distributed pamphlets to the voters urging them to support the Unionist Curtin and, through him, the national administration's war policies. The Union State Central Committee, under the chairmanship of Cameron's son-in-law, West Chester resident Wayne MacVeagh, circulated a long statement of their party's principles in the months just prior to the state election. The document reminded voters of the importance of their decision for the major state offices of governor and state supreme court judges. The Unionists stressed that "in other days we prudently occupied our minds with questions of State policy; local alike in their interest and influence." These were not "other days," however.[23]

The manifesto issued on behalf of the Central Committee betrayed a strong concern for the views of Democrats and other non-Republicans concerned about the amount of money and men expended in the war effort. The Union men sought to turn the tables on Democrats, who argued against the Lincoln administration's use of the draft and new forms of taxation to fund the war. In doing so, MacVeagh and his fellow Unionists tied Democratic victory to *"renewed conscriptions"* as well as an *"increase [in] the burdens of taxation"* well beyond anything the Curtin administration had done. The stakes were much greater than personal or even national interest: the current political contest in the state involved nothing less than "the destiny of free government throughout the world." Pennsylvanians, therefore, had to choose whether they wished to bring the war to a speedy end or leave it in the hands of those of questionable loyalty.[24]

Frustrated in their previous attempts to pass laws allowing soldiers to vote in the field or by being furloughed, some Unionist politicians tried once more prior to the gubernatorial election to secure this favorable voting bloc, but to no avail. George Hamersly, secretary of the Union State Central Committee, informed Thaddeus Stevens that the party could not push to implement his proposals for permitting soldiers to vote. The problem, Hamersly wrote, was that the army "is now generally believed to be on the march, [and thus] we fear there would be great difficulty in carrying out" Stevens's plan. "Indeed," he confessed, "it is very doubtful whether many of those in command of the Army Corps would allow their men to vote at present." The good news, however, was that "in some of the Regiments votes have already been taken, which exhibit great unanimity in favor of Gov. Curtin." Even though Stevens failed to obtain the use of a more liberal furlough policy for soldiers to vote, the instances of soldiers casting their ballots for the Union Party and Curtin must have proved heartening to Unionists.[25]

The last-minute personal intervention into the campaign of Major General George B. McClellan in the form of an Election Day letter of support for Woodward did not turn the tide for the Democratic nominee. But the final tally showed that Democrats could remain a force to be reckoned with in Pennsylvania. The results of the gubernatorial contest gave Curtin the advantage over Woodward by a margin of less than 3 percent. Though Curtin, still in ill health, successfully retained his executive chair, the breakdown of votes by county likely gave some of his supporters pause. Eight of Pennsylvania's sixty-six counties went from supporting Curtin in 1860 to supporting his opponent in 1863. Curtin's victory came largely from a switch in his favor in just one county, Philadelphia County. Woodward generally performed well in the southwestern, central, and northeastern sections of the state, which included the more rural and many traditionally Democratic-leaning counties. In contrast, Curtin drew his support primarily from northwestern and southeastern urban centers such as Pittsburgh, Erie, and Philadelphia. Most telling of the erosion in Curtin's popular support came in the fact that Curtin's majority over his Democratic challenger actually decreased by half, from just over thirty thousand in 1860 to a little more than fifteen thousand three years later. While the Republicans did regain control of the state legislature, they held control by just one seat in the senate and only four seats in the house. The very narrowness of the margin of victory impressed upon Unionists the importance of redoubling their efforts to pass a bill in favor of counting the soldier vote in the upcoming November presidential election.[26]

Reflecting the disarray within their party, Democrats' response to Curtin and the Unionist victories ranged from an increased determination to win next year to simple resignation and assertions of outright fraud. Yet in a number of letters, one finds the recognition among Democrats of the importance of the formation of the Union Party and its auxiliary, the Union League, in providing the margin of victory for Curtin. Democrat James Potts believed the cause of Democrats was hopeless given that "254 thousand unbought and unbribed democrats of Pennsylvania" had to compete with the "Secrete [*sic*] Union Leagues" and other Unionist organizations in order to win elections. Worse still, he maintained that Unionists employed "every decree to get timid democrats to join them, under the false but plausible plea, that they don't belong to any party, but are merely an organization to sustain the government in putting down the rebellion." Ultimately, he wrote, "when the war is over, they will all return to their respective parties." Indeed, the late election furnished ample evidence that the Unionists had "induced some timid democrats already to join them" and would persist in this strategy "until after the Presidential Election." Thomas W. Grayson complained that the Democratic defeat resulted from "weak and wicked men [being] bought like sheep." Grayson did not necessarily favor a recount, though, allowing that "if a majority of that body [State Democratic Central Committee] should determine otherwise, I will spare no effort in cooperating with them."[27]

In such a close contest, the importance of War Democrats to the Unionist state victories was not lost on the Unionists, either. The Philadelphia newspaperman and former Buchanan loyalist John Forney confessed to Pennsylvania Union Party chairman Wayne MacVeagh that "the result of the election in Penn[sylvani]a carried New York and it ought to be the source of extreme gratification to yourself and Gov. Curtin to know that in all quarters the highest compliments were bestowed upon the State Committee and on the matter in which our governor made his canvass." In a letter to Edward McPherson, a Pennsylvania Unionist saw the Union state victories in 1863 as clearing the way for President Lincoln's eventual reelection. General George B. McClellan, this Unionist believed, had irreparably harmed his chances when he opted to endorse Woodward instead of Curtin in the final days of the gubernatorial campaign. Still, it was essential to keep the Union Party coalition together, as the coalition that supported both the current state and national leaders achieved victory only because the votes of "the Union democrats" and a high turnout of Republicans worked to its advantage. The candidacy of a popular conservative Democrat like McClellan posed a real threat to the continued success of this formula.[28]

Aware of the popularity of McClellan within the ranks of the common soldier, Unionists carefully coordinated the national campaign for Lincoln with the state organizations like the one in Pennsylvania to distribute campaign literature. One secretary of the Union League from West Findley Township in Washington County came and spent "several days" among the troops of the Second Corps before they paraded for Vice President Hamlin and other national leaders. Declaring that "the importance of the pending contest for the Presidency cannot be exaggerated," Unionist brochures exhorted Unionists

to "aid in the election of Lincoln and Johnson and the general strengthen-
ing of the Union" through a "judicious distribution of PROPER DOCUMENTS
AND SPEECHES." These pamphlets would circulate within soldier camps and
in no small part shaped the perceptions of the conflict that historians investigating common soldiers have found within the armies.[29]

Paying little heed to Democratic denunciations of the supposedly "nonpartisan" Union Leagues, Unionists continued to stress that those organizations actually placed the preservation of the Union above mere party
considerations. In January 1864, the Philadelphia Union League tried to assure voters of its independent stance in politics by publishing an address that
described the league's purpose as "to unite men of all parties in the cause
of the country, that the loyal North might present an unbroken front in the
face of the traitors who are seeking our destruction." To this end, members
of the Union League pledged their unanimous support for Abraham Lincoln
in the upcoming presidential contest. The Unionists hoped that a show of
"unanimity so unexampled" would guarantee victory over the rebels and the
restoration of the Union to its former glory. This reliance on a nonpartisan
appeal grounded in national unity, while frustrating to the Democrats, enabled Unionists to extend fellowship to War Democrats in support of state
and national policies.[30]

Democrats gathered at their state convention in March 1864 to announce
their support for George B. McClellan, a native Philadelphian and one-time
Union commander. McClellan's endorsement of Woodward kept him in
good standing among Pennsylvania Democrats. There was little surprise at
the selection of McClellan for the state's Democratic endorsement. Seeking
to foster a sense of party unity, most Pennsylvania Democrats saw little reason to complain publicly about the elevation of a military man to the White
House. A prime reason for this acquiescence, according to one historian, was
that the former commander of the Army of the Potomac represented "an
unknown quantity" into which various groups could project their hopes and
aspirations. Democrats could then craft their platform around a man who
had not made many public speeches on political matters that would make
him a liability to the party.[31]

When Unionists finally assembled at their first national convention in
Baltimore in early June 1864, they prepared to nominate an executive ticket
in the midst of slow advances by both major Union armies. The situation in
the West saw William T. Sherman still inching toward Atlanta, while Confederate general Joseph E. Johnston managed to keep his army in front of the
Union commander and largely intact. The two major armies spent much time

in entrenchments, with Johnston waiting for Sherman's attack on his positions. Events in the eastern theater did not inspire Northerners very much, either. There, Ulysses S. Grant squared off with Robert E. Lee in a series of flanking maneuvers toward Richmond. The terrible news of Cold Harbor had just started to reach most Northerners, and Democratic cries for an immediate peace settlement grew even louder. It was in this atmosphere that Unionists stood together and declared their unanimous endorsement of Abraham Lincoln as well as a Tennessee Union Democrat, Andrew Johnson, for vice president.[32]

Some Unionists fretted about native son George McClellan winning the state's electoral votes unless pro-Union soldiers could have their ballots included in the final totals. During the campaign, the members of the Pennsylvania Union Party selected Simon Cameron as the Union State Central Committee Chairman to replace his son-in-law Wayne MacVeagh. One of his first actions as the new chairman was to quickly prepare an address entitled "The Soldier's Vote." "It is of the utmost importance," he wrote, "to get a full vote of our gallant soldiers in the army for our county tickets at the November election." In order to do this, Cameron asked all local Unionist officials to find out "who are enabled to vote, and of attending to the necessary work," adding that all the work "devolves upon you." The legislature had recently passed, on a strict party-line vote between Unionists and Democrats, a proposal for permitting soldiers who paid their ten-cent county poll taxes to vote, subject to a new popularly ratified amendment to the state constitution. Nevertheless, Unionist soldiers had to obtain documentation from their tax assessors in order to cast their ballots. Since the Unionist legislature in Pennsylvania had "secured to the soldier the right to vote," Cameron noted, any man loyal to the Lincoln administration should "see to it that he has every possible opportunity of exercising that right at the November election." Union Party members went busily to work appointing men to canvass and conduct the soldier vote.[33]

Despite the appeal contained in Cameron's circular, military leaders sometimes complained of the lack of attention the Union Party showed to men in the ranks. General Samuel Crawford, a native of Franklin County, found the leadership in Harrisburg strangely unreceptive to his pleas for assistance in getting soldiers to the polls. Representing the desires of his men in the Fifth Corps, Crawford reminded Wayne MacVeagh in mid-October that his "seven or eight Pa regiments" were ready to vote but said that "I do not think the proper attention has been paid to these men by their friends at home in regard to their assessment & I do not believe that half of them are qualified voters." He had tried to get a copy of the new law on soldier voting from Cameron but still waited for a response. Although Democrats came into camp trying to win over soldiers to McClellan before the election, Crawford complained that he had yet to see any men "of the loyal side of the question." Without any support from the home front to get soldiers to the polls, these valuable votes would be lost to the Pennsylvania Union Party.[34]

For all their hope in the soldier vote, though, prominent Unionists of Democratic extraction, such as John W. Forney, appealed to the national administration to offer patronage and policy concessions to the Union or War Democrats whose votes had allowed Unionists to carry close contests in states like Pennsylvania. Forney implored President Lincoln and other Republicans to recognize *"your bounden duty to take the earliest opportunity to recognize and to distinguish leading Union Democrats in every part of the country."* In particular, Forney deplored the way in which the Bell and Everett men had received a larger share of the offices than loyal Democrats had. Similarly, Governor Curtin worried that the upcoming presidential election might interfere with his attempts to pacify Democrats like Forney in the Union coalition. As Republicans and Democrats vied for the president's ear in attempting to shape the patronage policy toward the Pennsylvania Union Party, the seeds of a bitter contest after the war were already being sewn.[35]

By focusing on the need to support the Lincoln administration and the war for Union, Pennsylvania Unionists tried to overcome the criticism lodged at them for their support of conscription and emancipation as a war measure. Incumbent U.S. representative Henry W. Tracy endorsed Lincoln and Johnson and called upon his fellow citizens to join him. Pennsylvanians, he argued, must understand the "great and all-absorbing questions, whether the Union shall be preserved in its integrity, and whether our nationality shall be maintained." Significantly, the ex-Democrat Tracy pointed to the threat of "an organized and armed rebellion seeking to establish a Southern Confederacy, based upon an aristocracy, built upon slavery as its cornerstone," and seeking the destruction of the national government. With the national platform of the Union Party advocating a constitutional amendment against slavery, Democrats in the Union Party coalition like Tracy drew a dividing line between preserving slavery and preserving the Union.[36]

Another former Democrat, state legislator George F. Train, wrote to the editor of the *Philadelphia Age,* a Democratic-leaning newspaper, to explain his political course. In his estimation, the current national Democratic platform held just "three planks: STATE RIGHTS, that is SECESSION; FREE TRADE, that is DESTRUCTION; REPUDIATION, that is INFAMY. " He could not consent to being part of such an organization any longer. "The difference between us is," Train stated, that "you have party on the brain—I have country. . . . You despond when Sheridan beats Early—I cheer. . . . Your party has no opinions—mine has." The National Union City Executive Committee of Philadelphia presented a nightmarish image of a loyal North in the wake of a McClellan victory. Any armistice contemplated by the Democratic candidate "would enable the rebels to collect new supplies and munitions of war, to recruit their wasted armies, and again to take strong positions upon our *immediate borders,* ready, upon the resumption of hostilities, to desolate the North." To end the war, Pennsylvanians would have to shun those who emboldened the slaveholding enemies of the Republic.[37]

For all the Democratic appeals to racism and Lincoln's despotic rule, they could not prevail in Pennsylvania on Election Day in November. State elections in October had returned Union majorities, but the closeness of many of the individual contests made the November election very tight. For his part, McClellan won majorities in thirty-five of the sixty-six counties in the Keystone State. Every one of the fourteen counties whose state representatives opposed giving the vote to absentee soldiers went to McClellan and the Democrats. Indeed, the final total gave Lincoln a majority of only 20,075 votes out of 572,707 cast. This was only slightly better than Curtin's performance in 1863. Lincoln had also managed to gain almost 28,000 votes over his 1860 total, with over 26,000 coming from the soldiers themselves. In his study of the election, Arnold Shankman credited Lincoln's narrow victory entirely to the soldier vote, for Lincoln "received about two-thirds of the 39,000 army ballots, which gave him a 20,000 majority of the state's total vote." The Unionist strategy of 1864, which built upon the earlier efforts to win over a segment of Union Democrats and the Bell and Everett men, added soldiers to the coalition. Pennsylvanians, with the timely assistance of thousands of soldiers, had spared themselves from Copperhead rule and would now see the war conclude under both Union national and state governments.[38]

While the Union coalition had endured an uphill battle to victory, events after 1864 would see the resurgence of factional disputes concerning the proper policy of Reconstruction. The conclusion of the war and the process of Reconstruction raised divisions among Unionists over the status of newly freed African Americans in the reunited nation. While the Pennsylvania Union Party, despite the obvious tensions within that group, brought together various War Democrats, Constitutional Unionists, and Republicans, it did so with silence regarding racial readjustment issues. To be sure, Union men did talk about emancipation and accepted it as a necessary war measure, but there the agreement stopped. Once President Johnson and Radical Republicans in Congress began to argue over the future of the newly freed slaves, the Pennsylvania Union Party began to split internally along pro-Johnson and anti-Johnson lines. In part because of his efforts to cultivate alliances with Democrats during the war, Curtin found himself marginalized by his former Republican associates. Eventually he would leave the party altogether during the Liberal Republican bolt of 1872 and later made his way into the Democratic Party, where he would have a moderately successful career as a U.S. congressman.[39] Although he had tried to pursue policies as governor to broaden the base of the original Pennsylvania People's Party of 1860, in the end, Curtin left the governor's chair as a man embittered at national authorities for their insensitivity to his own electoral needs.

In time, a generation of Progressive reformers, including Henry Charles Lea, would carry on the reformist, antiparty ethos of the wartime Union Party into their political battles with Pennsylvania's Gilded Age party bosses. He and other reformers sought to purify the ballot box as well as regulate what they viewed as the excesses of a democratic system of mass partisanship too often susceptible to the control of "wire-pulling" politicians. All of these ideas had been expressed before—in the formation of the Pennsylvania Union Party. So while the Union Party ultimately had a short life, its intellectual impact on the course of Pennsylvania politics would prove enduring.

Notes

1. In this essay, I use the term "Union coalition" to indicate the informal alliance between Democrats, Constitutional Unionists, and Republicans that existed before the formal creation of the Pennsylvania Union Party in August 1863.

2. James M. McPherson, *Battle Cry of Freedom: The Civil War Era* (New York: Oxford University Press, 1988), 716–17. Michael Les Benedict's earlier study of the impeachment of Andrew Johnson also joins McPherson's stance on the meaning of the Republican/Union name change. Early on he writes, "During the war, Republicans had ostensibly submerged their party organization in a broader Union party. Although many former Democrats did join this new, expanded organization, it clearly retained its Republican character, and by 1865 the term 'Republican' was in general use again." Benedict, *The Impeachment and Trial of Andrew Johnson,* (New York: W. W. Norton, 1974), 2n2. For a similar evaluation, see Michael S. Green, *Freedom, Union, and Power: Lincoln and His Party during the Civil War* (New York: Fordham University Press, 2004), 289.

3. Michael F. Holt, "Abraham Lincoln and the Politics of Union," *Political Parties and American Political Development from the Age of Jackson to the Age of Lincoln* (Baton Rouge:

Louisiana State University Press, 1991), 330. For earlier studies that emphasize the possibilities of forming a national Union party both during and after the war, see William A. Dunning, "The Second Birth of the Republican Party," *American Historical Review* 16 (October 1910): 55–63; Roy F. Nichols, "A Great Party Which Might Have Been Born in Philadelphia," *Pennsylvania Magazine of History and Biography* 57 (October 1933): 359–74; and Christopher Dell, *Lincoln and the War Democrats: The Grand Erosion of the Conservative Tradition* (Rutherford, NJ: Fairleigh Dickinson University Press, 1979).

4. In highlighting interactions between state and national leaders, the present essay joins with recent attempts to call for a reevaluation of the ways federalism shaped the course of the Civil War. For instance, see Rachel A. Shelden, "Measures for a 'Speedy Conclusion': A Reexamination of Conscription and Civil War Federalism," *Civil War History* 55 (December 2009): 469–98; and William A. Blair, "We Are Coming, Father Abraham—Eventually: The Problem of Northern Nationalism in the Pennsylvania Recruiting Drives of 1862," in Joan D. Cashin, ed., *The War Was You and Me: Civilians in the Civil War* (Princeton, NJ: Princeton University Press, 2002), 183–208.

5. Herschel Johnson to Richard Vaux, November 28, 1860, Richard Vaux Papers, box 7, Historical Society of Pennsylvania, Philadelphia (hereafter HSP).

6. Duff Green to John Bell, January 16, 1859, John Bell Papers [microfilm], Library of Congress (hereafter LC); Jacob Dewees to Alexander Robinson Boteler, February 10 and 23, 1860, Alexander Robinson Boteler Papers, box 2, Duke University, Durham, NC; "The First Duty of the Citizen," [July 1862], Henry Charles Lea Papers, University of Pennsylvania, Philadelphia. Indeed, this case study of Pennsylvania's Union Party agrees in part with Adam I. P. Smith's recent analysis of the nonpartisan dimension of the Union Party appeal, while at the same time seeking to understand how local and state politicians helped channel the development of the Union Party movement. For an excellent statement of Smith's central thesis, see Adam I. P. Smith, *No Party Now: Politics in the Civil War North* (New York: Oxford University Press, 2006), 3–8. Another important work that stresses the ideal of antipartisanship in the Civil War is Mark Neely's *The Union Divided: Party Conflict in the Civil War North* (Cambridge, MA: Harvard University Press, 2002). Neely's work is particularly helpful in stressing the ways in which Unionists framed the debate between one's loyalty to country and one's loyalty to party. Finally, Joel Silbey has usefully characterized Pennsylvania on the basis of his analysis of its national and state elections, as one of only two "intensely competitive" states in the North for Democrats during the Civil War Era; see his *A Respectable Minority: The Democratic Party in the Civil War Era, 1860–1868* (New York: W. W. Norton, 1977), 152, table 6.2. For the position that voting alignments remained stable throughout the 1860s, see ibid., passim.

7. Israel Gutelius to Eli Slifer, August 26, 1861, Slifer-Dill Papers, box 5, Dickinson College, Carlisle, PA (hereafter DC).

8. William McCandless to Richard Vaux, August 26, 1861, Vaux Family Papers, box 7, HSP; James Buchanan to Lewis S. Coryell, September 18, 1861, Lewis S. Coryell Papers, HSP; Minutes of the Bell and Everett Association of the 15th Ward of Philadelphia, [ca. 1861 or 1862], HSP (third quote); *Philadelphia Inquirer,* October 5, 1861, and January 8, 1862.

9. J[ohn] B. Linn to Eli Slifer, September 12, 1861, Slifer-Wallis Papers, Bucknell University, Lewisburg, PA; B. R. Plumby to Simon Cameron, Simon Cameron Papers, reel 8, LC.

10. *Harrisburg Weekly Patriot and Union,* January 9 and 30, 1862; *Philadelphia Inquirer,* January 18, 1862; J. Glancy Jones to Lewis S. Coryell, June 5, 1862, Lewis S. Coryell Papers, HSP; William H. [?] to Simon Cameron, July 21, 1862, Simon Cameron Papers, reel 9, Dauphin County Collection.

11. *The American Annual Cyclopædia and Register of Important Events of the Year 1862* (New York: D. Appleton, 1863), 705.

12. Edwin Stanley Bradley, *The Triumph of Militant Republicanism: A Study of Pennsylvania and Presidential Politics, 1860–1872* (Philadelphia: University of Pennsylvania Press, 1964), 158; *The American Annual Cyclopædia and Register of Important Events of the Year 1862* (New York: D. Appleton, 1865), 705; "The Diary of Sidney George Fisher, 1862," entries for October 11 and November 5, 1862, *Pennsylvania Magazine of History and Biography* 88 (July 1964): 360–61; W. J. Woodward to Charles R. Buckalew, October 17, 1862, Charles R. Buckalew Papers, LC; J. W. Blackburn to John Covode, October 24, 1862, John Covode Papers, LC.

13. R. B. M. Creecy to Edward McPherson, January 31, 1863, Edward McPherson Papers, box 48, LC; Col. Alexander Hamilton to Simon Cameron, February 23, 1863, Simon Cameron Papers, reel 9, Dauphin County Collection (emphasis in original); *Harrisburg Weekly Patriot and Union,* March 12, 1863.

14. Neely, *Union Divided,* 27–32; Dan M. Smyser to Edward McPherson, January 25, 1863, Edward McPherson Papers, box 48, LC. Hartranft later became a successful Republican gubernatorial candidate in 1872.

15. Thomas Morris to Lewis S. Coryell, April 13, 1863, Lewis S. Coryell Papers, HSP.

16. George W. Woodward to Lewis S. Coryell, June 1, 1863, ibid.

17. An indication of the success of the exertions on behalf of Governor Curtin prior to the Battle of Gettysburg is that Painter received numerous telegrams from party activists between May and June that mostly pledged their support for Curtin. See Uriah Painter Papers, box 2, HSP; and Israel Gutelius to Eli Slifer, May 27, 1863, Slifer-Dill Papers, box 5, DC; see also Joseph J. Lewis to Wayne MacVeagh, June 1, 1863, MacVeagh Family Papers, box 2, HSP.

18. Edwin B. Coddington, *The Gettysburg Campaign: A Study in Command* (New York: Touchstone, 1968), 3–29; Alexander K. McClure to Eli Slifer, June 9, 1863, Slifer-Dill Papers, box 7, DC. For a good discussion of the problems encountered by the Curtin administration in securing popular support for federal conscription policies see Blair, "We Are Coming," 185–86, 193–94.

19. Andrew Curtin to Alexander Henry, June 14 and 15, 1863, Alexander Henry to Andrew Curtin, June 15, 1863 (first quote), Alexander Henry to William Whipple, June 15, 1863, Andrew Curtin to Henry D. Moore, William Walsh, and others, June 16, 1863, Andrew Curtin to Alexander Henry, June 18, 1863 (second quote), Alexander Henry to Andrew Curtin, June 19, 1863, all in Alexander Henry Papers, box 2, HSP. The references to the six-month minimum requirement followed the first section of the July 22, 1861, Act to Authorize the Employment of Volunteers to Aid in Enforcing the Laws and Protecting Public Property, *Congressional Globe,* 37th Cong., 1st Sess., appendix, 27–28. After the war, Curtin would deprecate the "thankless unjust and unmanly conduct of the national authorities" in the heady days of the conflict in a letter to Eli Slifer, December 28, 1865, in Slifer-Dill Papers, box 3, DC.

20. William W. Woodward to Lewis S. Coryell, June 27, 1863, Lewis S. Coryell Papers, HSP; John Covode to Uriah Painter, June 28, 1863, Uriah Painter Papers, box 2, HSP; "The Diary of Sidney George Fisher, 1863," entry for June 16, 1863, *Pennsylvania Magazine of History and Biography* 88 (October 1964): 469; James Langstaff Dunn to wife, July 5, 1863, James Langstaff Dunn Letters, Albert and Shirley Small Special Collections, University of Virginia, Charlottesville.

21. Charles J. Biddle to George W. Woodward, July 7, 1863, Biddle Family Papers, box 38, HSP; John Covode to President of the National Union National Convention, August 5, 1863, John Covode Papers, LC; H. D. Maxwell to Wayne MacVeagh, August 8, 1863, MacVeagh Family Papers, box 2, HSP; Bradley, *Triumph of Militant Republicanism*, 164–68. The mutually shared prejudices held by Philadelphians such as James Dunn toward rural Pennsylvanians and vice versa constituted a challenge for politicians seeking to organize a united Democratic opposition against the Union Party in the summer of 1863. For contemporary recognition of the strong regional antagonisms between rural and urban Pennsylvania Democrats, see John Cessna to Richard Vaux, April 3, 1862, Vaux Family Papers, box 7 and C[hristopher] L. Ward to George W. Woodward, June 18, 1863, Biddle Family Papers, box 38, HSP.

22. Israel Gutelius to Eli Slifer, June 13 and 22, 1863, Slifer-Dill Papers, box 5, DC.

23. "To the People of Pennsylvania," [1863], Henry D. Gilpin Collection, HSP.

24. Ibid. (emphasis in original).

25. George Hamersly to Thaddeus Stevens, September 29, 1863, Thaddeus Stevens Papers, box 2, LC.

26. Bradley, *Triumph of Militant Republicanism*, 427–28. The eight counties that went from supporting Curtin in 1860 to supporting his Democratic opponent in 1863 were Bucks, Centre, Clinton, Juniata, Luzerne, Lycoming, Monroe, and Wayne. The foregoing analysis of the geographical patterns of voting is based primarily upon "Pugh's Political Map of Pennsylvania," 1864, Henry D. Gilpin Collection, HSP; and *The American Annual Cyclopædia and Register of Important Events of the Year 1863* (New York: D. Appleton, 1864), 739–40.

27. James Potts to Charles J. Biddle, October 28, 1863, and Thomas W. Grayson to Charles J. Biddle, November 19, 1863, both in Biddle Family Papers, box 38, HSP. Edwin Bradley also acknowledges the importance of the Union League in obtaining votes during the 1863 campaign; see his *Triumph of Militant Republicanism*, 174.

28. John W. Forney to Wayne MacVeagh, November 10, 1863, MacVeagh Family Papers, box 2, HSP; J. R. Donnellson to Edward McPherson, November 5, 1863, Edward McPherson Papers, box 48, LC.

29. P. Paul to J. L. Harrison, March 3, 1864, Letters from John Batcheler and 4 Other Union Soldiers, University of Virginia, Charlottesville; "Union Congressional Committee Rooms," June 29, 1864, Edward McPherson Papers, box 49, LC. Two of the best studies of soldier motivation and ideology, James M. McPherson's *For Cause and Comrades: Why Men Fought the Civil War* (New York: Oxford University Press, 1997) and Chandra Manning's *What This Cruel War Was Over: Soldiers, Slavery, and the Civil War* (New York: Alfred A. Knopf, 2007), find abundant evidence for a high level of political commitment on the part of soldiers, yet both tend to play down the extent to which politicians and party activists *during the war* contributed to the level of politicization observed. Exactly what sort of political pamphlets and political speeches these activists disseminated within the

camps and to what extent this literature actually altered the common soldier's sense of the ultimate meaning of the war remains open to further investigation.

30. "Union League of the Twenty-Forth Ward, Philadelphia," January 19, 1864, Wayne McVeagh Family Papers, box 2, HSP.

31. Arnold Shankman, *The Pennsylvania Antiwar Movement, 1861–1865* (Madison, NJ: Fairleigh Dickinson University Press, 1980), 181–82.

32. McPherson, *Battle Cry of Freedom*, 689–750.

33. "The Soldier Vote," [1864], LC; Wayne MacVeagh to Eli Slifer, September 29, 1864, Slifer-Dill Papers, box 7, DC; Josiah Henry Bunting, *Voting in the Field: A Forgotten Chapter of the Civil War* (Boston: privately printed, 1915), 189–203; *The American Annual Cyclopædia and Register of Important Events of the Year 1864* (New York: D. Appleton, 1866), 649–50. The vote on the soldier amendment in August 1864 also reflected a division along strict party lines, 199,855 to 105,352, with Democratic counties voting against the measure by a margin of 8,611 votes and Unionists embracing it by a margin of 42,487 votes. For further discussion of the amendment, see Bunting, *Voting in the Field*, 200.

34. General S[amuel] W. Crawford to Wayne MacVeagh, October 13, 1864, MacVeagh Family Papers, box 3, HSP.

35. John W. Forney to Abraham Lincoln, October, 24, 1864, Abraham Lincoln Papers, LC (emphasis in original).

36. Printed broadside, "To the Electors of the 13th Congressional District of the State of Pennsylvania," *Bradford Argus* (extract), October 6, 1864, LC.

37. Printed broadside, "Letter from George F. Train," *Philadelphia Age* (extract), October 29, 1864, LC (emphasis in original); " To Every Patriot Irrespective of Party," November 1864, Henry D. Gilpin Collection, HSP.

38. Bradley, *Triumph of Militant Republicanism*, 428–29; Shankman, *The Pennsylvania Antiwar Movement*, 201. While Shankman correctly states the margin of victory that soldiers gave Lincoln over McClellan, it is important to bear in mind that Lincoln also narrowly won the home vote by a margin of 5,712 votes. See, for instance, results reported in *Annual Cyclopædia for 1864*, 650. Thus the soldier vote, as authorized during the special session of August 1864, augmented what would otherwise have been an exceedingly narrow Lincoln triumph.

39. For brief references to Curtin's involvement in the Liberal Republican movement, see Andrew L. Slap, *The Doom of Reconstruction: The Liberal Republicans in the Civil War Era* (New York: Fordham University Press, 2006), 134, 197.

Alabama's Presidential Reconstruction Legislature

J. Mills Thornton

The South's Presidential Reconstruction state legislatures have not had a good press. Suspicious Radical Republicans at the time thought them dominated by the former slavocracy and secessionists. The Black Codes enacted by a number of them seemed to Radicals—and not without good reason—to represent an effort to re-create slavery in another form. Modern scholars, beginning with W. E. B. Du Bois, have echoed these charges and have joined the Radicals in regarding the legislatures' membership and actions as proof of the fecklessness and racism of President Andrew Johnson's postwar policies. Yet few of these scholars have subjected the legislatures to close scrutiny. An examination of the personnel and proceedings of Alabama's legislature, for instance, must cause one at least to question many of the Radicals' suspicions and may even lead the student to doubt the wisdom of the Radicals' response to President Johnson's endeavors.[1]

Studies of Presidential Reconstruction have universally failed to note the marked decline in the wealth and social standing of the men elected to the initial postbellum legislatures. But in Alabama, at any rate, nothing is more significant than this fact.

Until the final dozen years of the antebellum period, Alabama's legislators had generally been men of relatively modest means. I have elsewhere explored the changing socioeconomic composition of the legislature before the Civil War.[2] In 1830 the median legislative slaveholding was 9, and in 1840 it was 9.5. In 1830 half of the legislators were in the middle class of small slaveholders (owners of five to nineteen slaves), while planters (owners of twenty or more slaves) and members of the lower-middle and lower grouping (nonslaveholders and owners of one to four slaves) were each a fourth of the members. Large planters (owners of fifty or more slaves) were only 7 percent of the total. By 1840 the increased social polarization that came with the advent of two-party competition had eroded the middle class's numbers from both above and below, so that planters, the middle class of small slaveholders, and the lower-middle and lower class members were each a third of the legislators. The economic and geographical divisions within the state upon which the party system was built—focused as it was primarily on questions of banking and internal improvements—are apparent in the legislators' slaveholdings; throughout this period, the median slaveholding of Whig legislators was double that of Democrats. But large planters were still only 10 percent of the membership.

The rise of the Young America movement within the Democratic Party in the years after the Mexican War had a marked effect on the wealth of Alabama legislators in the 1850s. The exacerbation of sectional tensions in national politics that flowed from Young America's enthusiasm for territorial aggrandizement and Young America's openness to internal improvements and economic modernization showed themselves in an increasing representation of planters among Alabama's lawmakers in the final antebellum decade. By 1850 the median legislative slaveholding had risen to 12.5, and by 1860 it had reached 17. In 1850 the lower-middle and lower class and the middle class were again each about a third of the legislators, as they had been in 1840. But the proportion of large planters advanced from 10 percent of the members to almost 18 percent. And by 1860, the lower-middle and lower grouping and the middle class had fallen in each case to about a fourth of the legislators, while planters were now half of the membership, and large planters were a fourth of it.[3]

The devastation wrought by civil war effectively burst the bubble of increasing legislative wealth that had characterized the 1850s and returned the lawmakers to the humbler status they had occupied for most of the antebellum era, even if measured in antebellum terms. This development seems to have begun in the general election of 1863, when secessionists suffered a widespread electoral repudiation. The median legislative slaveholding for the legislators chosen in November 1865 (derived from the census of 1860) fell from seventeen to eight, even less than it had been in 1830 (see table 1). The median among representatives was seven and among senators was thirteen. The lower-middle and lower grouping now formed some 40 percent of the legislators and the middle class perhaps 30 percent (see tables 2 and 3). The percentage of members in the lower-middle and lower classes was the largest proportion for that grouping of any legislature for which I have developed figures. The percentage of large planters, from 13 to 15 percent, depending on the data used, was a bit above the comparable figure from 1840 but was substantially less than proportions from the 1850s. In general, the legislators of Presidential Reconstruction were poorer than they had been since the early antebellum years. Of course all slaveholders were substantially poorer after emancipation, but the essential point is how much poorer the legislators of 1865–67 were than those of the final antebellum years, even when judged by 1860 standards.[4]

TABLE 1 Median slaveholdings among legislators, 1829–1867

	Total	House	Senate	% large slaveholders
1829–31	9	8	12	7
1839–41	9.5	8	19	10
1849–50	12.5	11	16	18
1859–60	17	14	19.5	23
1865–67	8	7	13	13

TABLE 2 Economic groupings in the legislatures, 1829–1850

	1829–31 (% by slaveholding)	1839–41 (% by) slaveholding)	1849–50 (% by) slaveholding)	1849–50 (% by) real estate)
Lower middle/lower	25	34	35	21
Middle	50	34	29	34
Small planters	18	22	18	28
Large planters	7	10	18	18

TABLE 3 Economic groupings in the legislatures, 1859–1867

	1859–1860			1865–1867		
	% by slave-holding	% by real estate	% by personal property	% by slave-holding	% by real estate	% by personal property
Lower middle/lower	31	22	30	41	34	43
Middle	25	28	21	31	36	27
Small planters	21	21	24	15	16	15
Large planters	23	29	25	13	13	15

Of course, the legislature did still contain a significant number of wealthy members. The counties of the eastern Black Belt seem to have been especially unchastened. Montgomery representative Tristram B. Bethea had owned 221 slaves, and his colleague Henry M. Caffey had owned 89. Senator Americus C. Mitchell of Barbour had owned 220 slaves. Macon County representative John C. Judkins had owned 84 slaves, and Senator James W. Castens of Russell had owned 83. Representative Gardner H. Davis of Barbour had owned 53 slaves, and Representative Nathan L. Brooks of Lowndes had owned 54. In the western Black Belt, Wilcox County also returned a wealthy delegation; Senator Aaron B. Cooper had owned 91 slaves, and Representative J. Richard Hawthorn had owned 110. Two of Perry County's representatives had owned 30 slaves, and the third had owned 36. But other counties in the area showed new doubts about planter leadership. Dallas County elected two Selma physicians, Drs. Albert G. Mabry and James T. Reese, each of whom had owned 4 slaves—although when Dr. Reese resigned, voters selected a young attorney, William Craig, whose father had owned 90 slaves.[5] Greene County, a center of the state's plantation agriculture, returned Senator Caswell C. Huckabee, a farmer who had owned 11 slaves, though his two colleagues in the house were both from large slaveholding families.

The plantation counties of the Tennessee Valley, where the war had been particularly destructive, showed similar ambivalence. One of Limestone's representatives, attorney William Richardson, had owned 30 slaves, but the other, Charles W. Raisler, was a cabinet maker who had owned only 1. Morgan County was represented in the senate by Dr. James M. Jackson, a physician who had owned 14 slaves, and in the house by Zenas F. Freeman, a nonslaveholding schoolteacher who was born in New York. Franklin County's senator was future governor Robert B. Lindsay, an attorney born in Scotland—the legislature's only foreign-born member—who had owned 14 slaves; its representatives were young attorney F. LeBaron Goodwin, who owned no slaves, and farmer Thomas Thorn, who had owned 11. Madison County was represented in the senate by farmer John N. Drake, who had owned 18 slaves, and in the house by planter William D. Humphrey, who had owned 44 slaves, and Huntsville merchant J. W. Ledbetter, who had owned 3.

The bulk of the legislature's poorer members came, of course, from the hill counties and the Wiregrass. Henry R. McCoy of Tallapoosa had been an archetypal yeoman farmer; a nonslaveholder, he had owned real estate valued at $425 and personal property worth $250. It was very likely the events of the war that elevated McCoy to the legislature; he had become a major in the Confederate army. But other members of the yeomanry had no such claims:

Henry McBee of Calhoun, Winston Steadham of Marion, Joseph D. McCann of Talladega, Henry F. Smith of Jackson, and W. C. Menefee of Pike had all been nonslaveholding farmers with property values comparable to McCoy's. All of the delegation from Randolph County, where resistance to the war had been strong, were nonslaveholders. Dr. Middleton R. Bell, who represented the county in the senate, was a physician and a close associate of Wedowee attorney William H. Smith, who in 1868 would become Alabama's first Radical Reconstruction governor; Dr. Bell too became a Republican. Randolph's three house members were a store clerk, a schoolteacher, and a farmer, all of them with very modest property holdings. The representative from Winston County, where resistance to the war had been even more intense, was also a nonslaveholder, carpenter John Wilhite, who also would become a Republican. Two other future Republicans were Elba physician Dr. John G. Moore and Rockford minister Rev. James Vansandt, both of whom were also nonslaveholders. George P. Plowman, who would become the leader of Talladega County's Republicans and the county's probate judge, had been the operator of a leather tannery and the owner of eight slaves.

Fayette County's delegation consisted of Senator Elliott P. Jones, a lawyer and farmer who had owned three slaves, and a merchant and two farmers in the house, the merchant a nonslaveholder and the farmers the owners, respectively, of one and two. Cherokee County's delegation was typical of the Appalachian counties. Senator Augustin L. Woodliff was a farmer who had owned two slaves. Thomas B. Cooper, an attorney who had owned ten slaves, became Speaker of the House. His colleagues were farmer John Lawrence, who had owned fourteen slaves, farmer John W. Brandon, a nonslaveholder, and Methodist minister John Potter (grandfather of the distinguished historian David M. Potter), who had owned two. Blount County, similarly, was represented in the senate by William H. Edwards, a schoolteacher who had owned no slaves, no real estate, and only $500 in personal property, and in the house by attorney A. M. Gibson and the young schoolteacher Solomon Palmer Jr.—a future state superintendent of education—both of whom were also nonslaveholders. The legislature was, in short, more fully representative of the general white population of the state in economic terms than any had been in perhaps two decades.

Another instructive insight into the effect of war and defeat on the electorate is the legislators' occupations. In the early antebellum decades, attorneys had been no more than 12 to 16 percent of the legislators, compared with 70 percent or more who were engaged in agriculture. But by the 1850s this balance had changed. In the final antebellum years, farmers fell to some

57 to 59 percent of the legislators, and lawyers rose to 26 or 27 percent of them. This tendency reached its high point in the secession convention, when only 43 percent of the delegates were in agriculture, and 37 percent were attorneys. And this rise in the proportion of lawyers had a most baleful effect: opponents of immediate secession were a majority both among delegates who were farmers and among delegates who were neither farmers nor attorneys, but lawyer delegates favored immediate secession by two to one.[6] This differential reflected the extensive tendency of ambitious young attorneys to associate themselves with the increasingly influential faction within the Democratic Party led by William Lowndes Yancey, doubtless in part in an effort to further their careers.

This disposition did not escape public notice. The same resentment that led to a decline in the wealth of the legislators chosen in November 1865 led also to new suspicions of attorneys. Though lawyers continued to be almost 29 percent of the senate, they fell to only about 15 percent of the house, returning to a proportion comparable to that usual before the 1850s. However, doubts about planter influence kept legislators engaged in agriculture to only about half of the members in each house, far below their early antebellum proportion. The result, especially among the representatives, was a sharp increase in the diversity of the occupations to be found among the members. Physicians were 8 percent of the house and 14 percent of the senate. Ministers were another 8 percent of the house, and merchants and related occupations were 9 percent of it. Thus, despite the continued power of the bar in the senate, attorneys' influence in the lower house was less than it had been for many years, and the diversity of occupations represented there was greater than at any previous time in the state's history.

Two final aspects of the legislature's membership are also significant. The first is nativity. Essentially all of the members were Southerners. Only five representatives and three senators had been born in nonslaveholding states. Georgians and native Alabamians together constituted a majority of each house, and they along with members native to the Carolinas and Tennessee accounted for more than 80 percent of the legislators in each body. Thus virtually all of the members had grown up amid slavery and had known no other world. The second is the number of novice lawmakers in the legislature. The substantial electoral repudiation of legislators from the 1850s and early 1860s had necessarily brought into the body many men who were new to it. Some 45 percent of the senators and 73 percent of the representatives had never served in the legislature before. Both of these factors are important to remember as we turn to the legislature's struggles to adjust to emancipation, which had come to Alabama just seven months before the members' election.

The constitutional convention that had met in September 1865 had formally abolished slavery in Alabama. Ironically, this very fact formed the principal argument against the ratification of the proposed Thirteenth Amendment, forbidding slavery in the United States, once the new legislature convened in November. As Senator John N. Drake of Huntsville, who led the senate opponents of ratification, told the upper house, because slavery had already been abolished in the South by the various state constitutional conventions, abolition could not have been the real goal of Congress in proposing the amendment. The actual intention of the congressional sponsors of the amendment, he argued, was to gain for the Congress, through the amendment's enforcement clause, the power to enact federal legislation governing the status of the freedmen and according them civil rights. The result would be to "establish the black race on a firmer and broader basis than will be allowed to the white race."[7] To deal with this objection, the house amended the ratification resolution by adding a reservation specifying that in ratifying, the legislature did not intend to confer on Congress the power to legislate upon the political status of the former slaves. With this proviso, the ratification resolution passed the house 75–17 and the senate 23–5. Alabama's ratification proved the crucial one, bringing the number of ratifying states to three-fourths and thus making the amendment a part of the Constitution.[8]

The fifteen representatives who voted against the addition of the reservation to the ratification resolution and the legislators who voted against ratification despite the reservation provide insight into the two extremes on the question of emancipation. The fifteen who preferred an unqualified ratification were generally poorer members from North Alabama. Twelve were from the hill counties and only three from plantation areas. No large planters and only two small planters were in the group; seven of them had been nonslaveholders. Three of them were among the nine representatives who would become Republicans. Four were so opposed to the reservation that they proceeded to vote against the ratification resolution itself once the reservation had been added to it. Excluding these four produces a group of eighteen legislators (thirteen representatives and five senators) intransigent in their opposition to emancipation. This group was substantially more diverse than the opponents of the reservation. Seven of the eighteen were from plantation counties, and eleven were not. Six had been planters, four of them large planters, but four had been nonslaveholders, and an additional six had owned fewer than ten slaves. The group included future U.S. Senator John H. Bankhead of Marion—only twenty-three years old and just out of the Confederate army—and Greensboro attorney John G. Pierce, both of them from large slaveholding families. But it also included Dr. John G. Moore of Coffee, a future Republican, and Stockton merchant George W. Robinson, a nonslaveholding native of New York, who represented Baldwin. The group was small, but the considerable diversity of those utterly unwilling to accept the outcome of the Civil War constitutes an index to the surprises that the roll calls would hold as the legislature turned to consider the condition of the freedmen.

Though the opponents of the Thirteenth Amendment had worried that it might transfer authority over the freedmen to the federal government, it is clear that the members of the legislature regarded the status of the freedmen as a concern principally for the former planters in their body. The adjustment of the former slaves to free labor was a matter of desperate anxiety for large landowners, as it was for the freedmen themselves, of course. But for most of Alabama's whites, the war had left far more pressing matters in its wake. Substantial numbers were living on the food parcels given out by the U.S. Army; even in late 1866, some 21,700 Alabamians—perhaps 10 percent of the state's families—were receiving federal relief supplies each month, with whites outnumbering blacks among them by two to one.[9] All of the state's banks had suspended specie payments, and only two had any prospect of resuming; their banknotes in circulation were nearly worthless as a result.[10] Debtors were in dire straits, with virtually no way to meet their obligations; creditors consequently were in almost equally difficult circumstances. The state government had very little income, and its institutions were struggling to function; the schools had ceased to do so at all. Railroads lacked the credit to rebuild their track and turned to the state for endorsement of their corporate bonds. The legislature had before it proposals to try to meet each of these predicaments—a stay law to delay suits for debt; internal improvement schemes; bills both to authorize specie suspension and to punish suspended banks; various suggestions for attempting to operate the schools, or simply closing them; ideas for how to re-create the state's revenue system now that the principal source of antebellum taxes, the slaves, had been eliminated; radical proposals for retrenchment; and a proposal to issue state bonds to relieve the widespread destitution among the citizenry. All of these issues produced deep divisions among the legislators, and all of them seemed much more urgent to most poorer white Alabamians than did the labor system on the plantations. As a result, in the early months of the new legislature's first session, the freedmen seem to have been the focus of attention chiefly of better-to-do members.

The committees on the freedmen established in each house reflected this situation. The chairman of the house committee was the wealthy Montgomery planter Tristram B. Bethea, whose 221 slaves had made him the legislature's single largest slaveholder. Five of the committee's twelve members were substantial slaveholders, and seven were from plantation counties. Similarly, the chairman of the senate committee was Aaron B. Cooper of Wilcox, who had owned ninety-one slaves. Five of its nine members had been extensive planters. Most of the bills reported from these committees—a ferocious bill to compel the freedmen to enter into labor contracts; a bill declaring any stubborn or refractory servant or any laborer who loitered away his time or refused to comply with a labor contract without just cause a vagrant, subject to being hired out to work on the county chain gang; an equally severe bill regulating black apprentices; a bill extending to every freedman all the highly discriminatory provisions of antebellum criminal law applying to free blacks—passed with little discussion, by voice vote. The one bill that generated conflict—because it was the one with general implications for poorer whites—opened the courts to freedmen on the same basis as all citizens and permitted black testimony in cases in which a freedman was a party.

Early efforts to get the legislators to take the rights of freedmen seriously gave little cause for optimism. Senator Francis W. Sykes of Lawrence, though he had owned forty-seven slaves in 1860, was one of the legislature's most racially liberal members and would become a founder of the state's Republican Party. At the outset of the session, he had introduced a bill to repeal all existing laws making a distinction of color. Senator Martin L. Stansel of Pickens, a Carrollton attorney, in an effort to convey his contempt for this proposal, moved to amend it to say "except the distinction which has existed since the days of Japhet and the curse of Ham." In the face of such scorn, Senator Sykes's bill was tabled, 16–11. Three of the eleven who opposed tabling were future Republicans, while none of the sixteen for tabling was.[11]

Yet, though the chances initially looked bleak for an enlightened racial policy, the outcome would be very different. The reversal turned upon the intervention of Governor Robert M. Patton. Patton, a Florence merchant and planter, had strongly opposed secession, but he had owned 117 slaves in 1860, and he was certainly not moved by any sense of racial egalitarianism. In his inaugural address, he told Alabamians, "It must be understood that, politically and socially, ours is a white man's government. In the future, as has been the case in the past, the state affairs of Alabama must be guided and controlled by the superior intelligence of the white man." And in his annual message in November 1866, he emphasized that the freedmen "should be especially taught the utter absurdity of expecting or aspiring to a condition of social equality with the white race. To do so would be to struggle against a palpable and inexorable decree of Providence."[12] Nevertheless, Patton was deeply committed to paternalist ideals. "We have a high moral duty to perform toward the freedmen," he said in the same annual message. "Let them be convinced that we are their friends and that we feel an interest in their prosperity and welfare. They should be assured of our firm purpose to give them all of their legal rights." And in his initial annual message he had lectured the legislators, "Surely no good, law-abiding citizen will desire laws for the government of the unintelligent negro which he himself is unwilling to abide by. No good to the country can result from having one code of laws for the whites and another for the blacks in their new relations, so far as concern the rights of persons and property."[13]

It was against this background that Governor Patton approached the mass of legislation regulating the former slaves that had passed the legislature with so little dissent. Patton was inaugurated on December 13, 1865, and two days later the legislature adjourned for its Christmas recess, leaving the bills on the new governor's desk. When the lawmakers returned just after the new year, Patton greeted them with a flurry of veto messages. The bill governing black apprentices was class legislation, he told the house; the general provisions of the code on apprenticeships were ample regulation for all persons of both races. No legislation governing the labor contracts of the freedmen was necessary, he said to the senate; the state already had general laws governing contracts, and the freedmen should be able to look to the courts to protect their natural rights without any discriminating statutes. And the bill extending the antebellum laws governing free blacks to the freedmen would create absurd or inoperable results; one of them, for instance, would require almost all freedmen to leave the state.[14]

The gubernatorial objections had an electric effect. The bills that had passed with essentially no dissent now suddenly provoked the deep divisions that questions surrounding banking, internal improvements, and social reform always had. The house sustained the governor's veto of the black apprenticeships bill, 42–51. Of the 51 voting to sustain the veto, 23 had been nonslaveholders, and an additional 15 had owned fewer than 10 slaves. Just 5 had been planters. Eight came from plantation counties, while 43 were from nonplantation counties. Of the 42 voting to override the veto, 15 had been planters. Only 7 had been nonslaveholders, and an additional 13 had owned fewer than 10 slaves. Twenty-two came from plantation counties and 20 from nonplantation counties. The economic and geographical divisions in the voting thus are clear. In addition, 8 of those voting to sustain the veto would become Republicans, while none of those voting to override would. The senate sustained the governor's veto of the bill to compel freedmen to enter into and abide by labor contracts, 15–18. Here the divisions of wealth were less clear; 6 former planters voted to override the veto, and 6 to sustain it. But of the 18 voting to sustain the veto, 13 were from North Alabama and only 5 from South Alabama, while of the 15 voting to override the veto, 9 were from South Alabama and 6 from north Alabama. Only one senator—John Drake of Madison, who had led the fight against the Thirteenth Amendment—voted to override the veto of the bill extending antebellum laws governing free blacks to all freedmen.[15]

Throughout the antebellum era, legislators from the small-farm counties had been on their guard against the specter of planter domination. Certain questions, such as taxation, had always aroused such feelings. Indeed, in the session of 1865–66, as legislators searched for some revenue source to replace the tax on slaves and thus to allow the real property tax to remain low, planter legislators had hit upon the scheme of placing a high tax on the stills that throughout the hills turned the corn crop into liquor. The Revenue Act of 1866 placed a property tax on every still of two dollars for every gallon of its capacity and in addition a production tax of fifty cents for every gallon distilled. Representative James Williams from the Appalachian county of Jackson railed at this levy. Planters, he said, "have shaped the legislation of this session" and were half the membership of the Ways and Means Committee (an accurate allegation). Rather than tax the "great staple commodity, cotton," they had "shifted the burdens on other men's shoulders—on my constituents, and on North Alabama generally, by imposing an onerous capitation tax and by taxing their little distilleries. . . . If the poor pay the tax, fight the battles, hew the wood and draw the water, certain it is, a poor man in Alabama is not to be envied now." As Williams predicted, the tax on distilling created an uproar across the hills and the Wiregrass, and when the legislature reconvened the following fall, at the urging of Governor Patton, it repealed the Revenue Act altogether and substituted a new one, eliminating the property tax on stills completely and reducing the production tax from fifty cents a gallon to five cents.[16]

It was struggles such as this one that had formed Alabama's antebellum political culture, and the electorate fully understood their implications of culture and class. But these beliefs had not heretofore been extended across the barrier of race. In the days of slavery, black people, as property, were an element of wealth, to be envied or resented, perhaps, but merely a symbol in the conflicts over white political equality. And the persistence of such attitudes toward blacks is apparent in the feeling widespread among less well-to-do legislators early in the session, as we have said, that the regulation of plantation labor was a concern of planters but essentially irrelevant to the rest of the electorate. Governor Patton in his veto messages, however, had placed the matter in a different light. He had called the bills class legislation because there were already general laws governing apprenticeships and contracts, and these additional bills sought to carve out a portion of the citizenry, at least as newly defined, to whom different, and harsher, regulations would apply. This was a logic that reached back to Jacksonian denunciations of special privileges for chartered corporations, and legislators from the small-farming areas immediately grasped the threat. Planters who sought special regulations for their labor force were only too ready to seek special advantage in tax policies, for instance, as their actions as to the revenue bill clearly showed. Suddenly the racial legislation became a matter of general concern.

The one piece of legislation regulating the freedmen that did become law was the vagrancy bill, declaring all stubborn or refractory servants vagrants, subject to the county chain gang. It had been signed by provisional governor Lewis E. Parsons before Governor Patton's inauguration. But even this act was not long for the statute books. Later in the session the legislature passed a new state penal code, drafted by former and future state supreme court justice George W. Stone. The new penal code contained its own, nonracial vagrancy provisions, and it provided that all laws in conflict with it were repealed. The courts generally held therefore that the provisions of the new code had superseded the vagrancy statute, and to clarify the situation, the legislature at its second session formally repealed the vagrancy law.[17]

The only piece of legislation then left with restrictions on the freedmen was the law opening the courts to them and permitting them to testify if a black person were a party to the case. But this act, which passed only after a considerable struggle and no less than two conference committees, had actually represented a victory by more progressive members over more racially conservative ones. Future Republicans had supported it overwhelmingly through all of its versions, against determined planter opposition; eleven of the twenty-eight representatives who voted against the bill on final passage were planters, and every future Republican voting favored it.[18] Governor Patton regarded the bill as such a success that he urged the legislature at its second session to eliminate all restrictions on black testimony, though the lawmakers were unwilling to reopen the question.[19] The legislature enacted one other statute with clear implications for the freedmen, a law making it a misdemeanor punishable by a fine of up to $500 for one employer to lure away a worker under contract to another employer. But though this act certainly limited the ability of freedmen to seek better pay, its criminal penalties were only directed at whites.[20]

The essential defeat of the Black Code in Alabama is too seldom emphasized. And the failure to emphasize this defeat is especially regrettable because the circumstances that produced it also formed the background to the rejection of the Fourteenth Amendment at the legislature's second session. Let us now turn to that half of the story.

As the first session of the legislature was coming to an end in February 1866, a joint committee cochaired by future Republican attorney general Joshua Morse of Choctaw submitted an angry report denouncing "the falsehoods propagated in the North and in Congress" about Southern racial conditions, which it said were "circulated only for the basest political purposes." It then submitted, and the legislature adopted unanimously, resolutions opposing the proposed Fourteenth Amendment; stated one, "Alabama will not voluntarily consent to change the adjustment of political power as fixed in the Constitution of the United States, and to constrain her to do so in her present prostrate and helpless condition, with no voice in the councils of the nation, would be an unjustifiable breach of faith."[21] By the time the legislature reconvened for its second session the following November, the Fourteenth Amendment had been formally submitted to the states for ratification. In his annual message, Governor Patton condemned it. Its provisions would vastly increase the power of the federal courts and would subject state court decisions to the review of federal judges, he told the legislators, quite correctly. And unless the Southern states agreed to enfranchise the freedmen, they would lose half their representatives in Congress. For those and other reasons, Patton urged the legislature to refuse to ratify it.[22]

Two different lines of response to the amendment quickly emerged. In the senate the racially liberal Lawrence County planter and physician Francis W. Sykes, seeking to save the amendment from Governor Patton's assault, proposed resolutions submitting the amendment to a popular referendum. A committee headed by future governor Robert B. Lindsay reported adversely to the resolutions, and they were tabled, 21–9. Three of the nine opponents of tabling filed a statement saying that they had voted nay merely to allow Senator Sykes to speak in support of his resolutions but that they were opposed to them. Of the remaining six, four were among the five members of the senate who would become Republicans.[23]

Early in December 1866, just before the legislature was to take its Christmas recess, Governor Patton sent both houses a special message saying that it had now become apparent that the Congress considered ratification of the amendment a prerequisite to readmission of the Southern states to the Union. Under these circumstances, Patton suggested that the legislature might ratify to regain membership in Congress and then hope that the state's readmitted members could mitigate the amendment's effects in the future. To emphasize its contempt for this advice, the senate formally voted to reject the amendment, 28–3, with only three future Republicans—Middleton R. Bell, Adam C. Felder, and Francis W. Sykes—supporting ratification. Sykes once again sought a popular referendum on the amendment, but his proposal was tabled by voice vote.[24]

The senate resolution refusing ratification then went to the house. The future Republican attorney general Joshua Morse took up Sykes's idea and proposed a popular referendum on the amendment. But the proposal was rejected, 49–24, and the resolutions refusing to ratify were then approved, 71–9. Only one of the nine supporters of ratification had been a significant slaveholder, Prattville attorney Charles S. G. Doster, who would become a Republican. Of the other eight, six had been nonslaveholders and the other two owners of ten and two slaves, respectively. The twenty-four representatives who had supported a popular referendum included only two owners of twenty or more slaves, Doster and Nathan L. Brooks of Lowndes, about whom I will have more to say shortly. Nine of the twenty-four had been nonslaveholders, and another nine had owned ten or fewer slaves. With these votes the idea of submitting the Fourteenth Amendment to a popular referendum died, as did any prospects for ratification.[25]

In the meantime, however, another line of response to Radical Republican demands was developing in the house. The leader of this effort was Nathan L. Brooks, a Lowndes County planter and antebellum legislator who had owned fifty-four slaves. Brooks's idea reached back to events at the state constitutional convention in September 1865. Alabama's constitution of 1819 had provided that membership in both houses of the state legislature would be apportioned among the counties on the basis solely of white population, and under this constitutional mandate the small-farming counties had dominated the legislature throughout the antebellum period, to the great chagrin of the plantation counties. But with the emancipation of the slaves, delegates to the 1865 constitutional convention from the plantation counties had seen the prospect of changing this situation. Now that blacks were free, they argued, legislative representation should reflect their numbers. Plantation county delegates pushed hard for apportionment on the basis of total population. But the constitutional convention was itself apportioned on the basis of white population, and the Black Belt efforts had proven futile. The constitution of 1865 repeated the apportionment provisions of the constitution of 1819.[26]

The Fourteenth Amendment's section reducing the states' congressional representation by the proportion of their disfranchised male population offered Representative Brooks the chance to reopen this question, however. His initial proposal was to amend the state constitution to permit literate freedmen to vote. This change would have the immediate effect of blunting the reduction of congressional representation under the Fourteenth Amendment and in the longer term could provide the foundation for seeking increased legislative membership for the Black Belt counties. The house tabled this amendment, 72–16. Four of the sixteen opposed to tabling filed statements saying that they had voted against tabling because they were so completely opposed to the amendment that they wanted to vote against it on the merits. Of the remaining twelve, six were from the Black Belt and had been large slaveholders, and five of the other six (four nonslaveholders and two small slaveholders) were from the hill counties. Despite its overwhelming defeat, therefore, Brooks's proposal had begun to draw together the sort of coalition for which he clearly was aiming: Black Belters who sought greater legislative influence for their area and hill county progressives sympathetic to the ideas of the emerging Republican Party. Brooks and his allies therefore pressed on.[27]

Their next effort came after the legislature's return from its Christmas recess, when they advanced a proposal to submit to the voters the question of whether to call a new constitutional convention. A convention, of course, would allow the reconsideration of both the suffrage and the legislative apportionment provisions. The house tabled this resolution, 51–30.[28] Of the 30 members who supported Brooks's position, 11 were planters, and 14 were either nonslaveholders (four of them) or owners of ten or fewer slaves. Twelve came from plantation counties and 18 from nonplantation counties. But in fact, Brooks's opponents represented the coalition that Brooks was attempting to build almost as well as his supporters did. Eight of the 51 members who voted to table were planters, 17 were nonslaveholders, and 18 more owned ten or fewer slaves. Nineteen were from plantation counties and 32 from nonplantation counties. It is clear that Brooks had failed both to unify the plantation county representatives behind his strategy and to draw many of the poorer members to his cause. Moreover, though three of the future Republicans in the house supported him, five voted with his opponents.

The challenge that Brooks faced was twofold. He had to convince the planters that they would be able to control a literate black vote in their counties, so that in gaining additional representation for their areas, they would not find themselves voted out of office. This evidently was Brooks's own belief, so he could make this argument to his Black Belt challengers with sincerity. At the same time, however, probably in quieter conversations with representatives from the hill counties and the Wiregrass, he presumably would have had to have made the case that enfranchised blacks would vote with poorer whites in defense of egalitarian policies and in opposition to planter hegemony. This for Brooks was certainly a more disingenuous claim. But the fears felt by many planters of the enmity of their former slaves was exceeded only by small farmers' general conviction that the planters would be able to manipulate the votes of their black dependents. Thus Brooks was placed in the position of having to advance to the different constituencies precisely contradictory predictions of blacks' possible behavior if he were to draw them both to the support of his bill. Unless he could overcome both sets of white fears simultaneously, he had no hope of building the coalition he sought. And without such a coalition, he had no prospect of allaying the suspicions of the Radicals in Congress and forestalling their plans for draconian measures.

Brooks's third and final effort came at the end of the legislative session. By that time Military Reconstruction was pending in Congress, and Brooks clearly felt that the changed circumstances might lead enough legislators to reconsider their position that his ideas might now be accepted. Thus in mid-February 1867, Brooks rose to seek a suspension of the rules to permit him again to propose a referendum on summoning a new state constitutional convention. He did do a bit better on this try, but the house again voted him down, 34–45.[29] The number of planters who supported Brooks's position fell from eleven to seven, while the number of nonslaveholders who voted with him rose from four to ten. Apparently the growing strength of Radical sentiment in the North had increased both planters' fears and at least some small farmers' confidence in the prospects for an independent black electorate. The support of nonplanter slaveholders remained about the same, 15 on the earlier vote and 17 on this one. Eleven of the 34 members supporting Brooks came from plantation counties and 23 from nonplantation counties. Only 12 of the 30 members who had voted with Brooks on the earlier roll call remained with him on this one. Eleven planters voted against Brooks now, along with 14 nonslaveholders and an additional 14 members who had owned ten or fewer slaves. Sixteen of his opponents came from plantation counties and 29 from nonplantation counties. As in the earlier vote, 3 future Republicans supported Brooks and 5 opposed him. And so Brooks's last effort failed and, with it, any prospect that the legislature might seek to accommodate Radical demands.

It is surely an irony of the darkest hue that the same social attitudes that had produced the legislature's rejection of a Black Code produced also its inability to compromise with the Radicals' suspicions. But that is the case. When Governor Patton warned that acts imposing disparate regulations on the freedmen constituted class legislation, poorer legislators joined overwhelmingly to sustain his vetoes. They fully understood the danger of creating special exceptions to general provisions of law to benefit the planters or other wealthy elements. This fear had been the central emphasis of Jacksonian politics, and the consequences of excessive planter influence had been starkly accentuated by the death and destruction of the war, which had produced the extensive repudiation of late antebellum leadership in the election of this very legislature. On the other hand, the dread of planter domination was equally at work in the prospect of eliminating the white basis for legislative apportionment and the resultant transfer of seats from the hill counties and the Wiregrass to the Black Belt. Even an independent black electorate would have interests substantially different from those of white small farmers. But it was not independence that most hill county legislators actually expected; they foresaw—and the history of Alabama in the latter decades of the nineteenth century fully substantiated their fears—a black vote subject to planter manipulation, whether through economic pressures or physical intimidation. The hostility to planter power underlay both small-farmer legislators' rejection of the Fourteenth Amendment, with its provisions intended to push the Southern states into enfranchising the freedmen, and the repudiation of the possibility of such an enfranchisement itself, in the form of Nathan Brooks's efforts to summon a new constitutional convention or to amend the constitution to authorize it.

There can be no doubt that the Radicals in Congress had no real understanding of the subtleties of social conflict in the Lower South. A great many of them were afflicted with a romantic faith in democracy that led them to believe that black enfranchisement would solve the region's problems at a single stroke. Virtually none of them appreciated that the addition of blacks to the electorate would represent for a state like Alabama a massive intrastate sectional shift in legislative and political influence from the small-farming to the plantation counties. Indeed, almost all Radicals thought that planters controlled Southern politics already and understood themselves to be attacking, rather than threatening to strengthen, planter influence. But legislators from Alabama's hills and Wiregrass were under no such illusions. We can certainly imagine measures that might have established an independent black electorate. But that would have required a permanent occupying army sufficient to protect black voters from reprisals and an implacable refusal of amnesty for the planters' leadership. The number of Northerners prepared to maintain such measures on a long-term basis was vanishingly small. And since the number of Southern whites who accepted the legitimacy of independent black electoral participation was almost equally minuscule, it was by no means unreasonable for small-farmer legislators to regard the enfranchisement of the freedmen as a step toward planter rule of the state.

It is impossible today not to sympathize with those greathearted Americans who sought full citizenship for the freedmen. But however noble their goals, they reckoned without a sufficient appreciation of the force of history. A society that had assumed the naturalness of slavery for more than two centuries and that had experienced black freedom for only a matter of months could hardly have been expected to grasp the full possibilities of emancipation. And it is surely that chasm of white incredulity that, more than any other single factor, condemned Radical Reconstruction to failure. The widespread violence and fraud that suppressed the black vote during Radical Reconstruction itself and the electoral machinations of the Redeemers to crush white small-farmer resistance thereafter both reflected the general white conviction that blacks were not—and were incapable of becoming—authentic partners in democratic decision making. Theirs was, as they said repeatedly, a white man's government.

Nevertheless, the voting in the Presidential Reconstruction legislature emphasizes another, equally significant truth. Though the legislators from the small farming counties were certainly not open to any recognizable notions of racial equality, their strong sense of class conflict and the threat posed by their planter rivals could bring them to positions that had positive racial implications. This outcome was an especially important element of the populist revolt.[30] But as the defeat of the Black Code demonstrated, this potential had been present from the beginning. Its sources stretch back to the battles of the Jacksonian era. The white small farmers' beliefs very rarely extended to an acceptance of black social equality. But when racial discrimination encompassed behavior that threatened the equal citizenship of poorer whites, wealthier political forces could very suddenly find themselves confronted with incensed small-farmer opposition. The emergence of the one-party system after Reconstruction deprived these attitudes, except in the brief period of populism, of the institutional structure that could otherwise have given them full scope for their expression. But they had always been there. A recognition of this fact is essential to a complete understanding of the patterns of Southern history.

Notes

1. By far the most careful examination of the Southern state governments under Presidential Reconstruction is Dan T. Carter, *When the War Was Over: The Failure of Self-Reconstruction in the South, 1865–1867* (Baton Rouge: Louisiana State University Press, 1985). Also useful is Michael Perman, *Reunion without Compromise: The South and Reconstruction, 1865–1868* (Cambridge: Cambridge University Press, 1973). On the period in general, the standard work is Eric Foner, *Reconstruction: America's Unfinished Revolution, 1863–1877* (New York: Harper & Row, 1988); see also W. E. B. Du Bois, *Black Reconstruction . . . in America, 1860–1880* (New York: Harcourt, Brace, 1935). On President Johnson, see Eric McKitrick, *Andrew Johnson and Reconstruction* (Chicago: University of Chicago Press, 1960); and La Wanda and John H. Cox, *Politics, Principle, and Prejudice, 1865–1866: Dilemma of Reconstruction America* (New York: Free Press, 1963). On the Black Codes, see Theodore B. Wilson, *The Black Codes of the South* (University: University of Alabama Press, 1965). On Alabama, see Sarah Woolfolk Wiggins, *The Scalawag in Alabama Politics, 1865–1881* (University: University of Alabama Press, 1977); Peter Kolchin, *First Freedom: The Response of Alabama's Blacks to Emancipation and Reconstruction* (Westport, CT: Greenwood, 1972); Margaret M. Storey, *Loyalty and Loss: Alabama's Unionists in Civil War and Reconstruction* (Baton Rouge: Louisiana State University Press, 2004); and Michael W. Fitzgerald, *Urban Emancipation: Popular Politics in Reconstruction Mobile, 1860–1890* (Baton Rouge: Louisiana State University Press, 2002).

2. See my *Politics and Power in a Slave Society: Alabama, 1800–1860* (Baton Rouge: Louisiana State University Press, 1978), 60–68, 296–99. The determination of class status is of course a very tricky business, especially before the census of 1850, when slaveholding is the only indication we have of an individual's wealth. In the work cited, I adopted the approximate relationships between class and slaveholding suggested by Ulrich B. Phillips in his *Life and Labor in the Old South* (1929; Boston: Little, Brown, 1963), 339. Phillips calls twenty slaves "roughly a minimum for the plantation method" of agriculture. He ranks owners of five to nineteen slaves "as a middle class of large farmers and comfortable townsmen." Holders of four or fewer slaves, including the vast numbers of nonslaveholders, Phillips thus presumably places in a lower-middle and lower grouping. To these divisions I added a final boundary not suggested by Phillips, letting fifty slaves mark the division between small and large planters. With the census of 1850 we gain the value of the household

head's real estate and, in 1860, both his real estate and his personal property. I formed scattergrams to relate legislators' slaveholdings with these figures and derived boundaries in dollars from them. In 1860, the upper limit for the poorest group was $3,000 in real estate and $10,000 in personal property; for the middling group, $10,000 in real estate and $27,500 in personal property; and for the small planters, $20,000 in real estate and $55,000 in personal property. I have carried all of these figures forward to the legislature elected in 1865. Of course all slaveholders were substantially poorer after emancipation, but my point here is how much poorer the legislators of 1865 were than those of 1859–1860, even when judged by 1860 standards.

3. Thornton, *Politics and Power,,* 61–64, 296–99.

4. Wiggins, *Scalawag in Alabama Politics,* 6–7. President Johnson's policy had initially disfranchised persons who owned more than $20,000 in property unless they received an individual pardon. But the president granted these pardons freely, and that the limitation barred very few former large slaveholders from political participation is demonstrated by the fact that so many of them were chosen to represent the plantation counties. It was not presidential policy but the electorate that actually was responsible for the decline in legislative wealth.

5. In the case of young legislators who were residing with their parents at the time of the 1860 census, I have used the property holdings of the head of the household in the summary statistics.

6. Thornton, *Politics and Power,* 64, 299, 426.

7. Senate Journal (hereafter cited as SJ) 1865–66, 83–84.

8. House Journal (hereafter cited as HJ) 1865–66, 85–88; SJ 1865–66, 77, 79–80; *Acts of Alabama,* Sess. of 1865–66, 597–98.

9. HJ 1866–67, 26–27, 254–55.

10. Ibid., 16–17.

11. SJ 1865–66, 140–41.

12. HJ 1865–66, 159; HJ 1866–67, 25–26.

13. HJ 1866–67, 25–26; HJ 1865–66, 192.

14. HJ 1865–66, 206–7; SJ 1865–66, 162–64.

15. HJ 1865–66, 236, 237; SJ 1865–66, 188, 190. The initial recorded vote in the house was 40–51, but two additional members subsequently asked to be recorded as voting yea.

16. HJ 1865–66, 424–25; HJ 1866–67, 11–12; *Acts of Alabama,* Sess. of 1865–66, 3–36, Sess. of 1866–67, 259–96. On the general significance of tax policy in this period, see my "Fiscal Policy and the Failure of Radical Reconstruction in the Lower South," in J. Morgan Kousser and James M. McPherson, eds., *Region, Race, and Reconstruction: Essays in Honor of C. Vann Woodward* (New York: Oxford University Press, 1982), 349–94.

17. *Acts of Alabama,* Sess. of 1865–66, 116, 119–24, Sess. of 1866–67, 504.

18. HJ 1865–66, 100–101, 106–7, 113, 116–17, 120, 127–28; *Acts of Alabama,* Sess. of 1865–66, 98.

19. HJ 1866–67, 25–26; *Acts of Alabama,* Sess. of 1866–67, 435.

20. *Acts of Alabama,* Sess. of 1865–66, 111–12.

21. HJ 1865–66, 416–20; *Acts of Alabama,* Sess. of 1865–66, 606–7.

22. HJ 1866–67, 32–37.

23. SJ 1866–67, 154–56. The four future Republicans were Dr. Sykes himself, Dr.

Middleton R. Bell of Randolph, Montgomery attorney Adam C. Felder, and Dr. John T. Foster of Choctaw; three of the four were physicians. The one future Republican who consistently opposed the amendment was Tallapoosa farmer Alfred H. Slaughter, who shortly thereafter resigned from the legislature.

24. SJ 1866–67, 176–77, 182–83.

25. HJ 1866–67, 209–14.

26. Wiggins, *Scalawag in Alabama Politics*, 12–15. Professor Wiggins's account of these events, however, is marred by her apparent misunderstanding of the antebellum constitutional provisions. See also Malcolm C. McMillan, *Constitutional Development in Alabama, 1798–1901: A Study in Politics, the Negro, and Sectionalism* (Chapel Hill: University of North Carolina Press, 1955), 90–109, especially 104–5. In 1842, the white basis was extended to congressional districts as well, over the furious opposition of Whigs and Black Belters.

27. HJ 1866–67, 160–62.

28. Ibid., 395–96.

29. Ibid., 476–77.

30. On this point see, of course, the work of C. Vann Woodward, especially *Tom Watson, Agrarian Rebel* (New York: Macmillan, 1938), *Origins of the New South, 1877–1913* (Baton Rouge: Louisiana State University Press, 1951), and *The Strange Career of Jim Crow* (New York: Oxford University Press, 1955).

The Fate of Northern Democrats after the Civil War

Another Look at the Presidential Election of 1868

Erik B. Alexander

"Never before, in the history of the country have I been willing to see policy in any contingency, have any sort of dominion over principle," wrote Samuel M. Johnson, a Democrat from New York, to fellow Democrat Horatio Seymour in April 1868. "I think it possible," Johnson continued, "that in the coming canvass, we shall be called upon to consider not whether we shall sacrifice a principle, but whether we ought to select a candidate exclusively on the ground of his known qualifications. We may find it necessary, in other words, to take matters as we find them, and select a candidate pretty exclusively, on the grounds that he can be elected."[1]

In his note to Seymour, Johnson rather effectively summed up the dilemma Democratic Party leaders faced in the North heading into the presidential election of 1868. That year, as had been the case throughout the 1860s, bitter divisions existed among Northern Democrats over what they considered the best strategy to ensure the party's success in the elections that fall. Emboldened by success in the off-year elections of 1867, many Democrats advocated running a traditional campaign, continuing the party's strenuous opposition to Radical Republican policies. To those Democrats who endorsed this strategy, it seemed that Northern voters were finally tired of Radical Reconstruction and the Republicans. On the other hand, other party members in the North, men like Samuel Johnson, questioned the Democrats' continued defiance of the Republican agenda. These Democrats took a more pragmatic approach to the party's campaign strategies and wondered aloud if their party would do best to throw off the stigma of secession and betrayal left over from the Civil War by making a clean break from the issues of the past.

In short, as Northern Democrats entered the presidential campaign of 1868, competing groups of the party struggled over which direction the party's campaign would take that year, and to Northern Democrats, there was little that was new about this struggle. Ultimately, the more conservative elements of the party won out, as Democrats ran a relatively traditional campaign in 1868, nominating Horatio Seymour for president and continuing their heavy criticism of the Republicans' Reconstruction agenda.[2] Even as the Northern half of the party appeared to settle on a conservative campaign sharply critical of Republican policy, the internal squabbles of the party hardly subsided, however, as the campaign produced "a ticket and platform representative of a divided and floundering party."[3] In other words, on the surface it appeared that the Democrats were presenting a united front, but beneath the surface was a party full of bitter divisions.

Nonetheless, 1868 was more than just a recapitulation and rehashing of the same tired debates the Democratic Party had cycled through for nearly a decade. Rather, this essay argues that 1868 marked a significant turning point for Northern Democrats after the Civil War. Following that failed contest of 1868 in which the Democrats ran a traditionally conservative campaign, many Northern Democrats became frustrated with the direction of the party and blamed their defeat at the hands of Grant and the Republicans on a variety of factors. In particular, Northern Democrats were especially concerned about their susceptibility to Republicans waving the "bloody shirt"; the Republican reaction to vice-presidential nominee Francis Preston Blair Jr.'s infamous "Broadhead letter" that summer was the primary example.[4]

Ultimately, the defeat in 1868 helped to legitimize and push the arguments of moderate Democrats to the forefront of the party. Democrats in the North faced a crossroads. No longer, it seemed, could the party win standing on the traditional planks of its platform. Following the failure of 1868 and a pattern of electoral defeat throughout the 1860s, Northern Democrats shifted their rhetoric. They flirted with new issues, abandoned old ones, and engaged in political coalitions with third parties in order to reform the party's image. Northern Democrats thus emerged from the elections in 1868 convinced that the party could no longer win running on its traditional issues. Leaders in the party were eager to explore new campaign strategies and even to seek out new political alliances.

This turning point of 1868 of the Northern half of the Democratic Party is important for two reasons. First, the outcome of the 1868 elections resulted in a realization by Northern Democrats that the predominant strategies the party had used throughout the 1860s were simply not working. The subsequent willingness of Northern Democratic leaders to explore new campaign strategies and seek out new political alliances after 1868 would produce the so-called New Departure of the early 1870s, which, among other things, called for Democrats to "accept the natural and legitimate results of the war."[5] Aside from signifying a dramatic shift in the Democrats' public rhetoric, the New Departure also played a major role in precipitating the unlikely alliance between Democrats and the dissident Republicans who made up the Liberal Republican movement in the late 1860s and early 1870s.

As several historians have pointed out, including William Gillette, Michael Les Benedict, and most recently Andrew L. Slap, the Liberal Republican bolt was "the most crucial element in weakening Republican resolve on the Reconstruction issue," in part because of the strength the Liberals received at the hands of Northern Democrats.[6] In other words, what happened to Northern Democrats during the election of 1868 held major implications for the fate of Reconstruction in the South; the path Northern Democrats followed after 1868 produced the alliance with the Liberal Republican movement, and that alliance played a central role in Ulysses S. Grant and the Stalwart Republicans backing away from Radical Reconstruction. Understanding the Northern Democrats during this period helps us to better understand the larger political world of Reconstruction.[7]

Second, the turning point of 1868 and the path Northern Democrats followed after their defeat highlight the fluidity and flux of Civil War–era politics. For nearly a half century, political historians typically associated with the so-called New Political History have organized political developments in the nineteenth century around the idea of successive two-party systems. According to this model of political history, one can identify and characterize each two-party system through the stable behavior and voting loyalties of the electorate. Proponents of the New Political History have emphasized aggregate voter behavior, differentiating between different party systems by identifying voter realignments where large blocs of the electorate permanently shifted their allegiances over the course of several critical elections.[8] While this model is helpful in explaining some elements of the major voter realignments in American history, it assumes a certain rigidity or fixedness in American political history. As Michael F. Holt has recently observed, "No one living through realigning periods, either voters or politicians, knew for certain that they were in the midst of one."[9] For politicos and voters in the nineteenth century, partisan life was much more uncertain and unpredictable, and that perceived instability played a major role in influencing the decisions of political actors.

For example, even if there was no permanent voter realignment in the 1870s, the absence of an identifiable realignment does not change the fact that contemporaries fully expected there to be one. Such an expectation was especially relevant to Northern Democrats in 1868, as throughout the 1860s, Democrats in the North were convinced that the Republican Party was a temporary organization—an ad hoc coalition of sorts—that had come together with a specific purpose: to preserve the Union in the face of Southern extremism and secession. With that conflict now past, most Democrats believed that many white Northerners had grown tired of the Republicans' Reconstruction agenda and were ready to put the issues of the war to rest. Democrats were therefore certain that the Republican Party was bursting at the seams with voters ready to defect if given the slightest chance.

This belief, that the Republicans were on the verge of hemorrhaging Northern voters fed up with Reconstruction, coupled with Democratic electoral successes in 1867, helps explain the willingness of Northern Democrats to run a markedly conservative campaign in 1868. More important, it also explains why, after then experiencing defeat in 1868, the Democratic Party changed course and attempted to construct a more moderate public image and jettison the stigma of secession and copperheadism. In fact, moving closer to the political center was, in part, an effort by the Democrats to appear more attractive to Republican voters, and especially the Liberal Republicans once that movement appeared. When the Liberal Republican movement finally did emerge in 1869 and 1870, it simply reinforced the view of the Republican Party that the Democrats had already held for several years. Democrats believed that the Republicans were rife with dissent and that if the Democrats could simply find a way to capture those dissatisfied members of the opposition, they could, for the first time since 1860, finally shed their status as the minority party in the North.

In January of 1868, Northern Democrats began to look to the election cycle for that year. While the party had seen mostly defeat with a few bright spots during the 1860s, the Democrats entered 1868 with a degree of guarded optimism. In the off-year elections of 1867 Democrats had not only grabbed much-needed victories across the North, they had also increased their percentage of the vote over the elections of 1866.[10] The Democratic victories were so overwhelming that even Republicans declared that their party "must become more conservative if it expect [sic] the support of the people in [the] future, and that to that end it must not hesitate, if need be, to cut loose from the [Horace] Greeleys, the Wendell Phillpses, and the [Theodore] Tiltons altogether."[11] Particularly telling for Democrats, it seemed, was the defeat of several Republican referendums in Northern states on black suffrage.[12]

Democrats thus entered the campaign of 1868 "with *hope* as well as energy and courage" created by the momentum of the 1867 successes and a belief that Northern voters had grown tired of the Republicans' Reconstruction agenda.[13] For the upcoming presidential campaign, the field of candidates was wide open, ranging from Indiana senator Thomas A. Hendricks to Ohioan and former vice-presidential candidate George H. Pendleton to the wartime governor of New York, Horatio Seymour, and celebrated Civil War general Winfield S. Hancock. Montgomery Blair told anybody who would listen that his brother, Francis Preston Blair Jr., was "*the man* for the crisis," but in the spring of 1868, the primary candidates for the Democratic nomination appeared to be Hendricks, Pendleton, Seymour, and Hancock.[14]

Each of these candidates, however, represented a relatively traditional approach to the elections of 1868 for the Northern half of the Democratic Party, and some members of the party voiced concern that this approach is exactly what had held the party back during the 1860s. Discussing the slew of potential candidates already mentioned, one New York Democrat wrote Samuel J. Tilden and clamed that the "selection of any such names as those you mentioned would bring up *old issues* & prejudices and *insure* defeat." Rather, this Democrat hoped that the party might "cut loose from such old associations," as those men had "been worn out on antiquated platforms." Finally, he went on to suggest that the party should "cheerfully accord freedom to the negro, and equality before the law," arguing that "if such a platform could be put out and *stuck to,* not dragged out into *side* issues, or *dead* issues, success would be sure."[15] Despite this vocal dissent within the party, the Democrats nevertheless marched forward in 1868 behind the notion that "our position must be *the condemnation and reversal of negro supremacy*" and a resignation among many party members that despite objections, they could "scarcely look beyond Seymour or Pendleton for a candidate."[16]

Early in 1868, then, even as some Democrats expressed concern that running a conservative campaign would do more harm than good, much of the party remained convinced that the successes of 1867 suggested the Northern electorate was growing tired of Republican hegemony. Thus, central to the mind-set of key Democratic leaders was a belief in the fundamental instability of voter allegiances and shakiness at the base of the Republican Party. Referencing his earlier statement regarding "negro supremacy," Samuel Tilden argued, "On no other question can [we] be so unanimous among ourselves. On no other question can we draw so much from the other side & from the doubtful," as Tilden firmly believed that "the Republican party contains large numbers who are naturally revolted by its position on this question."[17]

Tilden, who was the chair of the Democratic State Committee in New York, reiterated this point in a circular letter to New York Democrats. The circular heavily emphasized the recruitment of fresh and new allies to the party, claiming that it "must strike the roots of its growth into fresh soils." Tilden further urged party organizers and committees to seek out "doubtful men," "moderate Republicans," "and all Republicans," concluding that "men are growing moderate and thoughtful, and many will hear our side who would formerly have refused."[18] August Belmont agreed, as he had suggested to Tilden "that an earnest appeal should be made to the conservative element throughout the Union which has not heretofore acted with the Democratic party."[19]

Elsewhere, George McClellan thought the party's primary concern should be recruiting "well meaning men who want to come over to the Conservative side," and one of Horatio Seymour's closest advisors believed that "with our own strength merely we cannot win. If we could make a breach in the other party & combine we could sweep the country."[20] Samuel Johnson of New York opined, "What we have to do is to get rid of the destructives. In order to do this we shall have to recruit from the republicans."[21] Finally, Robert J. Walker argued, "We must select the man who can secure the most votes, and who will be supported with enthusiasm by every Democrat, War, or Peace so-called, by every conservative democratic or republican Soldier, and by the thousands of new recruits and conservative republicans."[22]

For those Democrats who began to embrace a more moderate position in the 1860s, it was not just a matter of practicality or electability. Manton Marble, who was the editor of the New York World and a member of the elitist Swallowtail faction of moderate and hard-money Democrats in New York (along with Samuel Tilden, Samuel Barlow, and August Belmont, these Democrats were called "Swallowtails" because of the fashionable cut of the tails of the suit coats and white ties that they wore to monthly dinners at the Manhattan Club in New York City), realized that continuing to steadfastly resist and oppose Reconstruction simply played into the Republicans' hands. Accepting some of the achievements of Reconstruction instead allowed Democrats a chance to actually engage Republicans on their level and attempt to try to exert some control over Reconstruction policy. In other words, the process by which Northern Democrats embraced a more moderate position on Reconstruction was more than just a cynical ploy to restore the party's public image. For the eastern moderates, led by the hard-money wing of the party and typified by the Swallowtails of New York, there was a genuine ideological shift at work. That ideological shift would culminate with the New Departure in the early 1870s, and the election of 1868 played a major role in legitimizing the moderate wing of the party.

A perfect example of the ideological shift that moderate Democrats were undergoing in 1868 was the support that Chief Justice Salmon P. Chase received for the Democratic nomination during the first half of 1868. Even as George Pendleton, Thomas Hendricks, Horatio Seymour, and Winfield Hancock were the clear favorites among hard-line Democrats, a significant faction of moderate Democrats favored Chase. Pro-Chase Democrats were often hard-money men who had begun to lean toward a more moderate platform on Reconstruction, typified by the Swallowtails of New York. These Democrats saw in Chase congruence between his and their fiscal policies. Moderate Democrats also saw an opportunity to present a conservative Republican as their candidate who would (1) provide a means to attract moderate and conservative Republican voters and (2) help the Democrats neutralize the bloody shirt by presenting a more moderate candidate who had aligned with Lincoln during the war, not opposed him.

On the other hand, by 1868 a divisive split had developed between eastern and western Democrats over monetary policy. Eastern Democrats, representing business and banking interests, adhered to strict hard-money policies, while many western Democrats with farming constituencies favored soft-money policies. In 1867, Pendleton, a soft-money man, had campaigned for Ohio Democrats on the "Ohio Idea"—a soft-money plan that called for the redemption of federal bonds in paper money instead of specie.[23] Pendleton's "Ohio Idea" was anathema to eastern Democrats who favored Chase, and the Chase movement provided a suitable alternative to try to neutralize Pendleton's popularity in the Midwest.

Chase's own political ambitions are well known—he openly sought the Republican presidential nomination in 1860 and 1864.[24] With Grant appearing to have secured the Republican nomination as the summer of 1868 neared, Chase began to find the courtship of Democratic leaders appealing. In turn, Chase's friends—including Colonel John Dash Van Buren (a Democrat) and Hiram Barney (a Republican), both of New York—were feeling out on Chase's behalf the prospects of the Democratic nomination. Chase had the support of most of the prominent New York Democrats, including Belmont, Marble, Barlow, and Seymour, along with other hard-money men in the party. For many moderate Democrats, the primary appeal of Chase's candidacy was not only his hard-money views but also his status as a former

Republican who might serve as a linchpin in attracting moderate Republicans to the Democratic fold.

As the chief justice of the Supreme Court, Chase was in the midst of Andrew Johnson's impeachment trial in the spring of 1868. While Chase was very careful to avoid any public declaration of interest in the Democratic nomination, privately he was clearly aware of the support he was receiving among Democrats. By late May, August Belmont wrote privately to Chase, noting Chase's "sympathies with the broad principles of the Democratic party on the questions of finance, free trade & states rights." Belmont explicitly told Chase that "among many of the leading men of the Democratic party your name has been suggested as the most powerful one to be put into nomination as our Candidate for the Presidency. I concur fully in this view & shall most cheerfully use all of my efforts & influence to bring about your nomination & work arduously for your election, provided you will consent to become our Candidate." Belmont also addressed the issue of African American enfranchisement in the South. While Belmont and his allies had begun to move toward a more moderate view of the race question, embracing full suffrage for freedmen in the South would no doubt have been out of step with the majority of the Democratic Party. Chase, however, had been very public in his support for the rights of freedmen. Belmont attempted to reconcile this dilemma by telling Chase, "In regard to the Negro suffrage I take for granted that you would rather be in favor of allowing the States to vote on that question." As reassurance, however, Belmont indicated to Chase that he knew firsthand of many Southern Democrats willing to acquiesce on the issue. Finally, Belmont closed his letter by informing Chase that he was writing "without the knowledge of anybody, but after being fully convinced that most of the leading Democrats in our State are for you."[25]

Although Belmont's overtures to Chase were private, Belmont constructed his proposal very carefully in hopes of bypassing some of the major ideological divides between Chase and the Democratic Party while simultaneously highlighting their common ground. After all, Belmont faced a stark task in recruiting Chase without overstepping the bounds of Democratic conservatism. For his part, however, Chase ignored Belmont's careful approach and responded on May 30 with a lengthy, blunt, and straightforward letter that emphasized and reaffirmed his stance on the race question, especially as it pertained to Reconstruction. Chase began with an olive branch, noting that for "more than a quarter of a century I have been in my political views and sentiments, a Democrat; and I still think that, upon questions of finance commerce, and administration generally, the old democratic principles afford the best guidance." He then quickly dashed Belmont's hopes of playing down the suffrage issue, however, making it clear that "what separated me, in former times, from both parties was the depth and positiveness of my convictions on the slavery question." Tracing his views on slavery through the Civil War and into Reconstruction, Chase reiterated that he was "in favor of so much of the reconstruction policy of Congress as bases the reorganization of the State Governments in the South upon universal suffrage." Chase also stressed his belief "that if the democratic party will give such assurance in any way they can understand and rely on, a majority if not all the Southern States may be carried for the democratic candidates at the next election."[26] With his response, Chase put a major damper on any hopes that he or Belmont harbored for Chase to gain the nomination. Privately, Chase felt the same way, as he thought the nomination "never appeared to me as a thing likely to be really done." Chase echoed that he had no doubt that "on the question of currency there would perhaps be as little difficulty in reconciling my ideas with those of the party" but was especially soured by what he believed was the "almost universal commitment of the party to hostility to the colored people."[27] The door had seemingly closed on Chase's chances; yet, "despite his disclaimers," Chase still became "a major candidate for the Democratic nomination."[28]

Soon, the Democratic Party's national organ, the *New York World,* noticed the pro-Chase sentiments within the party and began in March to discuss the possibility of Chase's nomination. Initially unaware of Belmont's private correspondence with Chase, Manton Marble and the *World* continued to tout Chase's candidacy in the first half of June, just a month before the Democratic National Convention.[29] Recognizing the divide between Chase and the party over African American suffrage in the South, the *World* also attempted to bypass the issue, just as Belmont had done in his letter to Chase. Meanwhile, other newspapers and politicians came out in favor of Chase, including the independent (but conservative) *New York Herald* and Democratic congressmen Samuel Cox of New York and Daniel Voorhees of Indiana. The growing Chase movement was not lost among Republicans either, as Lyman Trumbull also observed that "Chase' [sic] chances for [the] democratic nomination seem to be growing."[30]

Support for Chase hinged on several factors. For hard-money Democrats like Belmont, it was Chase's well-known hostility toward greenbacks. Other Northern Democrats believed that Chase provided the best opportunity to woo dissident Republicans. Chase himself had grown increasingly disenchanted with the Republicans, and many Democrats were hopeful that Chase would appeal to other white Northerners with similar viewpoints. In other words, these Democrats believed Chase was "the only possible candidate who could rally enough conservative and moderate Republicans, which together with the Democratic organization would be strong enough to defeat Grant."[31] On May 28, Hiram Barney had reported to Chase from New York that many Democrats he had canvassed "supposed that neither Pendleton nor Seymour can be a successful candidate and neither would object to Mr. Chase," pausing to point out that Chase's "views on Negro suffrage are the point of hesitation."[32]

Chase recognized this problem, and as the Democratic convention approached, Chase "was now faced with watering down his position on suffrage to placate party leaders."[33] To this end, Chase began to backpedal rapidly on his views of suffrage that he had stated so unequivocally to Belmont just six weeks before. On July 1, Chase wrote a public letter to Thomas Ewing Jr. in which he made a vague affirmation of his belief in universal suffrage, with the qualification that the "practical disposition of the question of suffrage, as well as all other domestic questions, is for the people of the States themselves, not for outsiders. On this question I adhere to my old States rights doctrines."[34] Even more explicitly, Chase and John D. Van Buren prepared a platform for Chase's candidacy, and the first plank of that platform declared "universal suffrage is a democratic principle, the application of which is to be left, under the Constitution of the United States, to the States themselves."[35]

Chase's platform is interesting not only for the ideological accommodations Chase made to soothe the Democrats but also because it anticipated virtually every issue that would appear in the Liberal Republican–Democratic platforms of 1872. Most discussions of Chase's platform focus on Chase's backpedaling on the issue of black suffrage, but also important was Chase's insistence on restoring political rights to all disenfranchised Southerners, including former Confederates (a key issue the Liberal Republican movement would soon embrace). Finally, Chase's platform emphasized the acceptance of issues the Civil War had decided, the opposition to and desire to end military rule in the South, and opposition to a centralized national government. Notably underemphasized was any discussion of monetary issues.

As John D. Van Buren canvassed on Chase's behalf, he asked Horatio Seymour whether it was "worth proposing for the basis of a party with Chase at the head." Van Buren then proposed a compromise on the suffrage question; "the new party" under Chase would "take ground for *universal suffrage of whites and blacks in voting for new constitutions in the South* & refusing admission till the vote [has] thus [been] taken for *universal amnesty*. The constitutions only to be voted for by this universal suffrage; leaving to the constitutions of course to prescribe what restrictions they choose in each State."[36] Van Buren believed that this plan would allow the Democrats to concede universal suffrage to Chase and attract moderate Republicans to a new party but then, as a wink to Southern Democrats, allow the individual states to determine the shape of their new constitutions once those states had established universal suffrage.

Undergirding the Chase movement, then, was the belief of many Democrats in the fundamental instability of the two dominant political parties, the possibility of splitting apart the Republican opposition, and the "doubts whether any straight democrat" could be elected.[37] On June 1, the Republican *New York Times* discussed the possibility of the Democrats nominating Chase and fretted over Chase's appeal to the "elements of disaffection in the Republican ranks" and worried that "if their strength could be added to the full Democratic vote, it would give the Democracy a fair chance of carrying several important Northern States."[38] The *New York Evening Post* even declared "that Chase's nomination on a platform supporting his principles would bring about a dissolution of the parties."[39] The Chase movement represented the willingness of many Northern Democrats to begin exploring new strategies. Chief among those strategies were efforts to siphon off voters from the Republican Party and the belief that "Chase would get a large Republican vote."[40] Chase, some Northern Democrats believed, provided the best opportunity to do so.

Democratic Party delegates gathered for the National Democratic Convention at the newly constructed Tammany Hall in New York on July 4 in the midst of a sweltering summer heat wave. As the delegates turned to the business of the convention, Salmon Chase remained a solid underdog despite his growing support within the party. George H. Pendleton entered as the clear frontrunner when the proceedings convened. Pendleton came to national prominence in 1864 as the Democrats' vice-presidential nominee alongside George McClellan. In the years since that 1864 loss, Pendleton had gained a strong following in the West as arguably the preeminent western Democrat, gradually building momentum toward a presidential bid in 1868. Pendleton's popularity in the West hinged on his financial policies, the so-called soft-money Pendleton Plan. His financial proposals were especially appealing to western and midwestern Democrats, who were primarily poorer farmers.

While Pendleton's critics viewed his plan as "repudiation at worst and highly inflationary at best," Pendleton himself believed in both the legitimacy and importance of his plan as a solution to the fiscal problems created by Civil War debt.[41] For Pendleton, "greenbacks were a means to an end"; his ultimate goal was actually the resumption of specie payments (a fact his contemporary and modern critics frequently overlook), but in the meantime, he saw numerous benefits in the use of greenbacks to pay down the debt.[42] Moreover, Pendleton had an ulterior motive. Bitter from the opposition he had faced from eastern Democrats in 1864 and 1866, Pendleton faulted the party's internal divisiveness for Democratic defeats in those years. Instead, Pendleton believed midwestern and Southern Democrats shared similar economic interests that differed from those of their eastern brethren. By focusing on his Ohio Idea, Pendleton surmised he could shift political discourse away from the Reconstruction issues that Republicans had used to paint Democrats as treasonous and to focus instead on economic matters that he believed would unite Southern and midwestern Democrats in their common economic interests. The end result, Pendleton hoped, would "pressure the East to recognize a new regional leadership in the party, move the Democracy away from a dead past, address new issues popular with voters, and gain the presidential nomination for himself in 1868."[43]

As Pendleton vigorously campaigned on his Ohio Idea in 1867 and 1868, he succeeded in building a strong following. His well-known name combined with the appeal that pro-greenback policies had for midwestern Democrats made Pendleton the strongest western candidate in the field, evidenced by the fact that delegations from eleven different states—almost exclusively in the West and including Ohio, Kentucky, and Indiana—had committed to Pendleton before the 1868 convention got underway.[44] Pendleton's supporters, in fact, controlled more than one-third of the convention's 317 delegates. The rest of the support divided among a smattering of candidates, most notably Winfield S. Hancock and Thomas A. Hendricks.

Despite having more initial support than any other candidate, Pendleton's campaign was fatally flawed. The convention rules required a two-thirds majority to secure a nomination, and even though Pendleton entered with nearly 150 votes in hand, he was unlikely to achieve the necessary majority for two important reasons. First, the major Democratic leaders in Ohio disagreed over their support for Pendleton, and thus Pendleton's campaign lacked the necessary political leadership to broker the additional votes he required. In particular, Alexander Long thought the Ohio Idea was his issue and was bitter with Pendleton for having stolen it from him. Clement Vallandigham had mixed views as well and would ultimately throw his support to Chase. Without the full support of the Ohio Democratic machine, Pendleton found himself forced to defend his home turf rather than bartering for additional votes elsewhere.

Second, and most important, Pendleton had absolutely no chance of ever garnering support from the New York delegation, the largest and easily most powerful delegation at the convention. As already mentioned, the hard-money men of the eastern Democrats, led by August Belmont and Samuel J. Tilden, abhorred Pendleton's Ohio Idea. Furthermore, Pendleton's status as a prominent Peace Democrat during the war further stymied his chances, especially among the Swallowtails who maintained more moderate leanings: if nominated, moderate Democrats knew, Pendleton's history as a Peace Democrat would make him easy bait for Republican attacks.

The central theme of the 1868 National Democratic Convention was this standoff between the eastern, moderate, hard-money wing of the party and the more conservative, soft-money western Democrats who backed Pendleton. Not only was the standoff over the presidential nominee, but it also produced a vicious fight over the planks of the national platform, as the pro-Pendleton platform committee inserted a greenback plank in the platform. The existence of this plank of the platform infuriated Belmont and the other hard-money men and only pushed them to dig their heels in further on the matter of the presidential nominee. Balloting for the party's nominee began on the convention's third day and would continue for three more days and twenty-two ballots.

For much of the balloting, Pendleton maintained a sizable lead, garnering 105 votes on the first ballot and receiving as many as 156.5 on the eighth ballot. Pendleton, however, could never quite get over the hump without the support of the East. From the outset, the New York delegation had decided to cast its votes as a unit for fellow New Yorker Sanford E. Church—a placeholder of sorts. While most of the prominent New Yorkers favored Chase for the nomination, their strategy was to "let Pendleton, Hendricks, and Hancock run their course while New York held back." When the time was right, "Chase would be placed in nomination and a stampede would ensue."[45] The wildcard among the New Yorkers, however, was Tilden.

Tilden's own leanings regarding the Chase movement are difficult to decipher. Whatever the actual intentions of Tilden and the New York delegation, the momentum that the Chase movement built leading up to the convention never actually materialized on the floor. Pendleton maintained a heavy lead through eight ballots, but once it became clear that he would not be able to garner the two-thirds majority required for the nomination, cracks began to appear in his support. First, Indiana split its votes between Pendleton and native son Thomas A. Hendricks. Other delegations followed suit, some voting for Hendricks, others for Winfield Hancock. Pendleton's support rapidly faded, and after the eighteenth ballot, he withdrew. Pendleton's withdrawal, however, did little to solve the dilemma of selecting a nominee. After support for Pendleton dropped off, the convention split between Hendricks and Hancock. Through twenty-one ballots and three days of balloting, Hendricks had 132 votes, and Hancock had 135.5. The delegates had reached an impasse.[46]

At this point, the moment for Chase's supporters had arrived. Unfortunately for Chase, however, any attempt at his nomination fell completely flat. As the balloting marched on, Chase received only a handful of votes. When it became clear that Hancock and Hendricks were deadlocked, and with the delegates exhausted after several days of balloting in the midst of the oppressive July heat (many attendees had given up and gone home before a nomination was decided), Clement Vallandigham—the infamous wartime copperhead from Ohio—supposedly hatched a plan to swing the convention in Chase's favor. The plan was for the Ohio delegation to formally nominate Horatio Seymour, who would clear the field of the other favorites, followed by Seymour declining the nomination. Vallandigham assumed Seymour would decline, as Seymour had repeatedly stated throughout the weeks leading up to the convention and at the convention itself that he held no interest whatsoever in receiving the party's nomination.[47]

Midway through the twenty-second ballot, the Ohio delegation paused to nominate Seymour. Seymour then immediately gave a speech once again vehemently denying that he had any interest in the nomination, declaring that "when I said here at an early day, that honor forbade my accepting a nomination by this Convention, I *meant* it."[48] What followed next, however, did not go according to Vallandigham's plan. Seymour left the stage to discuss the latest turn of events with his home delegation (according to one account, he attempted to propose Chase instead, when his friends forced him off the stage).[49] While he was absent from the floor, support for his nomination snowballed as the increasingly excited delegates saw an end to the proceedings in sight. Every state that had already voted on the twenty-second ballot changed its votes unanimously in favor of Seymour.

When it was apparent that Seymour would suddenly have the unanimous support of the convention, his colleagues from New York refused to allow him to turn down the nomination.[50] The final nail in the coffin came when Tilden himself walked out on to the floor and declared that New York would swing its votes to Seymour, finishing the stampede. The convention then unanimously declared Seymour the party's nominee, going against Seymour's own wishes. Exactly why Chase's name fell off in favor of Seymour is not entirely clear. Vallandigham later told Chase himself that he had tried to persuade Tilden to vote for Chase, but Tilden refused.[51] On the other hand, others reported that a gathering of the New Yorkers at the Manhattan Club the previous evening had produced a unanimous decision to nominate Chase the next day.[52] Most likely, it seems, the New Yorkers would have turned to Chase but had not expected the massive groundswell for Seymour once his name was proposed. Either way, Chase's nomination never had a chance to get off the ground. The convention unanimously voted Francis P. Blair Jr. (originally lost in the shuffle of presidential candidates) the vice-presidential nominee, almost as an afterthought.

In the final analysis, instead of nominating Chase—a candidate many Democrats believed would help the party draw dissident voters away from the Republican Party and "break Radicalism all to pieces"—the convention nominated Horatio Seymour, a candidate the *Cincinnati Enquirer* called "a Democrat of Democrats."[53] Seymour was the ultimate compromise candidate, settled upon when the two warring factions of the Northern half of the Democratic Party failed to reach a consensus. Seymour's staunch hard-money views certainly represented a small victory for the eastern Democrats over the threat that Pendleton had posed. At the same time, Seymour also carried with him the heavy baggage of a reputation as the wartime governor of New York who had opposed Lincoln, sympathized with Clement Vallandigham, and sided with the mob during the New York draft riots in 1863. For those Northern Democrats intent on jettisoning the stigma of secession and copperheadism, Seymour represented a step in the wrong direction, as the "weaknesses of Seymour during the War & the riots" led them to "expect nothing from the nomination."[54] In sum, Seymour's nomination came because the party remained deeply divided over the best course of action for its future success.

Seymour's nomination produced, at best, mixed reactions among Northern Democrats. To be sure, some Democrats embraced Seymour as the Democratic nominee. Seymour's supporters believed that "Governor Seymour's course during the war was so nobly sound and Democratic that he attained a very strong hold upon the confidence and affection of the democracy of this and all Northern and Western States. His name will, I assure you, develop a hearty enthusiasm among Democrats that can be drawn out by no other."[55] Unfortunately for Seymour, most Northern Democrats did not feel that strongly in favor of his candidacy.[56] In private, few Democrats expressed any sense of satisfaction at Seymour's nomination. Samuel Barlow wrote Tilden to inform him that "our ticket *here* creates almost universal execration & despair."[57] Other Democrats found it "impossible to deny that every Democrat feels disappointed" and that the party "could have nominated no candidate who would have taken away fewer Republican votes than Seymour."[58] Supporters of Chase thought that "Blair's name will not strengthen the ticket," and while Seymour might "poll the entire democratic votes," he would do little to "take much from the dissatisfied portion of the Republicans," as "Chase was the only candidate who could draw off voters in any great numbers, from that party."[59] Lamentations over Seymour's nomination reflected the belief of many Democrats that the key to their success was recruiting within the ranks of the Republican Party.

Democratic fears that the failure to nominate Chase would amount to a lost opportunity to secure the votes of dissident Republicans were certainly legitimate. After the convention, Seymour acknowledged "that he knew the character of democratic Republicans—and that they would never go back on their principles and the only way to win them was to acknowledge the correctness of their view and by which a course alone could they divide the Republicans party & ensure the triumph of the democrats." In response, Hiram Barney told Seymour the Democratic convention had "acted and spoke[n] not to win republicans but to please southern democratic rebels," and Barney did not "believe he [Seymour] would get many votes from dissatisfied republicans." Rather, by nominating Seymour, Barney claimed, the Democrats "had shut their doors square in the face of Democratic Republicans" and had "rendered it improbable that men of our way of thinking would ever trust the present leaders of the democratic party."[60] The wailing over Seymour's nomination was not just contained to private letters. The press, too, pointed out what a listless campaign the Democratic Party subsequently faced. The *New York Herald*, for example, declared, "The Democratic Convention has decided that our next President shall be General Grant." The *Herald* believed there to be "nothing in his [Seymour's] record, nothing in his platform that will bring a single recruit to the democratic party, but everything to rally the whole floating vote of the United States, with all the conservative republicans, around the glorious banner of Grant."[61] Ultimately, most Northern Democrats believed that Seymour's nomination would make the party "a house divided against itself."[62]

Part of the consternation over the ticket had as much to do with Seymour's running mate as it did with Seymour himself. While the Democrats had selected Francis P. Blair Jr. as the vice-presidential nominee practically as an afterthought, Blair arguably ended up having more of an effect on the Democrats' chances than Seymour did. On July 1, Blair sent a public letter (dated June 30) through his brother Montgomery to James O. Broadhead, a Missouri lawyer. The letter acknowledged Blair's candidacy for the Democratic nomination and outlined his disagreements with the Radical Republicans' Reconstruction policies. The ideas in Blair's letter did not necessarily depart from the views of many Democrats, but what made his letter so inflammatory was its excessive and extreme language.

Blair argued, "There is but one way to restore the Government and the Constitution." For Blair, that way was "for the President elect to declare these acts [Congressional Reconstruction] null and void, compel the army to undo its usurpations at the South, disperse the carpetbag Southern governments, allow the white people to reorganize their own governments and elect Senators and Representatives." Blair concluded that "this is the real and only question which we should allow to control us: Shall we submit to the usurpations by which the Government has been overthrown, or shall we exert ourselves for its full and complete restoration?"[63]

As a biographer of the Blair family once noted, "No one letter has been more fatal to the interest of a political candidate or to a party than was the Broadhead letter of June 30."[64] Republican newspapers widely publicized Blair's letter immediately after the Democratic National Convention, and in the campaign that followed, the Republicans ensured that voters remembered it. Just as Democrats feared, the Republicans responded by using Blair's own words against him. Republicans asserted that if Seymour and Blair won the White House, the Northern Democrats would overthrow the new state governments in the South, reinstate their Southern brethren, and reignite the sectional conflict.[65] One Democrat reported that a Republican slogan for the election that fall warned voters, *"Seymour was opposed to the late war,"* while *"Blair is in favor of the next one."*[66]

Democrats were furious about Blair's letter. When the campaign got under way, one of Seymour's top political advisers reported that *"Blair's letter is hurting us seriously—the people fear any more war"* and that "Western papers & speakers in the Republican side make this Blair revolution doctrine the only issue."[67] Less than a week after Blair's nomination, another Democrat proclaimed "widespread disaffection and a very general giving up of the contest. Blair personally, and 'Blair's letter,' excite *violent denunciations,* the Democrats generally taking the worst." This Democrat feared that "it is the old war feeling still smouldering and about to burst against us."[68] Later,

Michael Crawford Kerr would attribute the Democrats' eventual loss in part to Blair, calling the Broadhead letter "foolish and indefensible."[69]

In sum, the results of the Seymour-Blair nomination left the Democrats "a divided and floundering party."[70] James Watson Webb, the U.S. minister to Brazil, summed up the dilemma perfectly. He predicted that the party would not "carry a single one of the old non-slaveholding states" because Seymour had "embraced all the leading Rebels" followed by the party having "nominated Blair, after the publication of his letter," and to top things off, the Democrats had "placed a *gold* candidate on a *paper* platform."[71] Party divisions between the East and the West were too strong to emphasize the money question, and Seymour's wartime reputation combined with Blair's letter practically waved the bloody shirt for the Republicans. The failure to pass a moderate platform or nominate a moderate candidate certainly shut the door on luring dissatisfied Republicans to the folds of the Democratic Party. Rather than making fresh strokes, "party leaders followed a predictable pattern already well laid out over a decade of opposition, repeated familiar themes, and moved in well-worn grooves."[72] Reluctantly, it seemed, Northern Democrats temporarily united behind a campaign that emphasized issues many within the party had hoped to avoid from the start.

The resulting campaign was "the last Presidential contest to center on white supremacy."[73] Northern Democrats were unable to claim Seymour's loyalty or service to the Union during the war, and the money question was out of bounds for fear of splitting the party apart, so the Democrats focused on race. In the Midwest, for example, local Democrats echoed the themes of Seymour's campaign, claiming the Republicans' Reconstruction goals were to "feed the blacks and fatten the white radicals."[74] For whatever qualms many moderate Democrats had about such a campaign, they got behind it as best they could. Samuel Barlow suggested to Tilden that "the most effective campaign document that can possibly be circulated in Pa., N.Y., & Ohio is the series of portraits of the negroes who now govern La."[75] Despite the undercurrents from within that had been pushing the party to change course, ultimately the 1868 campaign represented little that was new about the Northern Democrats.

Unfortunately for the Democrats, running on the same issues did not prove as effective as it had in 1867. Before the presidential contest, politicos looked to state and local contests in September and October to gauge what the outcome might look like in November. For Democrats, the results were bleak. In actuality, the party had polled very respectably. For example, Democrats did gain forty-two congressional seats over the 1866 midterm elections, but the results in September and October also revealed the party's base had not moved. Despite having captured nearly half of the popular vote in state and congressional elections in those states where they had made gains, Democrats were hoping to make inroads into Republican support. The day before the October elections, the *World* noted, "What the Democratic party needs in the States which hold elections to-morrow, is not victories in them all, but gains."[76] The Democrats saw no such gains. Instead, defeats in Pennsylvania, Ohio, and Indiana made "Grant's election certain."[77] In September, John D. Van Buren reported to Horatio Seymour that "our people are not confident nor even hopeful" and party leaders were "discouraged."[78]

The November results played out almost exactly as the September and October contests had. Seymour made a strong showing in the popular vote, winning 47 percent of the 5.7 million votes cast, but the Democrats saw their ticket trounced in the Electoral College, 214 to 80. Much like the state-level contests, the Democrats ran well in the Lower North, winning New York, New Jersey, Delaware, and Maryland, but failed to win any of the states in the Midwest (in fact, Seymour's support in each state frequently ran behind the state-level vote Democrats had received in September and October).[79] When the dust cleared, Northern Democrats found that there was nothing new about their all-too-familiar position at the end of 1868. While Democrats managed to make some gains in congressional seats over 1866, they lost two seats in the Senate, lost most of the gubernatorial races, and fell short in the race for the presidency. Just as important to many Democratic observers, it appeared that they had not made any significant gains among Republican voters.[80] A familiar campaign had produced a familiar result.

Partisan outrage at a series of close electoral defeats should certainly not come as any surprise. Yet there was a "deep and prevalent dissatisfaction" among Democrats over the results of 1868 that makes Democratic reactions that year especially palpable.[81] In particular, moderate Democrats were furious over a campaign they believed had only reinforced the public stigma of copperheadism, not to mention a platform that kowtowed to the soft-money wing of the party. After a campaign in which the Democrats could not agree on strategy and had struggled to maintain any semblance of party unity, Seymour's defeat opened the floodgates.

Not surprisingly, most Democrats thought that "the Democratic party lost their senses & lost their cause," and as a result, their party had "made several mistakes."[82] The *New York Herald* believed that "the democratic leaders flung their chances of success overboard when they made their feeble nominations in July, and more especially when they brought prominently forward as delegates and stump speakers men from the Southern States steeped to the lips in disloyalty to the government."[83] August Belmont confessed to Manton Marble that Seymour's nomination had been "a *great calamity* for the Democratic party" because he "always thought Seymour the weakest candidate except perhaps Pendleton." Moreover, Belmont was furious that Seymour had been saddled "with Blair and greenbacks" just as McClellan had been weighed down "with Pendleton and peace" in 1864.[84]

Ultimately, the chairman of the Democratic National Committee wished to "get rid of all the old rubbish of Vallandigham, Pendleton, Seymour and a dozen others, build up a new party, take hold of new issues, so as to get the people with us and not remain in the leading strings of old political hacks."[85] Michael Crawford Kerr railed on for several pages at the "stupid ignorance" and "madness" that led to Blair's vice-presidential nomination. Kerr concluded that it was "such folly, so often repeated, that gave us defeat this year," similar to "the vain attempt to carry this kind of load in 1864 that secured us defeat then" because "such conduct will always produce like results." Finally, Kerr "heartily approved" a "change of leaders" because it would make the Democrats "a more compact and better organized party."[86]

Kerr certainly did not know it at the time, but his comments foreshadowed some major strategic changes among the ranks of the Democrats in the immediate years to follow. Some Democrats looked at the results of 1868 and concluded "that they do not show such a change in the northern mind as we had expected."[87] In other words, Northern Democrats had pinned their success on the hope that a fundamentally conservative campaign would appeal beyond the ranks of Democratic voters. When that strategy failed, as it had essentially since 1860, Democrats had to search for a new strategy based on a new reading of the Northern mind-set. After nearly a decade of internal stalemate between two warring factions of the Democratic Party and a decade of frustrating defeat at the polls, many Northern Democrats threw up their hands in frustration. The election of 1868 marked a turning point in Democratic strategy after the Civil War. One strategy that would become central to the party's plan of action in the wake of Seymour's defeat was the recurring belief that, as one Democrat put it, "we must have a division of parties. A fraction of our party and of the Republican party ought be brought into harmonious action" and "the extremes of both parties should be cast off." This particular Democrat concluded, quite prophetically, "that before another Presidential Campaign there will be a very great change in parties."[88]

Democrats had entered the campaign in 1868 convinced that there were masses of dissatisfied voters in the ranks of the Republican Party fully prepared to abandon ship if given the right opportunity. While 1868 did not provide that opportunity, it did not change the fact that many Democrats were certain of the existence of those dissatisfied Republicans. Rather, the election of 1868 provided evidence for Northern Democrats that a starkly conservative campaign would not woo those dissident Republicans over to the folds of the Democratic Party. Instead, Northern Democrats determined that they would have to move closer to the political center in order to capture those elusive Republican voters they had sought since the secession crisis. Northern Democrats did just that, adopting the New Departure in 1870 and 1871. Moreover, the near-simultaneous appearance of the Liberal Republican movement in 1869 and 1870 confirmed for many Democrats what they already believed about the splintered nature of the Republican Party and provided the perfect opportunity to make their move to the political center. That move to the center, prompted by the Democrats' failure in 1868 after running a conservative campaign, led to political fusion between Democrats and Liberal Republicans between 1870 and 1872. Ultimately, that fusion between Democrats and dissident Republicans spelled disaster for federal Reconstruction policies in the South as President Grant and other Stalwart Republicans rapidly abandoned Reconstruction in order to undercut the Democratic-Liberal alliance, an alliance whose seeds were sewn by the election of 1868.

Notes

The author would like to thank Gary W. Gallagher, Michael F. Holt, Sean Nalty, Cynthia Nicoletti, George Roupe, Rachel Shelden, and reviewers for University of Virginia Press, for valuable advice and assistance with this essay.

1. S. M. Johnson to Horatio Seymour, April 17, 1868, Washington, DC, autograph letter signed (ALS), Horatio Seymour Papers, New-York Historical Society.

2. See Joel H. Silbey, *A Respectable Minority: The Democratic Party in the Civil War Era, 1860–1868* (New York: W. W. Norton, 1977), 210, where he argues, "The Democrats ran a clear, crisp, and united campaign echoing their past." Although the book suffers from its organization, Silbey's study remains the best on the Democrats during this period. For a recent reappraisal of the most conservative Northern Democrats during the war, see Jennifer L. Weber, *Copperheads: The Rise and Fall of Lincoln's Opponents in the North* (New York: Oxford University Press, 2006).

3. Thomas S. Mach, "George Hunt Pendleton, The Ohio Idea and Political Continuity in Reconstruction America," *Ohio History* 108 (Summer–Autumn 1999), 125–44, quote on 142.

4. In the summer of 1868, Blair released a public letter dated June 30 to Missouri lawyer James O. Broadhead that was extremely critical of the Republicans' Reconstruction agenda. Almost immediately after the Democratic nominating convention, Republicans focused on the Broadhead letter and attacked the Democratic ticket, labeling it disloyal and traitorous. On Blair and the background behind the letter, see William E. Parrish, *Frank Blair: Lincoln's Conservative* (Columbia: University of Missouri Press, 1998), 254–60; and William Ernest Smith, *The Francis Preston Blair Family in Politics*, 2 vols. (New York: Macmillan, 1933), 2:405–30. The Broadhead letter and reaction to it are discussed in greater detail near the end of this essay.

5. Quoted in the *New York Herald*, May 20, 1871.

6. See Michael Les Benedict, "Reform Republicans and the Retreat From Reconstruction," in *Preserving the Constitution: Essays on Politics and the Constitution in the Reconstruction Era* (New York: Fordham University Press, 2006), 168–85, quote on 169. On this point, generally, see also William Gillette, *Retreat from Reconstruction, 1869–1879* (Baton Rouge: Louisiana State University Press, 1979), 71–72; and Andrew L. Slap, *The Doom of Reconstruction: The Liberal Republicans in the Civil War Era* (New York: Fordham University Press, 2006).

7. Along these lines, it is also worth noting that we know next to nothing about the Northern Democrats during this period, and the election of 1868 has received minimal attention from historians of the period.

8. An excellent summary of realignment theory and its use by the New Political History can be found in Peter H. Argersinger, "American Electoral History: Party Systems and Voting Behavior," in *Structure, Process, and Party: Essays in American Political History* (New York: M. E. Sharpe, 1992), 3–33, esp. 3–14.

9. Michael F. Holt, "A Time of Uncertainty: The Civil War Era and America's Two-Party System," 42nd Annual Robert Fortenbaugh Memorial Lecture (Gettysburg College, 2003), 15. For Holt's discussion of realignment theory and its implications for Civil War politics, see esp. 4–16.

10. Silbey, *A Respectable Minority*, 215.

11. *Baltimore Sun*, November 8, 1867.

12. For a detailed discussion of the elections of 1866 and 1867, see Silbey, *A Respectable Minority*, 212–17. Also helpful is Michael Les Benedict, "The Rout of Radicalism: Republicans and the Elections of 1867," in Benedict, *Preserving the Constitution*, 23–43.

13. A. G. Thurman to Samuel J. Tilden, January 31, 1868, Columbus, OH, ALS, box 6, Samuel J. Tilden Papers, Manuscripts and Archives Division, New York Public Library. Emphasis in original.

14. Montgomery Blair to Samuel L. M. Barlow, January 29, 1868, Washington, DC, ALS, box 65, folder 19, Samuel L. M. Barlow Papers, Henry E. Huntington Library, San Marino, CA. Emphasis in original.

15. R. C. Root to Samuel J. Tilden, February 10, 1868, New York, ALS, box 6, Samuel J. Tilden Papers. Emphasis in original.

16. Samuel J. Tilden to William Bigler, February 28, 1868, New York, draft, box 6, Samuel

J. Tilden Papers; Richard Taylor to Samuel L. M. Barlow, March 29, 1868, New Orleans, ALS, box 68, folder 28, Samuel L. M. Barlow Papers. Emphasis in original.

17. Samuel J. Tilden to William Bigler, February 28, 1868, New York, draft, box 6, Samuel J. Tilden Papers.

18. Circular letter, Samuel Tilden (chair, State Committee) to New York Democrats, March 31, 1868, ibid.

19. August Belmont to Samuel J. Tilden, February 1, 1868, ibid. Also cited in Silbey, *A Respectable Minority*, 199.

20. George B. McClellan to Samuel L. M. Barlow, March 13, 1868, Nice, France, ALS, box 67, folder 19, Samuel L. M. Barlow Papers; John D. Van Buren to Horatio Seymour, May 1, 1868, New York, ALS, Horatio Seymour Papers.

21. Samuel M. Johnson to Samuel L. M. Barlow, May 5, 1868, Washington, DC, ALS, box 67, folder 7, Samuel L. M. Barlow Papers.

22. Robert Walker to Samuel J. Tilden, May 30, 1868, Washington, DC, ALS, box 6, Samuel J. Tilden Papers. Walker believed Winfield Hancock was the nominee who best met his criteria.

23. See Mach, "George Hunt Pendleton."

24. John Niven discusses Chase's political ambitions throughout, in *Salmon P. Chase: A Biography* (New York: Oxford University Press, 1995). For Niven's discussion of Chase's flirtation with the Democratic nomination in 1868, see 426–32.

25. August Belmont to Salmon P. Chase, May 29, 1868; quoted in Irving Katz, *August Belmont: A Political Biography* (New York: Columbia University Press, 1968), 168. Katz cites Belmont's letter in Jacob W. Schuckers, *The Life and Public Services of Salmon Portland Chase* (New York, 1874), 584–85. The only letter between Chase and Belmont that appears in Schuckers's volume, however, is Chase's well-known response to Belmont of May 30, for which Katz cites a "private Belmont collection." More than likely, it seems, Katz mixed up his citations: Belmont's letter to Chase is found in the private Belmont collection, and Chase's reply of May 30, discussed below, comes from Schuckers's volume on Chase. See Katz, *August Belmont*, 168–69nn8 and 9.

26. Salmon P. Chase to August Belmont, May 30, 1868; in John Niven, ed., *The Salmon P. Chase Papers*, vol. 5, *Correspondence, 1865–1873* (Kent, OH: Kent State University Press, 1998), 221–24.

27. Salmon P. Chase to Milton Sutliff, June 3, 1868, in *Salmon P. Chase Papers*, 5:226–28, quotes on 226.

28. Niven, *Salmon P. Chase*, 428. On Chase's support among Northern Democrats, also see Michael Les Benedict, "Salmon P. Chase and Constitutional Politics," in Benedict, *Preserving the Constitution*, 129–51, esp. 145–51. Also helpful is Jerome Mushkat, *The Reconstruction of the New York Democracy, 1861–1874* (Rutherford, NJ: Fairleigh Dickinson University Press, 1981), 133–38.

29. Irving Katz claims that Belmont wrote to Chase without anyone's knowledge and that as late as June, even Marble was not aware of Belmont's overtures. See Katz, *August Belmont*, 168–70. There is nothing in Marble's manuscript collection or in his biographies to suggest that he was aware of Belmont's letters to Chase.

30. Lyman Trumbull to Charles Henry Ray, June 3, 1868, Washington, DC, ALS, box 3, folder RY 192, Ray (Charles Henry) Papers, Henry E. Huntington Library.

31. Niven, *Salmon P. Chase*, 428.

32. Hiram Barney to Salmon P. Chase, May 28, 1868, quoted in George T. McJimsey, *Genteel Partisan: Manton Marble, 1834–1917* (Ames: Iowa State University Press, 1971), 127.

33. Niven, *Salmon P. Chase*, 429.

34. Salmon P. Chase to Thomas Ewing Jr., July 1, 1868, in *Salmon P. Chase Papers*, 5:246. The letter also appeared in the *New York Herald*, July 6, 1868.

35. For the platform, see Schuckers, *Life and Public Services of Salmon Portland Chase*, 567–70, quote on 567. Chase's platform also ran in the press. John Dash Van Buren was a New York attorney, Democratic politician, and the private secretary of Governor John Hoffman. His son, John Dash Van Buren Jr., served in the Engineering Corps of the navy during the Civil War. Neither was the famous "Prince John" Van Buren, Martin Van Buren's son, who died in 1866.

36. John D. Van Buren to Horatio Seymour, May 20, 1868, New York, ALS, Horatio Seymour Papers. Emphasis in original.

37. Jerome B. Stillson to Samuel L. M. Barlow, June 30, 1868, Washington, DC, ALS, box 68, folder 21, Samuel L. M. Barlow Papers.

38. *New York Times*, June 1, 1868.

39. McJimsey, *Genteel Partisan*, 127.

40. James F. Noble to Samuel L. M. Barlow, July 1, 1868, Cincinnati, ALS, box 67, folder 35, Samuel L. M. Barlow Papers.

41. Thomas S. Mach, *"Gentleman George" Hunt Pendleton: Party Politics and Ideological Identity in Nineteenth-Century America* (Kent, OH: Kent State University Press, 2007), 128.

42. Ibid., 121.

43. Ibid., 117.

44. See Charles H. Coleman, *The Election of 1868: The Democratic Effort to Regain Control* (New York: Columbia University Press, 1933), 188. Convention proceedings are in the *Official Proceedings of the National Democratic Convention Held at New York, July 4–9, 1868* (Boston: Rockwell & Rollins, 1868). At the outset, Indiana supported Pendleton rather than native son Thomas A. Hendricks but would switch support to Hendricks beginning with the seventh ballot.

45. Niven, *Salmon P. Chase*, 431.

46. Balloting results in *Official Proceedings of the National Democratic Convention*, 75–162.

47. Seymour's only biographer affirms his disinterest in the nomination. See Stewart Mitchell, *Horatio Seymour of New York* (Cambridge, MA: Harvard University Press, 1938), 411–42.

48. *Official Proceedings of the National Democratic Convention*, 152–53. Emphasis in original.

49. Alexander C. Flick, *Samuel Jones Tilden: A Study in Political Sagacity* (New York: Dodd, Mead, 1939), 177.

50. One biography of August Belmont claims that Seymour literally had to be dragged off of the convention floor by his New York friends and forced to wait out the proceedings in the Manhattan Club to keep Seymour from denying the nomination and prolonging the

proceedings. See David Black, *The King of Fifth Avenue: The Fortunes of August Belmont* (New York: Dial, 1981), 304.

51. Edward Gambill notes that Vallandigham approached Tilden to urge the New Yorkers to support Chase, but Tilden claimed that a caucus of the New York delegation prevented him from doing so. See Edward L. Gambill, *Conservative Ordeal: Northern Democrats and Reconstruction, 1865–1868* (Ames: Iowa State University Press, 1981), 142.

52. Flick, *Samuel J. Tilden*, 177–78. The Manhattan Club was founded in 1865 by August Belmont as an elitist Democratic refuge for those wealthy Democrats who found themselves unable to make the ten-year waiting list at the Republican Union Club. It served as an unofficial headquarters of sorts for the Swallowtail Democrats. See Edwin G. Burrows and Mike Wallace, *Gotham: A History of New York City to 1898* (New York: Oxford University Press, 1999), 954, 1103; and McJimsey, *Genteel Partisan*, 82–83.

53. Quoted in Silbey, *A Respectable Minority*, 202; *Cincinnati Enquirer*, July 10, 1868, also quoted in Silbey, *A Respectable Minority*, 206.

54. John Henry Dillon to Samuel L. M. Barlow, July 25, 1868, Albany, NY, ALS, box 66, folder 3, Samuel L. M. Barlow Papers.

55. Arphaxed Loomis to Samuel J. Tilden, June 8, 1868, Little Falls, NY, in John Bigelow, ed., *Letters and Literary Memorials of Samuel J. Tilden*, 2 vols. (New York: Harper & Brothers, 1908), 1:229–30, quote on 229. Also cited in Silbey, *A Respectable Minority*, 205–6.

56. Jerome Mushkat also notes the lukewarm reaction Seymour received in Mushkat, *Reconstruction of the New York Democracy*, 137–38.

57. Samuel L. M. Barlow to Samuel J. Tilden, July 10, 1868, New York, ALS, box 6, Samuel J. Tilden Papers.

58. Samuel Ward to Samuel L. M. Barlow, July 16 and 20, 1868, Washington DC, ALS, box 68, folder 40, Samuel L. M. Barlow Papers.

59. William Davis Shipman to Samuel L. M. Barlow, July 11, 1868, Hartford, CT, ALS, box 68, folder 15, ibid.

60. Hiram Barney to Salmon P. Chase, September 7, 1868, New York, ALS, box 2, folder 19, Barney (Hiram) Collection, Henry E. Huntington Library. Also printed in *The Salmon P. Chase Papers*, 5:275–77, quote on 276.

61. *New York Herald*, July 10, 1868.

62. Samuel Ward to Samuel L. M. Barlow, July 16, 1868, Washington, DC, ALS, box 68, folder 15, Samuel L. M. Barlow Papers.

63. Blair's letter appears in Smith, *Francis Preston Blair Family*, 2:406-07. Mark Summers also provides an extended discussion of the Broadhead letter and its impact on the election of 1868 in *A Dangerous Stir: Fear, Paranoia, and the Making of Reconstruction* (Chapel Hill: University of North Carolina Press, 2009), 227–43. Summers, however, errs in claiming Blair wrote the letter to Pennsylvania politician Richard Brodhead, who died in 1863.

64. Smith, *Francis Preston Blair Family*, 2:405.

65. See Katz, *August Belmont*, 180; and Eric Foner, *Reconstruction: America's Unfinished Revolution, 1863–1877* (New York: Harper & Row, 1988), 340–41.

66. Samuel Ward to Samuel L. M. Barlow, July 22, 1868, Washington, DC, ALS, box 68, folder 40, Samuel L. M. Barlow Papers. Emphasis in original.

67. John D. Van Buren to Horatio Seymour, August 23, 1868, Horatio Seymour Papers. Emphasis in original.

68. Sam Ryan Jr. to Horatio Seymour, July 14, 1868, Washington, DC, ALS, ibid. Emphasis in original.

69. Michael Crawford Kerr to Manton Marble, November 8, 1868, container 20, Manton Marble Papers, Manuscript Division, Library of Congress.

70. Mach, "George Hunt Pendleton," 142.

71. James Watson Webb to Samuel L. M. Barlow, October 24, 1868, Brazil, box 68, folder 42, Samuel L. M. Barlow Papers. Emphasis in original.

72. Silbey, *A Respectable Minority,* 210.

73. Foner, *Reconstruction,* 341.

74. *Quincy (IL) Herald,* October 3, 1868, quoted in Peter Ufland, "The Politics of Race in the Midwest, 1864–1890" (Ph.D. diss., University of Illinois at Chicago, 2006), 121.

75. Samuel L. M. Barlow to Samuel J. Tilden, September 21, 1868, New York, ALS, box 6, Samuel J. Tilden Papers. Barlow was referencing a portrait of the heavily black state legislature in Louisiana, which the New York Democrats reproduced and distributed widely during the 1868 campaign.

76. *New York World,* October 12, 1868.

77. John Henry Dillon to Samuel L. M. Barlow, October 15, 1868, Albany, NY, ALS, box 66, folder 3, Samuel L. M. Barlow Papers.

78. John D. Van Buren to Horatio Seymour, September 22, 1868, ALS, Horatio Seymour Papers.

79. See Coleman, *The Election of 1868,* 363. On the 1868 results, see also Silbey, *A Respectable Minority,* 217–27.

80. That each party's voting base was solidly in place for the 1868 election is one of Silbey's main observations about 1868 and part of his larger argument that voter loyalty during the Civil War era, especially between 1860 and 1868, was decidedly stable. Lex Renda also supports Silbey's conclusions, finding that very few voters switched parties in 1868 in Connecticut and New Hampshire. See Lex Renda, "The Polity and the Party System: Connecticut and New Hampshire, 1840–1876" (Ph.D. diss., University of Virginia, 1991), 1085.

81. Allen C. Beach to Manton Marble, November 25, 1868, container 20, Manton Marble Papers. Irving Katz has also observed the difference in the tenor of Democratic reactions to 1868, noting that "after the Democratic losses of 1860 and 1864, bygones were bygones," but after 1868, Democrats "looked around for a likely victim on whom to vent their spleen." See Katz, *August Belmont,* 185.

82. Ferdinand Suydam to Samuel L. M. Barlow, November 4, 1868, Paris, ALS, box 68, folder 24, Samuel L. M. Barlow Papers; Hiram Ketchum to Samuel J. Tilden, November 12, 1868, New York, ALS, box 6, Samuel J. Tilden Papers.

83. *New York Herald,* November 4, 1868.

84. August Belmont to Manton Marble, November 6, 1868, container 20, Manton Marble Papers. Emphasis in original.

85. Ibid.

86. Michael Crawford Kerr to Manton Marble, November 8, 1868, ibid.

87. Thomas George Pratt to Samuel L. M. Barlow, September 18, 1868, Baltimore, ALS, box 67, folder 47, Samuel L. M. Barlow Papers.

88. Winslow S. Pierce to Manton Marble, November 10, 1868, ALS, container 20, Manton Marble Papers.

Consider the Alternatives

Reassessing Republican Reconstruction

Brooks D. Simpson

Scholars have long debated whether Reconstruction succeeded or failed, why it turned out as it did, and who or what was responsible for the outcome. Many have focused their efforts on exploring and assessing Republican policy makers and their handiwork—a major concern ever since historians began reevaluating Reconstruction in earnest in the wave of revisionist scholarship that appeared in the 1960s. Praise of Republicans' motives in many of these works soon gave way to more critical assessments of their performance and more skeptical treatments of their motives. Indeed, as Michael Perman once suggested, "There seemed to be so many indications that the proponents and agents of Reconstruction were flawed and deficient that it appeared unnecessary to look to external causes to explain the failure of the experiment."[1] In some cases, examinations of policy making took a backseat to passing judgment on the motives of policy makers, causing some critics of Reconstruction historiography to characterize it as a "morality play," a quest for villains and heroes, not understanding.[2]

It's reasonable to note that part of the problem is in assuming that Republicans agreed on ends as well as means, especially when some studies focused on the Radical Republicans, long the featured players in the story, and overlooked their more moderate colleagues. That is no longer the case. The scholarship outlining differences among Republicans themselves is so rich, in fact, that the Democrats are all too often relegated to the shadows. Who were the Radicals? Who were the moderates? What divided them? How did those differences shape the dynamics of policy making? Where could they find consensus? Much can be learned from these studies, particularly when it comes to the circumstances that shaped the give and take of framing legislation. But if politics is indeed the art of the possible, then we must ask what options were available to Republican policy makers. To answer that question, in turn, requires us to understand the context—ideological, institutional, and political—in which they acted. Perhaps Reconstruction did not achieve all of the goals envisioned by Republican policy makers in large part because such an outcome was beyond all reasonable expectation.

First, what were the general goals of Republican Reconstruction policy? Acknowledging that there were differences among Republicans, what common ground did they share? Three areas of general agreement stand out. First, Republicans looked to reunite the nation. Lincoln's call for "malice toward none, with charity for all" and Grant's terms at Appomattox aimed to heal sectional strife. Both men feared that should the Confederates resort to guerrilla warfare, the nation would be torn apart past reuniting, and the war for reunion would truly become a war of conquest and destruction. For all the talk of conquered provinces and state suicide, no Republican wanted to keep the former Confederate states out of the Union forever: rather, the debate was over how to balance reunion with other objectives and how best to go about the restoration of civil government in the South. Reunion meant reincorporation and restoration of the nation, albeit with some changes to secure the fruits of Northern victory. It might include some assistance for reconstructing the Southern economy, if for no other reason than to encourage stability and create opportunity for investment and development. Economic prosperity might make it easier for white Southerners to accept both defeat and Republicans' rule. Republicans might differ over how best to achieve this objective, but reunion, sooner or later, was a common goal.

Second, Republicans sought to provide justice for the freedpeople. While party regulars may have disagreed on how best to attain this goal, the vast majority of them pushed for equality before the law. Eventually this was augmented by the acceptance of the need to enfranchise blacks, although one must note that many Republicans thought that the ballot would empower blacks to defend themselves and to shape their own future (and thus obviate the need for more federal activity). Motives varied, but there was general agreement on the goal. Less agreement existed on the question of black rights in the North, where defections gave Democrats majorities, reminded Republicans of how far they could go, and led to the Fifteenth Amendment, which dodged popular referenda at the state level by choosing instead ratification by (Republican-controlled) state legislatures. More controversial were measures that would have promoted black economic opportunity, most notably proposals that would have taken the confiscated lands of former Confederates and redistributed them to the freedpeople.[3]

Finally, Republicans kept the welfare of their party in mind. Without possessing political power, they could not achieve what they wanted to do. Thus party leaders were always aware that they could not press too far in any direction lest they lose support at the polls. Even in 1864, when voters reelected Abraham Lincoln, they did so in the aftermath of a string of Union military victories. That was the high-water mark of voter support: during Reconstruction Republicans knew that it would be hard to muster similar majorities for less popular proposals. With the war at an end, many War Democrats who had been willing to side with the administration no longer had any reason to do so, and they would soon find themselves joined by conservative Republican voters who prized an early and easy reunion with minimal change in the relations of blacks and whites. Republicans' priorities were clear: they worked first to protect their own base in the North, second to protect their own power nationally, and third to expand their party southward. A truly national party would be the best of all worlds, of course, but events in the South should not be allowed to endanger the party in the North or in the nation. The Republicans had come to national power as a sectional party, and they realized that they could continue to exercise power under such conditions—provided they retained their majorities in the North.

What limits defined the boundaries of Republican Reconstruction policy? Ideological and institutional factors loomed large. Other historians have already explored the extent to which most Republicans maintained their faith in federalism and the limits of national power. This faith placed restraints on the scope of their solutions, although a good number of observers argued that the postwar amendments and other legislation represented a significant alteration of federalism. Few were willing to go further. Republicans were also uncertain about the best way to help blacks realize the full fruits of their freedom—and whether that was the responsibility of government in the first place.[4] Take the debate over confiscation and redistribution of planter lands. Confiscation would embitter Southern whites: redistributing land to blacks, critics asserted, might foster dependency instead of self-sufficiency. Indeed, considering the importance of federalism and the limits of national power, it is well to ask whether spotlighting national politics is the best way to explore the process of Reconstruction, given the role of state governments in proposing and pursuing policies that had a direct impact on people in the South, both white and black.[5]

Nor did many Republicans seriously consider setting aside the goal of restoring civil governments altogether until enough time had passed during which the federal government, acting through Congress, would have provided for a solid foundation for the future of the freedmen. To be sure, many congressional Republicans expressed their displeasure during the war with the haste with which Abraham Lincoln sought to resurrect civil governments in the South, but the theories of Massachusetts senator Charles Sumner and Pennsylvania congressman Thaddeus Stevens never found form in legislation that had a serious chance of passing Congress. The closest Republicans came to enacting legislation that would have retarded rapid restoration of civil rule, the Wade-Davis Bill of August 1864, fell victim to Lincoln's pocket veto. At best, congressional Republicans could refuse to seat congressmen and senators from states that had complied with Lincoln's own policy, which they did with some success. Even then, however, the debate was over how best to reestablish stable state governments loyal to the Union, not over whether Congress should set aside the enterprise altogether. That was also the case after the war: it was not until 1867 that Congress finally declared that the state governments set up in ten former Confederate states were provisional, and even then it did so in legislation that provided for the formation of new state governments where African Americans would play a role. Once Congress seated congressional representatives elected under its own plan, thus "readmitting" states to full representation, it surrendered whatever power it had over those states. Indeed, in enfranchising Southern blacks, one could argue that Republicans believed that they had armed the freedmen with a weapon with which they could shape their own destinies, leaving Republicans to pursue other policies, secure in the belief that they had done all they needed to do to protect blacks by empowering them to protect themselves.

Political considerations also restrained Republicans. While all Republicans shared an interest in all three goals of Republican Reconstruction, individuals' commitment to each varied. Much energy has gone into defining lines of division between various groups of Republicans as they debated over what sort of policy to pursue and how best to attain each of these goals. One need not detail these differences yet again to point out that they existed, creating the need for consensus and compromise. After all, congressional Democrats could exploit divisions among Republicans to block passage of significant measures by taking one side or the other as circumstances required.[6]

Party unity became even more essential once it became evident that President Andrew Johnson would do all in his power to obstruct the formulation and implementation of Republican Reconstruction in whatever form it took. That Johnson was an obstructionist is well known to Reconstruction scholars. But it is well to remember exactly how Johnson's behavior shaped Reconstruction. Those historians who stress the importance of the confiscation of plantations and the redistribution of land to the freedpeople often forget that such an option would never be implemented while Johnson resided in the White House. Presidential pardons and the restoration of planter lands to their owners indicated that a sustained program of confiscation and redistribution faced a hostile chief executive. Counterfactual speculations that chastise Republican policy makers for not doing more to realize this appealing vista of equality, opportunity, and power secured through confiscation and redistribution often overlook the blunt fact of Johnson's presence: there was no chance to realize this vision so long as he was president.

Johnson's vigorous use of the veto also shaped the environment of policy framing and the content of the policies framed. Congressional Republicans had to seek common ground if they were to forge the veto-proof supermajorities needed to override expected vetoes. This gave the edge to moderate Republicans in the ensuing debate; it also allowed opportunistic Northern Democrats to promote intraparty divisions in Republican ranks by siding with dissatisfied Republicans to vote down proposals. Johnson may not have promoted Republican harmony, but he made Republican unity essential as a matter of survival. That Reconstruction policy veered in a radical direction had more to do with continuing white Southern intransigence and presidential obstruction of moderate measures than with any inherent leanings toward more extreme measures. As it was, radicals never claimed that they had carried the day, and several of them expressed their reservations about the measures adopted in 1866 and 1867 even as they begrudgingly admitted that they were the best that could be achieved under the circumstances.[7]

The best evidence of Johnson's impact can be found in the legislative record. The most extreme legislation of congressional Republicans concerned not the postwar South but efforts to tie Johnson's hands as they struggled to establish a process independent of executive interference. It may not be too much to say that Johnson's behavior diverted Republicans' attention and energy from the problem of Reconstruction by replacing it with the problem of Andrew Johnson. Indeed, Ulysses S. Grant's oft-quoted statements about presidential power—such as his inaugural pledge that he might have policies to recommend "but none to enforce against the will of the people"—reflected not a passive conception of his office but a reassurance that he was not his predecessor, for Grant had seen firsthand how Johnson abused constitutional interpretation and executive power to free himself from the constraints of the very document he so often claimed to protect. Johnson's acts also reminded Republicans of the importance of having the White House in friendly hands, thus promoting the candidacy of the moderate Grant as the Republican most likely to win election.[8]

There were other political considerations. Northern Republicans were all too aware of the limited interest of the Northern electorate in Reconstruction. The electoral majorities of 1864 and 1866, impressive though they might look at first glance, were forged by exceptional circumstances not likely to persist for long. In contrast, the Democratic resurgence in the elections of 1867 reminded Republicans that while a majority of their followers might well support measures to secure and protect full black citizenship, a critical and decisive minority did not. Most Northerners wanted an end to Reconstruction, and this did not augur well for the patience required to secure fundamental changes in American society and polity.[9]

Reconstruction policy options were also intrinsically limited by the tension among the three goals of reunion, racial justice, and party welfare. Wooing whites meant deemphasizing issues of importance to blacks, sometimes to the point of pandering to prejudices; policies to promote and protect black rights and aspirations aroused white protests of preferential treatment and burdened white taxpayers. It proved especially difficult to seek both sectional harmony and racial justice when observers perceived one as coming at the expense of the other. Northern voters were more concerned about their own futures; intense outbursts of indignation about Southern affairs alternated with expressions of hope that before long peace would be restored and people could get on with their business. Under such circumstances, to undertake simultaneously the supervision and shaping of a social revolution, the reestablishment of sectional harmony, and the preservation of electoral majorities in the North was a daunting prospect. To establish the foundations for a self-sustaining Southern Republican Party presented an even greater challenge.

Such were the problems facing Ulysses S. Grant when he assumed the presidency in 1869. "To bind up the wounds left by the war, to restore concord to the still distracted Union, to ensure real freedom to the Southern negro, and full justice to the Southern white; these are indeed tasks which might tax the powers of Washington himself, or [one] greater than Washington, if such a one is to be found," noted one English observer.[10] Yet few historians have been kind to the eighteenth president's conduct of Reconstruction. William Dunning, Claude Bowers, and John Burgess charged him with being too hard on the white South, too willing to resort to federal power, too interested in not letting white Southerners resume "home rule," that charming euphemism for the restoration of native white supremacy. Then the pendulum of historical judgment moved in the opposite direction, and a new generation of historians claimed that Grant did too little. William Gillette and William S. McFeely offered the most sustained indictments, Gillette assaulting Grant's handling of policy while McFeely assailed Grant's commitment to black equality.[11] Occasionally, such swings in historiographical fashion entangled established scholars. In 1957, one historian labeled Grant a tool of Radical Republicans; nearly twenty-five years later the same historian claimed that Grant shared Andrew Johnson's sentiments and preferences.[12]

Those historians who focus on Grant overlook the context in which he struggled to frame a policy. "If reconstruction ever had a chance," Gillette declared, "it was during Grant's administration, when the Republicans controlled—in fact, not just in form—both the presidency and Congress."[13] This assertion is open to serious question. First, it is important to remember that 1869 was not 1865. Certain policy options—including confiscation and redistribution or prolonged federal governance of the conquered Confederacy—were not available to Grant. Instead, he inherited the outcome of previous Republican initiatives—the erection of state governments in which blacks were empowered to shape their own fate by casting ballots. With the readmission of reconstructed state governments, federal opportunities for intervention and influence narrowed considerably. Second, most Republicans thought that with Grant's election and the ratification of the Fifteenth Amendment in 1870, all that could be done for blacks and the South by the federal government had been done. George W. Julian later declared that the ratification of the Fifteenth Amendment "perfectly consummated the mission of the Republican party, and left its members untrammeled in dealing with new party questions."[14] Indeed, with the end of Reconstruction, some Republicans pondered whether the party still had a purpose as they found themselves divided over what to do next. Perhaps it was time for a realignment over new issues. At a time when the Northern electorate was growing weary of old issues, some Republican voters might very well be receptive to new arrangements that looked to the future rather than to the past. If, as Michael F. Holt says, the 1850s saw "the forging of a majority," Grant and the Republican Party in the 1870s faced the task of reforging a majority.[15]

Thus, Republican strength during the first two years of the Grant presidency was somewhat illusory and attributable to temporary conditions. As the party addressed issues of economic development, civil service reform, and financial policy, it was inevitable that some defections would result. With a Republican in the White House, party unity suffered, for opposition to Johnson and fear of his veto had helped to maintain congressional unity. After years of passing measure after measure of Reconstruction policy, many Republicans wondered whether it was time to let Southern blacks and their white allies fend for themselves. Finally, the party had aged and changed.

Members of the original cadre were now passing from the scene, and new leaders were staking claims to power and party leadership. The transition proved awkward, as new leaders battled each other and members of the old guard for control.

Compounding these problems was Grant's most significant effort to offer an innovative approach to Reconstruction: his proposal to annex the Dominican Republic. This much-ridiculed idea was rooted in part in his concern to offer the freedmen some form of economic leverage consistent with laissez-faire principles. What confiscation and redistribution might have achieved would, Grant thought, be secured by the opportunities that annexation would open to Southern blacks. "What I desired above all was to secure a retreat for that portion of the laboring classes of our former slave states, who might find themselves under unbearable pressures," he later remarked. The freedman, he argued, would be empowered "to demand his rights at home on pain of finding them elsewhere."[16]

This effort to create economic leverage for blacks won the support of far more Americans than it is customary to remember. Frederick Douglass, Benjamin F. Wade, and Samuel Gridley Howe, all committed to helping the freedpeople, supported it. But Grant failed to secure the support of Charles Sumner, and the division between the president and the senator had fateful consequences. Sumner justifiably raised questions about the negotiations: he also feared that annexation might compromise the independence of the black republic of Haiti. Other opponents raised less commendable objections, questioning the wisdom of incorporating more dark-skinned people in the United States. Senate Democrats, who would have embraced such a proposal had it led to the expansion of slavery, now rejected it. The resulting debate proved quite divisive to Republican unity and, in combination with other defections from the administration over civil service reform and financial policy, helped fuel the growing anti-Grant movement that culminated in the Liberal Republican coalition of 1872.[17]

In turn, the Liberal Republican movement damaged Grant's ability to frame and pursue a Reconstruction policy. Until recently most historians viewed the eighteenth president as a weak chief executive who fumbled with the levers of political power. Not so his critics within party ranks. True, they might question Grant's intelligence, but they charged that Grant was something of a tyrant. One dissatisfied Republican paper complained that Grant had "simply allowed himself to manage public affairs as if he was our master and not our servant—our landlord and not our steward." The dissenting Republicans who eventually found their way into open opposition battled against legislative proposals to protect African Americans from political terrorism as they called for an end to federal intervention in Southern affairs.[18]

Grant's role in this realignment within the Republican Party has not always received the attention it merits, and the president does not always get from historians the credit he deserves. His critics at the time understood far more clearly than do most historians today that the general, despite some rough and blunt edges, became rather skilled in the exercise of presidential power to forge support for the administration. But this process came at some cost to Reconstruction. Not all of the old guard bolted the party, and some of those who did had in any case lost interest in Reconstruction. Still, Grant's coterie of Senate supporters—including Roscoe Conkling, Oliver P. Morton, Simon Cameron, and Zachariah Chandler—understood that the primary purpose of electoral politics was to secure and retain office. Whatever their sentiments about Reconstruction, these men looked first to the home folk before they decided what to do. Yet their commitment to Reconstruction easily exceeded that of those who opted to join Horace Greeley in clasping hands across the bloody chasm.

Grant's other efforts to develop a Reconstruction policy addressed the interrelated problems of Southern Republicanism and the appropriate role of the federal government. It proved difficult if not impossible to address the problems of constructing a self-sufficient and durable Republican Party throughout the South in large part because the composition and thus the concerns of the party varied from state to state. While each state's Republican contingent was composed of carpetbaggers, scalawags, and blacks, the proportions shifted from state to state. In those states where native white Southerners formed a significant part of the party, many Republicans favored policies designed to solidify white support, most notably through the promise of economic development. In those states dominated by an alliance between blacks and carpetbaggers, many Republicans sought federal support through patronage or intervention—which in turn hindered their efforts to attain legitimacy in the eyes of their opponents and eroded their chances of attaining self-sufficiency. Furthermore, Southern Republicanism was plagued by factional disputes, usually concerning whether it was better to broaden the base of the party's support among whites or shore up its core constituency of blacks. These varied conditions made it impossible for Grant to formulate an overall policy that would serve both approaches equally well; it proved difficult to advocate different approaches for different states simultaneously.[19]

The Panic of 1873 and the resulting depression ruled out both alternatives. Efforts at economic development collapsed in the wake of the economic downturn, as railroads went bankrupt. The "gospel of prosperity" turned into a mockery of Republican hopes. In those states where Republicans sought to shore up their core constituencies through state programs, the depression increased the economic burdens of taxpayers—mostly white landowners—and caused them to resent the beneficiaries of the programs paid for by tax dollars, usually the former slaves. Northern whites wondered why the federal government seemed more interested in helping Southern blacks than Northern white workers, which in turn raised the political cost of intervention by the Grant administration.[20]

Lyndon Johnson once said that the hardest thing about governing was not doing the right thing but discovering what was the right thing to do. One can apply this insight to Grant's dealings with Republican regimes in the South. What could he have done in states like Arkansas and Florida, where Republican factionalism proved self-destructive? Acquaint yourself with the Brooks-Baxter War in Arkansas, where the two principals switched constituencies during their struggle, and then decide what Grant might have done to change the outcome in favor of the Republican cause. Even in states like Mississippi, Louisiana, and South Carolina, where black votes formed the bedrock of Republican strength, divisions among Republican whites—again over whether to expand the electoral appeal of the party or to shore up its core constituency—made it difficult to find out what was the right thing to do.

It proved problematic for Grant to develop an approach to Southern politics that would have benefitted the party across the entire region. In states where he fostered conciliationist regimes, the Democrats co-opted them and came to power. When he protected Republican regimes against violence, the very act of intervention served to highlight these regimes' inability to protect themselves and eroded whatever claims to legitimacy they had. Intervention also enabled Northern Democrats to charge Grant with establishing a military despotism; those Republicans who were already lukewarm to Reconstruction claimed that it was time to let Southern Republicans fend for themselves.

Where Grant came up short was in his failure to choose which policy to pursue. This, in turn, reflected his desire to keep in equilibrium the goals of reconciliation and racial justice. In holding out both the sword and the olive branch to Southern whites, he failed either to woo them to accept the postwar order or deter them from attempting to overthrow it. Trying to maintain a balance is not always the best policy, and in this case it was not. Indeed, Grant's approach to Reconstruction embodied the dilemmas of Republican policy instead of resolving them. Of course, Grant made several mistakes, as he admitted, although they were ones of judgment, not intent. His selection of Joseph P. Bradley to the Supreme Court proved counterproductive when Bradley ruled against federal attempts to punish white supremacists in *U.S. v. Cruikshank.* Attorney General George H. Williams proved ambivalent about administering the Enforcement Acts, and his successor, Edwards Pierrepont, was downright hostile. Surely Grant could have done better, although it is doubtful whether better appointments would have altered the outcome significantly.[21]

Nevertheless, Grant should not have to bear the burden of criticism by himself. Congressional Republicans also reacted in conflicting ways as they framed the postwar amendments and supporting legislation. Even as they enlarged the potential power of the federal government, they did so with surprising restraint, seeking to honor notions of federalism. In several instances their legislation proved to be hastily and sloppily drafted—although remedying this shortcoming would not have meant all that much in the long run, for these Republicans understood the limited nature of white Northerners' commitment to protecting Southern blacks and their white allies. Many historians still refer derisively to "waving the bloody shirt" as a cynical Republican appeal to recall wartime hatreds, overlooking the fact that many Southern Democrats engaged in exactly the same practice. True, references to the bloody shirt might well be tinged with cynicism, despite the very real importance of the war to many Northern whites, but Northern Republicans knew that the appeal had a better chance of mobilizing electoral majorities than would a plea for justice to blacks, and it must not be forgotten that in many cases the shirt was still wet with the blood of those killed by white terrorists in Dixie.

Republican electoral setbacks in 1874 presaged the end of Reconstruction. With the House of Representatives in Democratic hands, Grant could no longer secure legislation to bolster intervention. Indeed, unless the party did something to regain majorities in several states, it stood to lose the presidency in 1876. For Grant, the year 1875 presented in stark terms the dilemmas of Reconstruction. In January, Louisiana Democrats attempted a coup d'état; only the intervention of federal troops saved Republican governor William P. Kellogg and his administration from overthrow. Democrats and some Republicans expressed outrage—not at the actions of Louisiana's Democrats but at the response of the federal forces on the scene. Overlooking the fact that it had been the Democrats, not the Republicans, who first called upon the military for assistance, critics of the administration waxed eloquent about the dangers such intervention presented to representative government.

In one of the most impassioned statements ever to emanate from a president, Grant lashed back. He reminded them that those Louisiana whites who had massacred some one hundred blacks at Colfax in April 1873 had yet to be convicted for their crime, in part because of a federal district court decision that hindered efforts to arrest and prosecute the murderers. "Fierce denunciations ring through the country about office holding and election matters in Louisiana," Grant declared, "while every one of the Colfax miscreants goes unwhipped of justice, and no way can be found in this boasted land of civilization and Christianity to punish the perpetrators of this bloody and monstrous crime." Such comments echoed those offered by Grant five weeks earlier in his annual message. Replying to critics of federal intervention under the Fifteenth Amendment and the Enforcement Acts, he observed that if he could not protect blacks, then those measures were "without meaning, force, or effect, and the whole scheme of colored enfranchisement is worse than mockery and little better than a crime."[22]

These are not the statements of an indifferent man, but they are the words of a disappointed one. For with the Democratic triumph in the 1874 elections came an end to the chance to pass additional legislation to empower the president to act decisively in the South. A final effort to draft a new enforcement act failed. The president was already aware that there were court challenges to prosecutions under existing legislation—*U.S. v. Cruikshank*, which concerned the Colfax massacre, and *U.S. v. Reese*, which involved efforts to block blacks from voting, were about to be heard by the Supreme Court (indeed, Attorney General George Williams opened the government's case in *Reese* on the day Grant sent his passionate message about Louisiana affairs to the Senate). The most Congress would do was pass a new civil rights act, but whether it would achieve anything was unclear in light of the crippling of enforcement legislation. Finally, Grant himself foresaw what would happen next: once Democrats regained control of state governments, they would commence drafting new constitutions that would compromise the gains of the war, emancipation, and Reconstruction. His warnings in this regard went unheeded: some Republicans, including members of Grant's own cabinet, were openly critical of the president's position.[23]

Grant realized that a majority of Northern voters would no longer support federal intervention when there were more pressing needs to be met at home. That September, when Mississippi governor Adelbert Ames called on him to dispatch troops to protect 1Republican voters, Grant, aware that such an act might jeopardize Republican chances for victory in the closely contested state of Ohio, a bellwether of the presidential race, declined the request. "The whole public are tired out with these annual, autumnal outbreaks in the South," he wrote Attorney General Edwards Pierrepont, "and there is so much unwholsome lying done by the press and people in regard to the cause & extent of these breaches of the peace that the great majority are ready now to condemn any interference on the part of the government." It was a pragmatic political decision. He would not sacrifice the party in the North to keep it alive in the South; to do so would be to ensure the election of a Democrat as president in 1876, which would surely bring an end to Reconstruction. Grant may have had qualms about his decision, but his choice suggested just how much of a politician he had become. Equally revealing was his effort in late September to rally voters and veterans around a new cause—that of defending the public schools from sectarian attacks by the Catholic Church. It was a concession that Reconstruction was no longer politically viable as an issue for the Republican Party.[24]

During the first three months of 1876, it became apparent that Reconstruction was coming to an end. Only Louisiana, South Carolina, and Florida remained in Republican hands, and terrorism chopped away at already slim Republican majorities. Supreme Court decisions in the *Cruikshank* and *Reese* cases narrowed the grounds for and the scope of intervention. Revelations of corruption in the Grant administration and the president's lame-duck status crippled the chief executive still more. To be sure, Republicans, led by James G. Blaine, once more waved the bloody shirt, but Blaine focused not on events in the South but on the fear of the Confederates and their stooges, the Northern Democrats, recapturing the White House. In the presidential contest the Republican standard-bearer Rutherford B. Hayes saw no contradiction between his plans to abandon intervention and his advice to campaigners to stress the threat of a resurgent Confederacy. Such reasoning drew upon an understanding of how the Republicans first came to power in 1860 by stressing the threat of enslavement posed by the Slave Power, not the immorality of slavery. Republicans simply substituted the bloody shirt for the Slave Power and spoke of how a Democratic triumph would reverse the verdict of Appomattox. In so doing, they reverted to the sectional strategy that had proved so successful before the war. Ironically, however, Republicans needed the votes of three Southern states to retain the White House; that secured, they left those states to fend for themselves. By then, of course, it was too late to revive Reconstruction. Hayes's efforts to forge a bisectional Republican Party by appealing to Southern whites never had a serious chance, and before long even he had to admit that he had failed.[25]

It is difficult to see what could have been done to salvage Reconstruction after 1873. It is also unclear that anyone could have done a better job than Grant, at least anyone who was electable. The electoral limits of radicalism led most Republicans to turn to Grant in 1868. His popularity exceeded that of his party, and his image as the candidate of justice and peace was reinforced by the Democrats' choice of Horatio Seymour and Frank P. Blair to head their ticket. The new president survived and even shaped the Republican realignment during his first term, building a coalition of loyal supporters and securing reelection in 1872. But the very success of Reconstruction in readmitting reconstructed Southern states led most white Northerners to declare the process at an end; in turn, this eroding commitment enhanced the efforts of Southern white Redeemers to regain control of state governments one by one. Grant tried attracting Southern whites; he also tried protecting Southern blacks. Halfway policies in both directions failed to achieve either objective. In the end, Grant, disappointed both by the intransigence of Southern redeemers and the antagonism of Northern Democrats and some Republicans, realized that he could not fashion a policy to achieve all three objectives of Republican Reconstruction policy. Forced to choose, he opted to conserve Republican power in the North and in the nation and accepted Redemption as the price. To the end of his life, he still sought the restoration of sectional harmony, but he could never forget that the nation owed it to its black population to make things right.[26]

Most historians today would agree that Reconstruction failed to provide justice for the freedpeople. While emancipation and the postwar constitutional amendments represented a significant step forward, they proved to be insufficient by themselves. On the other hand, the goal of sectional harmony was, after a fashion, achieved. In recent years historians have urged us to view emancipation in comparative terms; we might also do well to look at reconciliation after a civil war in a like light.[27] Finally, it is interesting to consider whether Republicans' party aims were not in fact met. If Reconstruction's purpose was, as Gillette insists, "to lodge national political power permanently in the North within the national Republican party and to republicanize the South," it was obvious which goal would give way when the two were in conflict. In light of Republican domination of national politics for over four decades after Grant left office, Reconstruction, applying Gillette's criteria, was a partial political success, for during it Republicans forged the foundation of their post-Reconstruction dominance.[28]

Politicians understand that their profession is the art of the possible. In order to assess the past, scholars, too, must understand what was possible. Those historians who continue to point to the shortcomings of Republican policy makers to explain the collapse of Reconstruction owe it to us to offer an alternative that was historically plausible and achievable.[29] In so doing, they must consider the same three considerations that Reconstruction Republicans found so hard to reconcile: the restoration of sectional harmony, the securing of justice for the freedpeople, and the preservation of Republican political power in the North and in the nation. They need to take into account how Andrew Johnson's presidency narrowed Republicans' options and shaped the legislation that emerged even as they examine the extent to which Republicans were willing to go in constitutional and institutional innovation. Nor should historians neglect how the majority of white Southerners, including those who participated in political terrorism, shaped the outcome of Reconstruction in their battle to preserve white supremacy. Those who like to issue moral indictments would do well to recall who should head the list. Perhaps one should also recall those whites, North and South, who did nothing to stop the terrorism. Surely their hands are not exactly clean: Republicans knew that they could not stray far beyond what their voters would support when it came to Reconstruction, lest an ensuing electoral defeat hand the national government over to the tender mercies of the Democrats. Finally, it is well for historians to take a look at the world around them today before they rush to judgment about the past. Perhaps we should not demand of Ulysses S. Grant and his fellow Republicans of the 1860s and 1870s what we today find so hard to ask of ourselves.

Notes

1. Michael Perman, "Counter Reconstruction: The Role of Violence in Southern Redemption," in Eric Anderson and Alfred A. Moss Jr., eds., *The Facts of Reconstruction: Essays in Honor of John Hope Franklin* (Baton Rouge: Louisiana State University Press, 1991), 137.

2. Gerald N. Grob, "Reconstruction: An American Morality Play," in George Athan Billias and Gerald N. Grob, eds., *American History: Retrospect and Prospect* (New York: Free Press, 1971), 191–231, esp. 191–96.

3. Herman Belz, *Emancipation and Equal Rights: Politics and Constitutionalism in the Civil War Era* (New York: W. W. Norton, 1978); Earl M. Maltz, *Civil Rights, the Constitution, and Congress, 1863–1869* (Lawrence: University Press of Kansas, 1990).

4. The classic statement of this position remains Michael Les Benedict, "Preserving the Constitution: The Conservative Basis of Radical Reconstruction," *Journal of American History* 61 (1974): 65–90. See also Benedict, "The Problem of Constitutionalism and Constitutional Liberty in the Reconstruction South," in Kermit L. Hall and James W. Ely Jr., *An Uncertain Tradition: Constitutionalism and the History of the South* (Athens: University of Georgia Press, 1989), 225–49; Benedict, "Laissez-Faire and Liberty: A Reevaluation of

the Origins of Laissez-Faire Constitutionalism," *Law and History Review* 3 (1985): 293–331; and Benedict, "Reform Republicans and the Retreat from Reconstruction," in Anderson and Moss, *The Facts of Reconstruction*, 53–77.

5. On this point, see Carl H. Moneyhon, "The Failure of Southern Republicanism, 1867–1876," in Anderson and Moss, *The Facts of Reconstruction*, 99–119; and the essays in Otto Olsen, ed., *Reconstruction and Redemption in the South* (Baton Rouge: Louisiana State University Press, 1980).

6. David Donald, *The Politics of Reconstruction, 1863–1867* (Baton Rouge: Louisiana State University Press, 1965), 58–60.

7. The most detailed exploration of the struggles between Johnson and Congress is Michael Les Benedict, *A Compromise of Principle: Congressional Republicans and Reconstruction, 1863–1869* (New York: W. W. Norton, 1974). See also Eric McKitrick, *Andrew Johnson and Reconstruction* (Chicago: University of Chicago Press, 1960); James Sefton, *Andrew Johnson and the Uses of Constitutional Power* (Boston: Little, Brown, 1980); and Albert Castel, *The Presidency of Andrew Johnson* (Lawrence: University Press of Kansas, 1979).

8. Ulysses S. Grant, First Inaugural Address, March 4, 1869, in James D. Richardson, ed., *A Compilation of the Messages and Papers of the Presidents*, vol. 6 (New York: Bureau of National Literature, 1912), 3960–62.

9. Maltz, *Civil Rights, the Constitution, and Congress*, 29–30; Robert D. Sawrey, *Dubious Victory: The Reconstruction Debate in Ohio* (Lexington: University Press of Kentucky, 1992); Michael Les Benedict, "The Rout of Radicalism: Republicans and the Election of 1867," in Robert P. Swierenga, ed., *Beyond the Civil War Synthesis: Political Essays of the Civil War Era* (Westport, CT: Greenwood, 1975), 137–48.

10. "General Ulysses S. Grant," *Edinburgh Review* 129 (January 1869): 230–69.

11. John A. Carpenter, *Ulysses S. Grant* (New York: Twayne, 1970), 86; William Gillette, *Retreat from Reconstruction, 1869–1879* (Baton Rouge: Louisiana State University Press, 1979); William S. McFeely, *Grant: A Biography* (New York: W. W. Norton, 1981).

12. Compare C. Vann Woodward's comments on Grant and Reconstruction in "The Lowest Ebb," *American Heritage* 8:3 (1957): 52–57, 106–9, with his remarks about William S. McFeely's *Grant: A Biography* in *New York Review of Books*, March 19, 1981, 3–6.

13. Gillette, *Retreat from Reconstruction*, xii.

14. George W. Julian, *Political Recollections, 1840 to 1872* (1884; New York: Negro University Presses, 1970), 330.

15. Brooks D. Simpson, "The Reforging of a Republican Majority," in Robert F. Engs and Randall M. Miller, eds., *The Birth of the Grand Old Party: The Republicans' First Generation* ((Philadelphia: University of Pennsylvania Press, 2002), 148–66.

16. *Responses to Toasts at a Banquet . . . in Commemoration of the Seventy-Fourth Anniversary of the Birth of Gen'l Ulysses S. Grant, Philadelphia, April 27, 1896* (Philadelphia: Times Printing House, 1896), 40–41 (remarks of Andrew D. White); Ulysses S. Grant, Eighth Annual Message, December 5, 1876, in Richardson, *Messages and Papers of the Presidents*, 6:4353–67, quotation on 4366.

17. Brooks D. Simpson, *The Reconstruction Presidents* (Lawrence: University Press of Kansas, 1998), 145–48; Eric T. L. Love, *Race over Empire: Racism and U.S. Imperialism, 1865–1900* (Chapel Hill: University of North Carolina Press, 2004), 43–72.

18. See Andrew L. Slap, *The Doom of Reconstruction: The Liberal Republicans in the Civil War Era* (New York: Fordham University Press, 2006), 108–25, quotation on 125.

19. Two books by Michael Perman highlight this dilemma: *The Road to Redemption: Southern Politics, 1869–1879* (Chapel Hill: University of North Carolina Press, 1984) and *Emancipation and Reconstruction, 1862–1879* (Arlington Heights, IL: Harlan Davidson, 1987). See also Brooks D. Simpson, "Land and the Ballot: Securing the Fruits of Emancipation?" *Pennsylvania History* 60 (April 1993): 176–88.

20. See Mark W. Summers, *Railroads, Reconstruction, and the Gospel of Prosperity* (Princeton, NJ: Princeton University Press, 1984); and J. Mills Thornton, "Fiscal Policy and the Failure of Radical Reconstruction in the Lower South," in J. Morgan Kousser and James M. McPherson, eds., *Region, Race, and Reconstruction: Essays in Honor of C. Vann Woodward* (New York: Oxford University Press, 1982), 349–94.

21. See Robert J. Kaczorowski, *The Politics of Judicial Interpretation: The Federal Courts, Department of Justice and Civil Rights, 1866–1876* (Dobbs Ferry, NY: Oceana, 1985).

22. Ulysses S. Grant, Annual Message, December 7, 1874, in Richardson, *Messages and Papers of the Presidents*, 6:4238–57, quotation on 4251; Grant, Message to the Senate, January 13, 1875, ibid., 6:4259–68, quotation on 4262.

23. Simpson, *The Reconstruction Presidents*, 182; Charles W. Calhoun, *Conceiving a New Republic: The Republican Party and the Southern Question, 1869–1900* (Lawrence: University Press of Kansas, 2006), 72–74.

24. John R. Lynch, *The Facts of Reconstruction*, ed. William C. Harris (Indianapolis: Bobbs-Merrill, 1970), 152–55; Grant to Edwards Pierrepont, September 13, 1875, in John Y. Simon et al., eds., *The Papers of Ulysses S. Grant*, 31 vols. (Carbondale: Southern Illinois University Press, 1967–2009), 26:312–13; Simpson, *The Reconstruction Presidents*, 186–88.

25. Simpson, *The Reconstruction Presidents*, 199–228.

26. See Brooks D. Simpson, "Butcher? Racist? An Examination of William S. McFeely's *Grant: A Biography*," *Civil War History* 33 (March 1987): 63–83, especially 82–83.

27. See C. Vann Woodward, "Emancipations and Reconstructions: A Comparative Study," in *The Future of the Past* (New York: Oxford University Press, 1989), 145–66; and LaWanda Cox's comments on Woodward's initial presentation of this essay in 1970 in *Lincoln and Black Freedom: A Study in Presidential Leadership* (Columbia: University of South Carolina Press, 1981), 157–59.

28. Gillette, *Retreat from Reconstruction*, xiii.

29. See C. Vann Woodward, "Reconstruction: A Counterfactual Playback," in *The Future of the Past*, 183–200.

Works by Michael F. Holt

BOOKS

Franklin Pierce. New York: Time Books, 2010.

By One Vote: The Disputed Presidential Election of 1876. Lawrence: University Press of Kansas, 2008.

The Civil War and Reconstruction. Rev. ed. Coauthored with Jean H. Baker and David Herbert Donald. New York: W. W. Norton, 2001.

The Rise and Fall of the American Whig Party: Jacksonian Politics and the Onset of the Civil War. New York: Oxford University Press, 1999.

Political Parties and American Political Development from the Age of Jackson to the Age of Lincoln. Baton Rouge: Louisiana State University Press, 1999.

A Master's Due: Essays in Honor of David Herbert Donald. Coedited with William J. Cooper Jr. and John McCardell. Baton Rouge: Louisiana State University Press, 1985.

The Political Crisis of the 1850s. New York: John Wiley & Sons, 1978; reprint, W. W. Norton, 1983.

Forging a Majority: The Formation of the Republican Party in Pittsburgh, 1848–1860. New Haven, CT: Yale University Press, 1969; reprint, Pittsburgh: University of Pittsburgh Press, 1990.

ARTICLES AND BOOK CHAPTERS

"Lincoln Reconsidered." *Journal of American History* 96 (September 2009): 451–55.

Introduction to *Prologue to Conflict: The Crisis and Compromise of 1850,* by Holman Hamilton. Repr. ed. Lexington: University Press of Kentucky, 2005. xi–xvii.

"Making and Mobilizing the Republican Party, 1854–1860." In Robert F. Engs and Randall M. Miller, eds., *The Birth of the Grand Old Party: The Republicans' First Generation.* Philadelphia: University of Pennsylvania Press, 2002. 29–59.

"Change and Continuity in the Party Period: The Substance and Structure of American Politics, 1835–1885." In Byron E. Shafer and Anthony J. Badger, eds., *Contesting Democracy: Substance and Structure in American Political History, 1775–2000.* Lawrence: University Press of Kansas, 2001. 93–115.

"The Primacy of Party Reasserted." *Journal of American History* 86 (June 1999): 151–57.

"An Elusive Synthesis: Recent Literature on Northern Politics during the Civil War." In

William J. Cooper Jr. and James M. McPherson, eds., *Writing the Civil War: The Quest to Understand.* Columbia: University of South Carolina Press, 1998. 112–34.

"Another Look at the Election of 1856." In Michael Birkner, ed., *James Buchanan and the Political Crisis of the 1850s.* Selingsgrove, PA: Susquehanna University Press, 1996. 37–67.

"From Center to Periphery: The Market Revolution and Major-Party Conflict, 1835– 1880." In Melvyn Stokes and Stephen Conway, eds., *The Market Revolution in America: Social, Political, and Religious Expressions, 1800–1880.* Charlottesville: University Press of Virginia, 1996. 224–56.

"Rethinking Nineteenth-Century American Political History." *Congress and the Presidency* 19:2 (Autumn 1992): 97–111.

"Abraham Lincoln and the Politics of Union." In John L. Thomas, ed., *Abraham Lincoln and the American Political Tradition.* Amherst: University of Massachusetts Press, 1985. 110–41.

"The Election of 1840, Voter Mobilization, and the Emergence of the Second American Party System: A Reappraisal of Jacksonian Voting Behavior." In William J. Cooper Jr., Michael F. Holt, and John McCardell, eds., *A Master's Due: Essays in Honor of David Herbert Donald.* Baton Rouge: Louisiana State University Press, 1985. 151–91.

"Winding Roads to Recovery: The Whig Party from 1844 to 1848." In Stephen E. Maizlish and John J. Kushma, eds., *Essays on American Antebellum Politics.* College Station: Texas A&M University Press, 1982. 122–65.

Sections on Presidents Harrison through Buchanan. In C. Vann Woodward, ed., *Response of Presidents to Charges of Misconduct.* New York: Dell, 1974.

"The Democratic Party, 1828–1860" and "The Antimasonic and Know Nothing Parties." In Arthur M. Schlesinger Jr., ed., *History of US Political Parties,* 4 vols. New York: Chelsea House and R. W. Bowker, 1973. 1:497–737.

"The Politics of Impatience: The Origins of Know Nothingism." *Journal of American History* 60 (1973): 309–31.

Contributors

ERIK B. ALEXANDER earned his Ph.D. at the University of Virginia. He has been the recipient of fellowships from the Gilder-Lehrman Institute of American History in New York and the Henry E. Huntington Library in San Marino, California. Alexander is currently Research Assistant Professor in History and an Assistant Editor of *The Papers of Andrew Jackson* at the University of Tennessee, Knoxville.

JEAN HARVEY BAKER is Bennett-Harwood Professor of History at Goucher College. She is the author of numerous books, including *Mary Todd Lincoln: A Biography; James Buchanan; Sisters: The American Suffragists;* and the recently published *Margaret Sanger: A Life of Passion.*

WILLIAM J. COOPER is a Boyd Professor at Louisiana State University. He received his A.B. from Princeton University and his Ph.D. from Johns Hopkins University. He has been a fellow of the Guggenheim Foundation and the National Endowment for the Humanities and was a recipient of the Los Angeles Times Book Award for Biography. He is also a past president of the Southern Historical Association. His books include *The South and the Politics of Slavery, 1828–1856; Liberty and Slavery: Southern Politics to 1860; Jefferson Davis, American;* and *Jefferson Davis and the Civil War Era.*

DANIEL W. CROFTS is Professor of History at The College of New Jersey and studies the Old South and the North-South sectional conflict. He is the author of *Reluctant Confederates: Upper South Unionists in the Secession Crisis; Old Southampton: Politics and Society in a Virginia County, 1834–1869;* and several other books.

WILLIAM W. FREEHLING is a Senior Fellow at the Virginia Foundation for the Humanities and the author of *The Road to Disunion* and *Showdown in Virginia: The 1861 Convention and the Fate of the Union.*

GARY W. GALLAGHER is John L. Nau III Professor of History at the University of Virginia and author, most recently, of *The Union War* and *Causes Won, Lost, and Forgotten: How Hollywood and Popular Art Shape What We Know about the Civil War.*

SEAN NALTY is a graduate student at the University of Virginia, working under the direction of Michael Holt.

MARK E. NEELY JR. is McCabe-Greer Professor of the History of the Civil War Era at Pennsylvania State University. He is author of, among other titles, *The Boundaries of American Political Culture in the Civil War Era; The Union Divided: Party Conflict in the Civil War North;* and *The Fate of Liberty: Abraham Lincoln and Civil Liberties,* which won the Pulitzer Prize for History in 1992.

RACHEL A. SHELDEN received her Ph.D. from the University of Virginia in 2011. She is Assistant Professor of American History at Georgia College and State University.

BROOKS D. SIMPSON is ASU Foundation Professor of History at Arizona State University. He is the author of several books, including *Ulysses S. Grant: Triumph over Adversity, 1822–1865; The Reconstruction Presidents; America's Civil War;* and *Let Us Have Peace: Ulysses S. Grant and the Politics of War and Reconstruction, 1861–1868.*

J. MILLS THORNTON is Professor Emeritus of History at the University of Michigan, Ann Arbor. He is the author of *Politics and Power in a Slave Society: Alabama, 1800–1860* (winner of the John H. Dunning Prize of the American Historical Association) and of *Dividing Lines: Municipal Politics and the Struggle for Civil Rights in Montgomery, Birmingham and Selma* (winner of the Liberty Legacy Prize of the Organization of American Historians).

Index

Argersinger, Peter H. (historian), 209n8

Aristocratic Order, 38

Arkansas, 105, 107n11, 120, 123, 223

Armstrong, Jack (gang leader), 53

Articles of Confederation, 117

Ashe, John (U.S. representative, Tenn.), 25, 26

Atchison, David (U.S. senator, Mo.), 106n11

Atkins, John DeWitt Clinton (U.S. representative, Tenn.), 94

Ayers, Edward L. (historian), 105

Badger, George E. (U.S. senator, N.C.), 92

Baker, Jean Harvey (historian), 3, 50, 63n76, 107n17

Baker, Lewis (killer of Pool), 36, 44, 50

balance-of-power politics, 106n11

ballot, the, 162

Balogh, Brian (historian), 6n5

Baltimore, Md., 46, 59, 91, 96, 100, 143, 158; Know-Nothings, 96

Bankhead, John H. (state representative, Ala.), 174

banks, 115, 168, 176; suspension of, 174

Barber, Ambrose, 29

Barlow, Samuel, 193, 194, 203, 205, 213n75

Barney, Hiram, 194, 197, 203

Barringer, Daniel (U.S. representative, N.C.), 16, 17, 24

Barrow, Alexander (U.S. senator, La.), 18

Bates, Edward, 99, 134

Bayard, James A. (U.S. senator, Del.), 87

Bayard, Richard (U.S. senator, Del.), 13

Beauregard, P. G. T., 118–19

Bedini, Gaetano (papal nuncio), 46

Bell, John, 92–93, 99, 101–2, 110n42; as senator (Tenn.), 91; supporters of, 144; as Unionist presidential candidate, 90–91

Bell, Joshua, 94

Bell, Middleton R. (state senator, Ala.), 171, 180

Bell, Bell and Everett: Association, 147; "Men," 160–61. See also Constitutional Union Party

Belmont, August, 193, 194, 195–96, 197, 200, 207, 210n25

benevolent: activists, 68, 69–72, 74, 75, 79; societies, 76

Benjamin, Judah P. (U.S. senator, La.), 87

Bensel, Richard Franklin (historian), 56, 59, 63n76

Benton, Thomas Hart (U.S. senator, Mo.), 51, 106n11

Berrien, John M. (U.S. senator, Ga.), 19, 21, 22, 24, 27, 29

Bethea, Tristam B. (state representative, Ala.), 170, 175

Blackburn, J. W. (Unionist), 150

Black Codes, 167, 184–85; defeat of, 179

Black Hawk War, 53–54

blacks. See African Americans

Blackstone, Sir William, 66, 73

Blaine, James G. (presidential candidate), 226

Blair, Francis P., Jr., 106n11, 189, 192, 202–5, 207, 227

Blair, Montgomery, 104, 192, 204

Blair, William A. (historian), 145, 163n4, 164n18

"bloody shirt," 189, 205, 224, 226

"blundering generation," 6n8

boardinghouses, 3, 23, 31, 32n8, 34n36; regional and sectional dispersal of boarders/houses (28th and 29th congresses), 14t, 15t, 23t, 24t, 30t, 31t. *Specific houses:* Mrs. Adams's, 14; Mrs. Carter's, 26, 29; Mr. Gilbert's, 13; Mr. Gurley's, 24; H. V. Hill's, 14; Mr. Hyatt's, 30; Dr. Mayo's, 24; Miss Polk's, 13; Mrs. Potter's, 26; Mr. Stettinius's, 30; Mrs. Ulrick's, 13

Border South, 88, 119, 123, 131, 135, 136

border states, 96–97

Boteler, Alexander R. (U.S. representative, Va.), 108n22

Botts, John Minor, 97

Bowers, Claude (historian), 219

Bradley, Joseph P., 224

Brandon, John W. (state representative, Ala.), 171

fire-eaters, 133, 135, 140

First Party System, 56

Fisher, Sidney George (diarist), 150, 154

Fitzhugh, George, 113–14

flags and nativism, 61n19

Flexner, Eleanor (historian), 73

Florida, 225, 226

Foner, Eric (historian), 6n8

force of history, 184

foreign policy, 15, 184

Forney, John W., 157, 160

Fort Sumter, 104, 121, 122, 137, 140, 146

Foster, Ephraim (U.S. senator, Tenn.), 26, 28

freedom, 118, 128. *See also* republicanism

freedpeople, 4, 150, 161, 223–24, 227; as apprentices, 175, 176; civil rights of, 173, 215; condition of, 174–85; economic leverage of, 215, 221; enfranchisement of, 179, 181, 183–84, 215, 217; equality of, 215; justice toward, 228; labor contracts of, 175–76. *See also* African Americans

Freehling, William W. (historian), 3, 32n2, 87, 88, 105, 139n17

Freeman, Joanne (historian), 3

Freeman, Zenas F. (state representative, Ala.), 170

free-soil, 78, 92, 96, 106n11, 144

free states, 85, 87, 101

Frémont, John, 69

fugitive slaves, 39, 117–18; laws, 39, 87, 113, 116, 120

furlough policy, 155–56

Gallman, Matthew (historian), 76

Gambill, Edward L. (historian), 212n51

gang culture, 37

Garrison, William Lloyd, 71

George III (king), 113, 119

Georgia, 20, 24, 25, 120, 131–32, 136, 172; legislature, 132

German: Americans, 106, immigrants, 96

gerrymanders, 93

Gibson, A. M. (state representative, Ala.), 171

Giddings, Joshua (U.S. representative, Ala.), 19, 27, 92

Gienapp, William E. (historian), 112–13, 114

Gilded Age, 57, 162, 185

Gillette, William (historian), 190, 219–20, 227

Gilmer, John A. (U.S. representative, N.C.), 82, 93, 100, 103–5, 110n46

Gilmer, Thomas, 14

Ginzberg, Lori (historian), 73–74

Goggin, William (Opposition candidate for governor), 94

Goodwin, Doris Kearns (historian), 2

Goodwin, F. LeBaron (state representative, Ala.), 170

Gordon, Anne (historian), 72

Gorn, Elliott J. (historian), 38

"gospel of prosperity," 223

Graham, William A. (N.C. Whig), 97

Grant, Ulysses S., 189, 203, 220–30; and anti-Grant movement, 221; as general, 215; image of, 227; as moderate, 218; and patronage, 224; as politician, 226; popularity of, 227; as president, 190, 208, 218–20, 222–23, 225; public schools and Catholicism, defending, 226; Reconstruction policy of, 221–26; as Republican nominee, 194; and Republican power in the North, 227; and Southern politics, 223

Grayson, Thomas W., 157

Greeley, Horace, 22, 40, 98, 100, 191, 222. See also *New York Tribune*

Green, Duff, 139n10

greenbacks, 196, 199, 207; plank, 200

Greenbank, Thomas (Douglas Democrat), 147

Greenberg, Amy S. (historian), 60n9

Grider, Henry (U.S. representative, Ky.), 26

Grimké, Angelina, 71

Grimstead, David (historian), 63n76

Grinnell, Joseph (U.S. representative, Mass.), 21–22

Grow, Galusha (speaker), 149

McFeely, William S. (historian), 219–20

McGuire (challenged by Pool), 37

McLaughlin, Patrick (thug), 39–40, 44, 50, 57

McMichael, Morton (Philadelphia newspaperman), 150, 154

McNeely, Robert T. (old settler), 53–54

McPherson, Edward (U.S. representative, Pa.), 150, 157

McPherson, James M. (historian), 143, 162n2, 165n29

Menefee, W. C. (state representative, Ala.), 171

Merrick, William (U.S. senator, Md.), 28, 29

Methodism, 38, 45

Mexican-American War, 31, 47, 52; Cession, 127–28

Mexico, 12, 14, 19, 25, 29

Michigan, 22

Middle South, 105, 119–20, 123

Midwest, 70, 71, 194, 205, 206; Upper, 68

Miller, Jacob (U.S. senator, N.J.), 72

Millson, John (U.S. representative, Va.), 108n22

missionary work, 72

Mississippi, 118, 223, 225; governor of, 120

Missouri, 97, 104, 106n11, 110n42, 119, 204

Missouri Compromise, 91, 127–28; line extension, 129, 134, 136

Mitchell, Americus C. (state senator, Ala.), 170

moderate: candidate, 205; men, 135; platform, 205

monetary: issues, 197, 205; policy, 194

Monroe, James (president), 137

Monroe Guard, 46. See also fighting clubs

Moore, John G. (future Republican), 171, 174

Morris, Edward (U.S. representative, Pa.), 24

Morris, Thomas (Democrat), 151–52

Morrissey, John (boxer), 37, 39, 43, 44, 50, 54, 60n3

Morse, Joshua (future Republican), 179

Morton, Oliver P. (U.S. senator, Ind.), 222

Moseley, William (U.S. representative, N.Y.), 13

Mott, Lucretia, 73

"Mountain Men," 39, 41

Murray, Michael (brawler), 40

Nalty, Sean (historian), 4

"Nancy men," 69

national: outlook, 116, 138; politics, 105, 216; slave code, 117

National Era, 94, 99–100

National Intelligencer, 17

nationalism, 63n77, 105, 116, 118; civic, 58; ethnic, 58–59

National Union Party, 143–66; affiliation, 98; convention, 143

National Woman Suffrage Association, 76

nativism, 36, 44, 91, 96; political, 45. *See also* Know-Nothings

Nat Turner Revolt, 119

natural rights, 117–20, 123; theory, 75

Neely, Mark E., Jr. (historian), 3, 151, 163n6

Netherland, John (Opposition candidate for governor), 95

Nevins, Allan (historian), 86

New Departure, 189–90, 194, 208. *See also* Democrats

New England, 68, 71, 76

New Hampshire, 77, 78

New Jersey, 87, 101, 106n11, 206; state constitution of (1776), 67

New Mexico, 128

New National Party, 86, 87

"New Political History," 1, 63n76, 64–66, 68–69, 190, 209n8

newspapers, 15, 40, 45, 47, 50, 55, 77, 90, 203; and Chase, 196; Northern, 23; Philadelphia, 147; Republican, 134, 204; Southern, 22, 121; western, 204; Whig, 22. *See also specific newspapers by name*

Newton, Willoughby (U.S. representative, Va.), 25, 26

new women's history, 79

Philadelphia Union League, 158

Philips, Wendell, 191

Phillips, Ulrich B. (historian), 185n2

Phoenix, J. Philips (U.S. representative, N.Y.), 13

Pierce, Franklin (president), 88

Pierce, John G. (state representative, Ala.), 174

Pierrepont, Edwards (attorney general), 224, 226

Pittsburgh, Pa., 134, 154, 156

Pius IX (pope), 91, 113, 124

planters, 131, 167–68; fear of, 182; power of, 170, 183, 184. *See also* slaveholders

"Plea for Woman, A" (Dickinson), 76

Plowman, George P. (judge), 171

pocketbook issues, 86

police, 37, 43, 45

policy, 75; platforms, 89

political: alliances, 189; anti-Catholicism, 45–46; center, 191, 208; culture, 1–5, 40, 50, 52–53, 58, 79, 134, 145, 199, 215; development, 6, 190; equality, 73; extremism, 104; force, 133; fusion, 208; identity, 69, 79, 131; institutions, 2, 214–15; integrationists, 68, 72–77, 79; leadership, 1–2, 4; parties, 1, 50, 64–65, 75–76, 110n43 (*see also specific parties by name*); science, 2, 107n17; violence, 38–39, 48, 50, 59, 63n72, 91, 222, 226, 228. *See also* rhetoric

politics, 2, 5, 37, 66, 74, 77, 79, 137; as art of the possible, 214, 227–28; formal, 67, 78; gendered, 67, 69; as usual, 146

Polk, James K., 20, 21, 24, 29, 53; as president, 90

Pool, William, 3, 36–61; death of, 40, 45, 47; politics of, 41–43; "Pool Association," 45–46; Victorian side to, 38

popular sovereignty, 109n33

populism, 185

Potter, David M. (historian), 87, 104, 138n2, 138n8, 171

Potter, John (state representative, Ala.), 171

Potts, James (Democrat), 156–57

pragmatism, 226

Prentice, George (editor), 99, 109n35

presidential power, 218, 225

Presidential Reconstruction, 167–87

Preston, Jacob (U.S. representative, Md.), 24

Princeton, U.S.S., 15

prizefights, 38, 40. *See also* pugilism

professional men, 146

"progress," 137

Progressive(s), 76, 144, 146; Era, 56; reforms, 162

proslavery, 113; extremism, 85, 88, 94; laws, 113; politics, 97; smears, 93; standpatters, 96

Protestantism, 91

public schools, 226

pugilism, 36, 37, 40, 60n3. *See also* prizefights

racial: discrimination, 185; equality, 175–76, 184–85; issues, 4, 114, 149–50, 161, 167, 178, 195, 205; justice, 219, 223; order, 115, 120; policy, 175–76; readjustment, 162

Radical(s), 128, 171, 182–83, 214; antislavery politics of, 147; electoral limits of, 227; Reconstruction, 184, 188; Republicans, 134, 136, 162, 167, 180, 188, 204, 220; suspicion of, 182; view of Southern politics, 184

Raisler, Charles W. (state representative, Ala.), 170

"Raleigh Letter," 16, 21

Rayner, Kenneth (U.S. representative, N.C.), 13

Ready, Charles (U.S. representative, Tenn.), 94

rebels. *See* Confederates

Reconstruction, 1, 3, 4, 161, 173–87, 190, 193, 195–96, 204, 214–30; carpetbaggers, 222; dilemmas, 199, 219, 223, 224, 227; end of, 220, 226, 228; legality of, 220; military, 182; policy, 191, 220; scalawags, 222; South, 4; success of, 227. *See also* Congressional Reconstruction;

130–31, 145, 188, 191, 202; convention (Ala.), 172; crisis, 3, 117, 208; evolution of, 119; immediate, 172; lawyers on, 172; movement, 129; popular support for, 133; threats of, 129; winter, 4, 105. *See also* disunion

secessionists, 3, 103, 117–25, 167; anti-, 102; initial, 119–20; militant minority, 105; motivation of, 115; and Republicans, 135

Second Party System, 1, 11, 38, 48, 53, 58, 68, 72–73, 77, 79, 86, 168, 190; fraud and force in, 52; political culture of, 49–50; and violence, 51, 55. *See also* antebellum era

sectionalism, 3, 11–13, 17–18, 23, 26, 29–30, 85–86, 95, 98, 112, 144; compromise of, 126–40; conflict from, 204; harmony between, 219, 227–28; strategy toward, 226

segregation, 71, 114. *See also* white supremacy

semiotics, 69

senate, state: New York, 76; Pennsylvania, 149, 156

Senate, U.S., 28, 87, 91, 110n40, 120, 122, 206, 225; cabal, 88; in December 1843, 13; and Grant, 222. *See also* Congress, U.S.

Seneca Falls Convention, 72–73, 75

Senter, William (U.S. representative, Tenn.), 25, 26

Seward, William Henry, 92, 103, 105, 130, 140n23, 140n28; as governor (N.Y.), 18; on higher law, 128; on "irrepressible conflict," 128; on progress, 137; prominence of, 129; radicalism of, 128; as secretary of state, 104; on sectional compromise, 134–38; as senator (N.Y.), 128; on slavery, 137; on territorial expansion, 129, 137; and Union Party, 136

Sewell, Richard H. (historian), 100

"sex contract, the," 66

Seymour, Horatio, 154, 188, 192, 193, 194, 197, 201–2, 206–7, 211n50, 227; baggage of, 202; as Democratic nominee, 189, 202–5; hard-money views of, 202

Seymour-Blair nomination, 205

Shaffer, Christian W. (Know-Nothing), 45

Shankman, Arnold (historian), 161, 166n38

Shay, Cyrus (Pool partisan), 50

Shelden, Rachel A. (historian), 3, 163n4

Sherman, William T. (general), 158–59

Shields, James (Democrat), 54

Short, James (old settler), 53, 54

"short boys" (thugs), 52

"shoulder hitters," 40, 55; and primary meetings, 55

Silbey, Joel H. (historian), 55, 62n55, 163n6, 208n2, 213n80

Simpson, Brooks D. (historian), 4

Skinner, James H. (regular Democrat), 108n22

Slap, Andrew L. (historian), 190

Slaughter, Alfred H. (future Republican), 187n23

slaveholders, 89, 95, 116, 167; anti-secession sentiment of, 104; Border South, 105; culture of, 119; enemies of, 161; former, 169; among legislators, 169t; politicians, 143. *See also* planters

Slave Power, 113–14, 124, 130, 144, 167, 226; anti–, rhetoric, 98. *See also* conspiracy

slave rebellion, 100, 119

slavery (African American), 3, 33, 76, 85–86, 88, 112, 114, 122–24, 137, 148–50, 172, 184, 226; decline of, 96; expansion of, 92, 94, 98, 99, 109, 127–28, 129–30, 145, 221; protection of, 3, 15, 96, 120; in Southern society, 131; and taxation, 95. *See also* emancipation; territories

slavery (white), 102, 112–14, 118, 120–24, 137. *See also* republicanism

slave states, 26, 85, 87, 92, 110, 129, 131, 136

slave trade (African), 95, 99, 109n33

Slidell, John (U.S. senator, La.), 87

Slifer, Eli (commonwealth secretary, Pa.), 147, 154

Smith, Adam I. P. (historian), 146, 163n6

Smith, Caleb (U.S. representative, Ind.), 24

Swallowtail Democrats faction, 193–94, 212n52
Sydnor, Charles S. (historian), 52
Sykes, Francis W. (state senator, Ala.), 175, 179–80
symbolism, 137

Tappan brothers, 71
tariffs, 95, 96, 99, 115, 116; of 1842, 14
taxation, 67, 159, 177; ad valorem, 95; policy, 186n16
Taylor, Zachary (president), 116
Teachout, Woden (historian), 58, 61n19
telegraph, 121
temperance, 42, 68, 72
Tennessee, 20–21, 24–25, 88, 89, 92–93, 101–2, 105, 110n40, 119, 123, 159, 172; East, 90; Middle, 94; politics in, 90
territories, 86, 117, 145; slave code of, 95; slavery in, 126–40, 168. *See also* Kansas-Nebraska Act (1854); slavery (African American): expansion of
terrorism. *See* political: violence
Texas, 133; debts of, 19; disputed boundary of, 25; governor of, 120; secession of, 130; settlers of, 15
Texas annexation, 3, 11, 12–35; Northerners and, 12; Southerners and, 12; treaty, 15–16, 18–20, 25, 33–34n24
Third Party System, 57
Thorn, Thomas (state representative, Ala.), 170
Thornton, J. Mills, III (historian), 4, 55
Tilden, Samuel J., 192, 193, 200–203, 205, 212n51
Tilton, Theodore (Republican), 191
Toombs, Robert (U.S. senator, Ga.), 87, 136
Train, George F. (state legislator, Pa.), 160–61
Trumbull, Lyman (U.S. senator, Ill.), 78, 196
Tucker, George, 27
Turner, Jim (cooper), 44
Tuscaloosa Independent Monitor, 20

Tyler, John (president), 12, 13, 14, 19, 20, 25, 33n24

Una, 77
Underwood, Warner (U.S. representative, Ky.), 92
Union, the, 12, 18–21, 31, 85, 92, 96–97, 104–5, 117, 120–21, 124, 126–40, 143–44, 191, 205, 215, 219; armies, 148, 158–59; breakup of, 130; coalition, 149, 150–51, 154, 161; as enslaving, 123; resolutions, 147; -saving compromise, 103
Union Democrats, 93, 159–61
Union League, 156–58
Union Party, 4, 136, 147, 157, 163n6; central committee, 155–56, 159; convention, 152; platform, 160, principles, 149
Unionist(s), 143–66; Club, 52, national convention, 158, officers, 159, party, 102–5; Seward and, 135; Southern, 3; strategy, 161; Virginia, 122–23
United Democrats, 98
United Opposition Party, 97–102
Upper South, 85, 86, 88–111, 115, 120, 121–23, 135, 136, 140
Upshur, Abel (secretary of state), 15, 33n13
urban: growth, 91; political culture, 53
Utah territory, 128

vagrancy bill, 175, 178
Vallandigham, Clement, 199, 201, 207; plan, 201
Van Buren, John Dash (colonel), 194, 197–98, 206, 211n35
Van Buren, Martin: as Democratic candidate, 20, 33n15; as secretary of state, 14; as president, 67
Vance, Joseph (U.S. representative, Ohio), 30
Vance, Zebulon (U.S. representative, N.C.), 94
Van Pelt, Charles (butcher), 44
Vansandt, James (future Republican), 171

Varon, Elizabeth (historian), 3, 68

Vaux, Richard (mayor, Philadelphia), 147

Verba, Sidney (historian), 66

Victorians, 38, 40; pre-, 38

violence, 3, 39–40, 50–51, 57, 59, 184. *See also* political: violence

Virginia, 20–21, 25, 27, 52, 88, 93–94, 102, 105, 108, 119, 122; conventions, 89–90, 119, 122, 123; majority in, 122; Piedmont, 89, Tidewater, 89, trans-Alleghany, 89

volunteer fire companies, 39, 42, 46, 52, 60n9

Volz, Harry (historian), 102

Voorhees, Daniel (U.S. representative, Ind.), 196

voting, 64, 76, 89, 96, 129, 182–83, 196, 228; backgrounds, 70, 103; divisions, 177; fraud, 56–57; Lincoln and, 114; in Pennsylvania, 145; property qualifications and, 90; realignments, 163n6, 190–91; and secession, 120; soldiers and, 159–60, 165–66n29, 166n33. *See also* elections; suffrage

Wade, Benjamin F. (U.S. senator, Ohio), 221

Wade-Davis Bill, 217

Wakely, J. B. (Methodist minister), 45–46

Walker, Robert J., 193

War Democrats, 143, 151, 154, 157, 158, 160, 161, 216

War Department, 144, 153

War of 1812, 47

Washington, George (president), 52, 137

Washington, D.C., 3, 11–13, 23, 32n3, 97, 104, 121, 135, 136, 144, 145

Washington National Intelligencer, 16, 22

Ways and Means Committee, 177

Webb, James Watson (minister to Brazil), 205

Webster, Daniel, 67, 92, 94; as secretary of state, 15

Webster, Noah (historian), 67

Weed, Thurlow, 103, 129–30, 134, 135, 136; ideas of, 135

West, the, 12, 17, 39, 158, 198, 205; states, 202

Whig Party, 11–35, 52, 85, 90, 98, 112; coalition of, 112; cohesion of, 11–12, 22, 30; decline of, 11, 87; economic agenda of, 12, 116–17; and electorate, 89; leaders of, 89; nationalism of, 116–17; Northern, 11; principles of, 20, 28, 78; Southern, 11

Whigs, 48, 51, 55, 69, 77–78, 85, 87, 89, 93, 135, 168; and American "People's Party" ticket, 101; Arkansas, 107n11; congressional, 20; dominating Republican Party, 145; former, 145, 148, 151; Kentucky, 91, 99; local, 20; loyalty, 105; New York, 41; Northern, 17–18, 21, 27, 31, 97, 113, 136; Southern, 16–19, 21, 24, 26–27, 31, 91; successor parties, 89

White, Hugh Lawson (presidential candidate), 90

White, John (state representative, Ala.), 171

White, Jonathan (U.S. representative, Ky.), 24

White House, 13, 145, 158, 204, 226

white supremacy, 184, 205, 228

Wiggins, Sarah Woolfolk (historian), 187n26

Willard, Frances, 69

Williams, George H., 224, 225

Williams, James (state representative, Ala.), 177

Wilmot Proviso, 31

Wilson, Henry (American Party supporter), 49

Winthrop, Robert (U.S. representative, Mass.), 22

wire-pulling, 144, 146

Wise, Henry A. (governor of Virginia), 90, 108n25

women('s), 3, 39, 64–81; convention, 74; culture, 65; middle-class, 67, 68; as minority, 65; movement, 73; public